Alan Hicken was born in Worcester in 1949 into a military background. After leaving school Alan had a short spell in the army, then worked in the hotel industry before settling in the Somerset village of Montacute with his wife Marcia and their children Emma and Luke. Alan ran the village post office in Montacute for thirteen years while he set up the TV, Radio and Toy Museum there, which has now been open for twenty years. Starting with a small collection of thirty vintage radios from his father-in-law, Alan went on to collect a further 500–600 radios and TVs. To this he added TV and Radio programme memorabilia which now consists of thousands of items. This manuscript was found by Alan in papers belonging to S.G. Hulme-Beaman, the creator of the popular radio series based on his *Toytown* series featuring Larry the Lamb.

Paul Begg has a career background in newspapers, television and publishing. He became a freelance writer in 1979 and has written extensively for publication in Britain and abroad, and was for many years a respected reviewer of computer software. As well as writing about Jack the Ripper, he is the author of *Into Thin Air*, *The Scotland Yard Files* (with Keith Skinner), and *Mary Celeste: The Greatest Mystery of the Sea*. His books about Jack the Ripper include *Jack the Ripper: The Uncensored Facts*, *Jack the Ripper: The Definitive History* and *Jack the Ripper: The Facts*. He is currently working on a book about Jack the Ripper for Yale

University Press. He was formerly editor of *Ripperologist* magazine and has both appeared and been historical adviser on numerous television programmes. He lives in Kent with his wife Judy and daughter Sioban.

'An account by someone who was there, was at least a witness to the scenes of the murders and was potentially the perpetrator of the Jack the Ripper murders . . . a text that will no doubt be debated for years to come'
Alan Hicken

'This is the autobiography of a man who claims that for a few short weeks when he was a young man he killed several women in Whitechapel. It is either a genuine confession by Jack the Ripper, or it's an extraordinary novel. Or it is something else, but what? Only you can decide'
Paul Begg

THE AUTOBIOGRAPHY
OF
JACK THE RIPPER

James Carnac

CORGI BOOKS

TRANSWORLD PUBLISHERS
61–63 Uxbridge Road, London W5 5SA
A Random House Group Company
www.transworldbooks.co.uk

**THE AUTOBIOGRAPHY OF JACK THE RIPPER
A CORGI BOOK: 9780552165396**

First published in Great Britain
in 2012 by Bantam Press
an imprint of Transworld Publishers
Corgi edition published 2012

Typeset in 11.5/15pt Schmutz by Falcon Oast Graphic Art Ltd.
Printed and bound in Great Britain by Clays Ltd, St Ives PLC

4 6 8 10 9 7 5 3

Contents

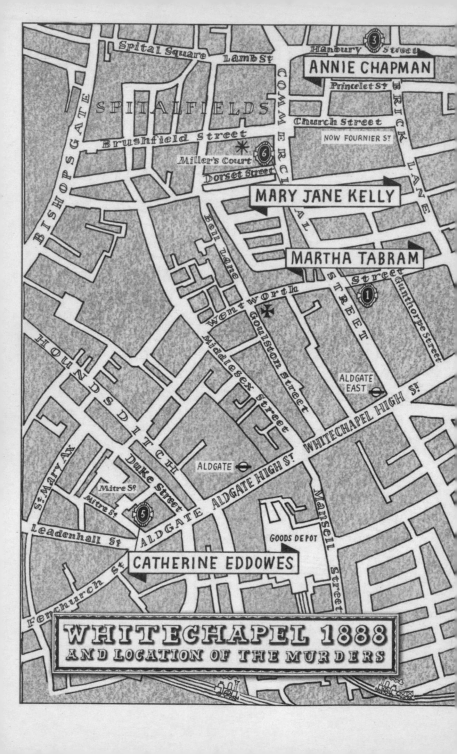

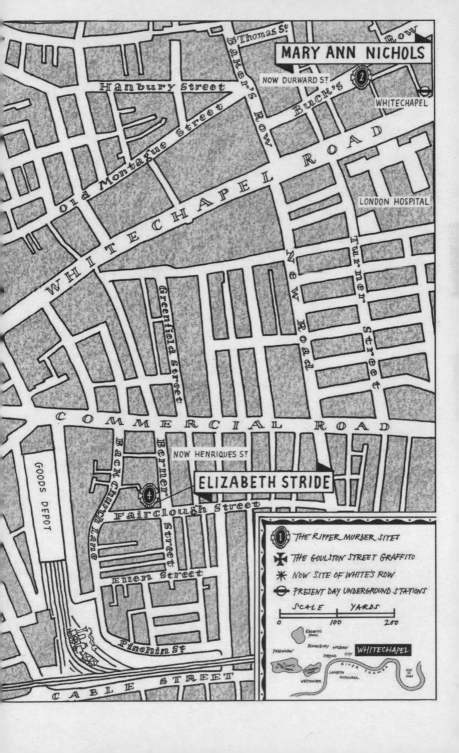

A Note on the Provenance
by Alan Hicken

I own and run Montacute TV, Radio and Toy Museum in the village of Montacute in Somerset. You may be wondering what on earth this has got to do with a manuscript purporting to be written by Jack the Ripper, so let me tell you how I came to be involved.

Just before Christmas 2007 I was contacted by Jean Caldwell. Her cousin Betty had recently moved into a home and had given her late father's memorabilia to Jean as she no longer had room for it. Neither had Jean but she wanted to keep her Uncle Sydney's collection together and preserve it in his memory. She initially approached an auction house with a view to selling it and they advised her to contact me. Jean's uncle was none other than S.G. Hulme Beaman. This name may not mean much to many people these days but many more will recognize the name of his most famous creation, Larry the Lamb. Sydney was born in 1887 and died far too young in 1932. However, he packed a lot into his short life. In the 1920s he became known as a versatile book illustrator and produced a daily cartoon strip called *Philip & Phido* in a newspaper, but he was best known for his creation of *Toytown*, broadcast on the radio on BBC's Children's Hour and starring the famous Larry the Lamb. Sydney even played the part of Dennis the Dachshund in these episodes as he was also a talented actor.

So of course I was extremely keen to have Sydney's memorabilia in my museum, and I said as much to Jean. Her uncle died shortly after she was born so she has no personal memories of him but family memories describe him as being extremely sensitive (he once fainted* when someone described a gruesome accident to him), introverted and a deep-thinker.

Jean gave me a list of the items and a description of the collection, which included some of her uncle's original work and some other materials, and we agreed a price for the entire collection. The day the large box arrived from Jean I was very excited; this was to be the first time I saw the items. I couldn't wait to unpack the contents, which included original paintings of Larry the Lamb and the other characters of Toytown, hand-carved bandsmen and soldiers, first editions of published books containing his illustrations and various other items. Then, almost at the bottom of the box, was a very old-looking manuscript. Intrigued, I picked it up and as I turned over the first few

* As told by Jean Caldwell when interviewed by Kate Smith.

pages the hairs on the back of my neck stood up and goose bumps appeared all over my body. After some explanatory remarks by, I assume, Sydney Hulme Beaman, I was reading an autobiography by someone called James Carnac, who claimed to be the world's most notorious serial killer, Jack the Ripper himself!

Needless to say as soon as I could I called Jean to ask her about the manuscript. She said she and Betty had discussed it and Betty believed it to be true but Jean had never read it as she felt it was too sinister. She did, however, hope that it would one day be published so that people could make up their own minds. This is the manuscript that you are about to read, an original historical manuscript from the 1920s that has never been published before.

Alan Hicken
Montacute TV, Radio and Toy Museum
www.montacutemuseum.co.uk

Introduction by Paul Begg

This book is the autobiography of a man who claims that for a few short weeks when he was a young man he killed several women in Whitechapel.

This book claims to be the autobiography of Jack the Ripper.

The alleged author is James Willoughby Carnac, a man whose name is otherwise unknown, who is untraceable, and who may not have existed.

This autobiography looks like a work of fiction. But things are never *that* simple.

The manuscript appears to have been written between 1928 and 1930. It is in three parts with an 'Explanatory Note' by SGHB and an Epilogue. Part 1 is about James Carnac's early life up to 1888. Part 11 concerns the events of 1888. Part 3 includes the Epilogue and does not seem to be written in the same style as the rest of the manuscript, in fact it feels like fiction, as I explain in greater detail in Appendix I. However, just because this part appears as fiction it does not mean the entire manuscript is fiction.

The manuscript is real enough. As stated by Alan Hicken, it was found by him in a box of memorabilia belonging to Sydney George Hulme Beaman. The simple answer would be to assume that this is the work of Hulme Beaman but it is very hard to credit this to him. Whilst he was undeniably a creative writer of ability, one can't easily imagine him in his office, an upstairs room in his home in Fulham, surrounded by illustrations and wooden carvings of figures from Noah's Ark and Larry the Lamb, trying to put himself into the cynical, offensive and unorthodox mind of a man who murdered and eviscerated helpless prostitutes in the slums of London's East End.

It's an image even more difficult to accept for those who know anything about Hulme Beaman. One anecdote told by his niece is particularly revealing about his character: 'He was a very sensitive man who could not bear horrors,' she said, and went on to describe how S.G. fainted at a family meal when someone described a gruesome local accident. So, do we really have an extraordinary novel written utterly against the character and entire literary oeuvre of Sydney George Hulme Beaman, or do we have something else, something genuinely intriguing? Did James Willoughby Carnac really exist, or is that a pseudonym chosen by the writer of the manuscript, or bestowed on him by Hulme Beaman?

Or are we looking at something more complex, such as

a genuine confession wrapped to look like fiction by Hulme Beaman or somebody else?

It is for you to decide.

Paul Begg is an eminent crime historian and a noted authority on Jack the Ripper. He was given the manuscript to read in 2010 and has written an extremely detailed analysis of it, going into details on the questions it raises as well as giving background information on the time and the characters involved. This analysis appears at the end of the book in Appendix I.

Explanatory Remarks.

As executor of the will of the late James Carnac I
feel it incumbent upon me to preface the
extraordinary narrative comprising the body of
this manuscript by a few words of my own. Primarily
I desire to emphasize that which will, no doubt, be
obvious; namely: that I can produce no evidence
touching the truth or otherwise of what Mr Carnac
calls his autobiography. I can accept no
responsibility whatever for his statements. His
confession, or claim, to the authorship of those
atrocities which horrified London in the year
1880* is not, I should imagine, susceptible to proof;
though one or two of the incidents he records —
apart from the actual atrocities — I know to be
true. And the confession — if it can be so regarded
— is valueless, I understand, from a legal
standpoint inasmuch as it is unwitnessed; I do not

* See discussion on this point on page 346–9.

feel constrained, therefore, to place it before the police authorities.

I must admit to great diffidence in even attempting to obtain publication of the manuscript; first, because it is not unlikely that any publisher to whom I submit it may regard the whole thing as a hoax either on my part or on the part of Mr Carnac – though it is difficult to understand why Carnac should have devoted the final periods of his life to a compilation designed to identify himself, untruthfully, with the most atrocious assassin of modern times; but secondly, and of more importance, is the fact that, in my estimation at least, the narrative is in very questionable taste. Had this been a confession couched in terms of contrition it would, I think, have been more acceptable, but it clearly is not. Throughout the whole runs a streak of cynical and macabre humour or facetiousness which I find rather distasteful. To me who knew the man this is typical of him, and I can appreciate that if he was 'Jack the Ripper' his terrible atrocities would have been carried out exactly in the spirit which his style of writing suggests.

My personal view, for what it is worth and after carefully studying the manuscript, is that James Carnac was in actual fact 'Jack the Ripper'; but with that belief I must couple the conviction that on one point at least he was insane. I will not labour this, but I feel sure that a similar opinion will be formed by other readers of the manuscript.

In common with other associates of Carnac I always regarded him as unpleasantly eccentric. He held, we were frequently reminded, unorthodox and peculiarly offensive views on certain vital matters. I know that to speak thus of a man recently dead is to be deplored, and I should not do so were it not that the statements made or implied in his own manuscript render any reservation on my part unnecessary.

As he shrewdly surmised, we ascribed his cynical outlook on life to his physical disability; for he had lost a leg in early manhood (as he explains in his manuscript) and on this account we made many allowances for his vitriolic tongue.

The manuscript came to me, as Carnac's executor, with his other effects; it was enclosed in a sealed packet and attached to the exterior of this was a letter requesting me to send the packet unopened to a certain firm of literary agents. Clearly I could not fulfil this wish blindfold; I could not accept the responsibility of parting with a package of unknown contents without sanction of the probate authorities. Such a course might have entailed unforeseen legal complications. I therefore opened the package and read the contents; and since it appeared to me to have little intrinsic value I

decided I could not shirk that other responsibility
imposed by my acceptance of the executorship.

I propose therefore to consult with the literary
agents whose names were specified by Carnac with a
view to at least attempting to fulfil his wishes
regarding publication.

In conclusion I should say that I have, after due
deliberation, removed and destroyed certain
portions of the manuscript which contained details
particularly revolting to me. I have little medical
knowledge, but these passages were, apart from the
general tone of the manuscript, sufficient to convince me that if the narrative is to be accepted as
a truthful autobiography the writer must be
regarded unquestionably as suffering from a form
of insanity.

Apart from the deletions to which I have referred
this narrative is presented exactly in the form in
which it came to me, even to the cynical dedication.

H.B.

The Autobiography
of James Carnac

Dedicated with admiration and respect to the
retired members of the Metropolitan Police
Force in spite of whose energy and efficiency I
have lived to write this book.

Part 1

Preface.

When a man has attained to any degree of note or notoriety he becomes afflicted by the itch to write his autobiography. I question whether the months of labour involved in carrying out such a task are often justified by the result, unless we regard as that result the mere satisfaction achieved by the autobiographer in writing continuously about himself to the extent of some seventy thousand words. So few of these autobiographers have anything of interest to say apart from the more or less technical interest attached to the narration of the steps and line of conduct which led the subject to eminence.

It is true that certain autobiographers may mildly amuse us by retailing the witty thing Sir Herbert Tree — or some such famous person — said to the autobiographer, and so forth; or it may pander to our love of scandal by vilifying the auto-biographer's contemporaries. But, on the whole, I feel that the frame of mind in which the autobiographer sets about his thankless task is the frame of mind in which the club bore button-holes me and tells me of the wonderful things he has done, the witty things he has said and what a clever fellow I must understand him to be.

Why then am I setting to work, at the age of nearly sixty-nine, to write my autobiography? Mainly, I think, because I have been nursing an exciting secret for forty years; I have had to guard that secret during my lifetime but there is a certain satisfaction in feeling that I can arrange for its disclosure after my death. And there have been so many speculations regarding the identity and motives of Jack the Ripper that I feel it to be almost a duty finally and definitely to put those questions to rest. And I may also be influenced by another matter. In several of the numerous articles which have appeared from time to time Jack the Ripper has been dogmatically described as a homicidal maniac; this statement has been made so often, in fact, that its truth seems now to be almost universally assumed. I recently observed an article in a popular encyclopaedia which refers to: 'Jack the Ripper, a homicidal maniac who . . .' etc. It may be that I grow touchy as the years increase, but I must admit that statements of this nature tend to irritate me.

The fact of this matter is that the writers of articles on Jack the Ripper — and I have heard that a story about him need never remain unsold — have either too much imagination or no imagination at all. In the former category are those who weave theories of extraordinary ingenuity; in the second are those who, being unable to apprehend any human actions which depart from their own standard of smug normality, fall back upon the old phrase — a homicidal maniac.

Forty years have elapsed since a mention of Jack the Ripper was sufficient to cause a shudder, not only in the East End of London, but in all parts of this country. A shudder based not altogether upon a horror of murder — as it is technically called — for many murders have been committed which have aroused no more than a rather pleasant excitement; but based more upon a shrinking awe of the unknown. For J.R. was not only a killer; he was a mysterious and bizarre killer, and in his efficiency (though I say it myself), his ubiquity and yet his uncanny invisibility, he appeared to the popular imagination to embody in his unseen personality the attributes of a ghoul. From my own recollection of the period I am able to say that, incredible as it may now seem, J.R. was actually regarded as a supernatural being by the less enlightened members of the community.

Now when a personality takes on this apocryphal aspect it is very difficult for the ordinary unimaginative person to conceive of him as a human man who was born, eats, loves and laces his boots. He cannot realize that that being has his thoughts and feelings and his own personal perception of the universe; being incomprehensible, the unknown must be a maniac.

And so it may come as a surprise to some that J.R. was a human man and that what he did was due to reactions which simply differed in some respects from the reactions of his fellows.

I need hardly say that my name is not Jack. I have given some thought to the question whether I should disclose my name at once or reserve it as a bonne bouche for the end of the record. But I have decided, mainly by the thought that I may never live to complete the work, to enjoy in imagination the sensation which the early mention of my name will afford to my associates. My name is James Willoughby Carnac.

'What, our Carnac!' I can hear old So-and-so saying at the club. 'It can't be!' And then he will scrabble over the pages until he perceives my portrait (which I hope will be reproduced in the book). 'Why it is!' he will cry. 'But it can't be! This is a joke. Why I have sat opposite Carnac in this smoking-room every day for years!'

But I assure you, my dear old friend So-and-so (I feel it would be unfair to specify your name and so fling your body to the reporters), that it is no joke. At least, not the kind of joke you have in mind. You may hardly be able to credit it at first, perhaps because you have read that J.R. was a homicidal maniac, and old Carnac was obviously sane. Why he could play bridge! But, leaving out this question of lunacy, surely you must realize that J.R. did actually exist? That he met people; sat next to them in trams and theatres; bought things in shops. And he became prominent only forty years ago, you know. What possible reason can you have for assuming that he did not live out his three score years and ten? People do; you are no spring chicken yourself, my dear So-and-so, if you will forgive my mentioning it.

When you have read this account and discovered that it contains nothing incongruous nor, in fact, anything you cannot yourself confirm with a little trouble, will you, I wonder, feel horrified? No; I suspect your sensation will be pride. You have had the extraordinary privilege of talking almost daily to J.R. for nearly fifteen years without knowing it; what a topic of conversation is now presented to you!

I think, by the way, I should enclose with my

manuscript a request that the six complimentary copies, which I understand are usually presented to an author by his publisher, be sent to the club. Otherwise my autobiography may never penetrate to that backwater.

Since this autobiography will not be published until after my death I can allow myself entire freedom in writing, bearing in mind, however, that convention has set certain bounds upon what is permissible. This book is not intended to be read aloud to the family circle, but on the other hand I do not want it impounded by the police. But although I may have to touch delicately upon one or two matters, there is this point: I have no relatives and no one need suffer, therefore, as a result of the obloquy which (society being constituted as it is) will attach to my name. And I have been careful not to refer by name to any person who is, to my knowledge, at present living.

As regards the ultimate publication of the manuscript: this has cost me much thought. But I am not without resource and a little ingenuity will, I think, overcome the difficulty. After all, there are such things as literary agents, and if my executor does not get involved over some difficulty with probate I see no reason why the plan which I have dimly evolved should not be successful. At least the manuscript should get as far as a publisher's office if my executor honourably fulfils my instructions and does not allow curiosity as to what it is he is dealing with to master him. As to any profits arising from publication, these must go with my other assets which, having no relatives, I am leaving to a charitable institution connected with animals. At least that has been my intention; but recently it has occurred to me to alter my will and to leave everything to the Police Orphanage. The idea rather appeals to me.

Before closing this somewhat rambling preface it is necessary for me to say a few words regarding conversations in this book. Truthfully to reproduce these verbatim after a lapse of forty or fifty years is obviously impossible; but a book devoid of conversational matter is, to my mind, dull; it lacks anything approaching vividness. The conversations here are therefore 'reconstructed', being based upon the gist of the matter spoken of and clothed in the characteristic dictions of the people concerned as I recall them. In some special instances, however, the words actually used have remained fixed in my memory despite the passage of years; Mrs Nicholl's remarks about her canary, for example. And when I mention Martha Tabron's

ejaculation of 'Oo Gawd!', which she managed to
utter through my clenched fingers when the light
caught the blade of my knife, I am reporting actual
fact. She said exactly that, no less and — no more.

And a last word to the general reader. This is not
put forward as a work of literature, but simply as a
record of the main incidents of my early life. I
make no pretence to any literary ability, and
skilled writers are not made at the age of
sixty-nine.

Chapter 1.

I was born at Tottenham, at that time a new suburb
— if, indeed, it could have been called a suburb of
London at all. My first childish recollections of
the place are associated with bricks and mortar and
muddy gashes cut into the green fields; our own
house was, I think, quite a new one. It was a double-
fronted, semi-detached house, the last of a row of
six; its left side adjoined a field owned by a dairy
farmer and into this field small parties
occasionally came to picnic, lighting furtive fires
in dangerous proximity to our wooden fence. When
detected, the picnic parties were chivvied from the
field by the farmer with whom my father was glad to
co-operate fearing, as he did, that sooner or later
his fence would be set on fire. This disaster never,
in fact, happened; but many were the arguments
carried on over our fence. Several of these ended by
my father dousing the illegal fire with a pail of
water and on such occasions I felt that only the

intervening fence saved my father from savage reprisals at the hands of the trippers. I learned to view with excited anticipation the advent of strange parties to our neighbour's field.

My father was a doctor who, no doubt, considered he was exercising wise foresight in renting a house in what appeared to be a rapidly expanding district. But in spite of this his practice was, I now know, but a small one for many years; not until relatively late in life was he ever free from grave financial anxiety.

Our house was built on the plan held, in those days, to be convenient. It contained three reception-rooms and a comparatively large number of bed-rooms of small size, the builder, presumably, being determined to make adequate provision for the results of the procreative enterprise common at that period. As our household was limited to myself and my parents, a large proportion of the rooms was never used.

The lower front room on the left-hand side of the entrance-hall, or 'passage', was utilized by my father as a surgery; the room behind it which communicated by folding-doors was fitted up as a dispensary. Into this room I was strictly forbidden to enter under any circumstances, but secret violation of orders had shown me that it contained shelves bearing innumerable bottles of varying size and fascinating appearance. The not unpleasant smell which proceeded from this Blue Beard's chamber permeated the whole of the lower floor and could occasionally be detected in the upper rooms.

My father, as I first remember him — if such a definite term can be applied to so indefinite a thing as the gradually dawning perceptions of a child — was a tall, thin man, wearing a fair moustache which extended into 'mutton-chop' whiskers. Later he adopted gold-rimmed spectacles, for his eyes were weak and his sight was probably affected by his habit of poring over a microscope during his periods of evening leisure. When I cast my mind back to those very early days I picture him crouching over the recently cleared tea-table, one side of his face red from the reflected light of the fire, the other green from the illuminated shade of an oil-lamp standing beside the microscope down which he was peering. Or I see him fiddling with small tweezers and little circles of almost incredibly thin glass, or, with a glass tube, drawing up drops of dirty-looking water from a collecting-bottle which, to my eye, contained nothing else but green weed. When, these drops being placed in a reservoir slide under the microscope, I was sometimes invited to look, I would never believe that the strange, moving creatures which swam across my field of vision had come from

the bottle. My father's proficiency in producing
these things from nothing at all astonished me and
yet, somehow, it did not carry with it increased
feelings of pride in him; in some curious way I
acquired the idea that the talent he displayed in
this magical procedure was one inherent in all
adults.

My father's microscopic hobby coloured the
Sunday morning walks which I took with him into
the country lanes near our house. A favourite walk
was to a place called Clay Hill, and my father
always carried with him on these occasions a
telescopic walking-stick which I considered a
miracle of ingenuity. To the extended end of this he
would attach, by means of a screwed-on ring, a
collecting-bottle and this he would dip into any
pond or ditch which lay along our course,
transferring the 'catch' to one of the other bottles
bulging in his pockets. He wore on these walks, in
place of his professional top-hat, a cap with ear-
flaps tied above the crown with tape: this headgear
he persisted in assuming in spite of the protests of
my mother who considered it to be unseemly for a
man in my father's 'position' to go out on a Sunday
morning in such a thing.

My mother's frequently expressed views as to
what was, or was not, respectable formed a large
part of my early home training. I am thinking now

of the time when I was about seven or eight years of age, a period during which the lower orders 'knew their place'; when those members of the middle-class community above the social status of the 'working man' (who, however, was a working man in those days) were oppressed by the fear that by a breach of conventional conduct the demarcation of class might become blurred. The 'lower orders' were largely uneducated — quite a large proportion were unable to read or write — they received, from their betters, tips of two-pence for casual services with apparent gratitude, and they lived, ate and bred like animals — though, on the whole, fairly respectful animals. And I believe that they were, in their unthinking animal way, more content than is the so-called working man of to-day.

To be guilty of any act or habit such as might be ascribed to the lower classes was, my mother drilled into me, a matter of special shame. She was more disturbed by conduct on the part of my father or myself which seemed 'low' than by any other manifestation; and her conventional religious views were, I think, based more upon what seemed 'respectable' than upon any conviction of divine benevolence. Her abhorrence of an atheist or free-thinker was due less to the realization that he might be an outcast from God than to the fact that his convictions were held to be not respectable convictions.

Strangely enough my mother was not, to me, such a definite personality as my father, although I was, I suppose, more in her company. She had little to say apart from her outbursts on matters of religion and convention to which I have alluded. She moved quietly about on her household duties in a mood which may have been either sullenness or apathy — I cannot say. And she was much given to furtive weeping. It was not until I reached the age of, I suppose, ten that I realized that my father's 'habits' were the cause of this, and some further years elapsed before I knew the habits in question were connected with drink. It is quite evident to me now that he drank steadily and persistently and this, no doubt, accounted to some extent for his lack of professional success.

I can touch but lightly upon these very early years for the memory of them is fitful, and the trivial incidents I am able to recall can have but little interest. I will pass over the period of my first schooling at what must have been, I think, a 'dame's' or church school, and try to describe my first boys' school to which I was sent at the age of about twelve.

Chapter 2.

'There is a fountain filled with blood
Drawn from Emanuel's veins—'

One of my earliest school recollections is the
yelping of that hymn (then a new one) in the
company of two or three dozen school-fellows; I
suppose it is safe to say that the words held for us
no religious significance whatever. In fact, I did
not then realize who 'Emanuel' was and only
learned later by a species of deduction. It seems to
me, looking back to those school-days, that most of
our time was given to the receipt of religious
instruction. The school was a small, private day-
school of the kind which, happily, is now rapidly
disappearing and the principal was, to all intents
and purposes, a religious fanatic.

He was an elderly man — to our boyish perceptions
he seemed a very old man — with a nearly bald head
and bushy white side-whiskers. A well-set-up man,

he took frequent opportunities of mentioning to us his practice of bathing each morning in cold water and following this with an earnest supplication to his Maker. One or both of these procedures had given him a ruddy and wholesome complexion and an upright carriage in spite of his years, but had failed to mellow his temperament, which was harsh and utterly lacking in imagination.

This Dr Styles prefaced the day's instruction by leading us through one or more hymns, which he followed by an hour's discourse of a religious character. Taking from the day's issue of the newspaper an item of news, and treating this as text, he would justify or condemn the occurrence recorded in the light of his dogmatic religious convictions. His vocabulary was, like that of the Cromwellian puritans, derived from the Old Testament, and his ideas were as rigid as theirs. Frequent references to biblical texts under his instructions necessitated the presence of a Bible on the desk of each boy, and it was our practice to relieve, to some extent, the boredom of these discourses by furtive search in the holy book for the more unsavoury and objectionable passages. These we would memorize and ultimately retail to each other with much boyish glee during the period of the mid-morning recess.

What a hateful, narrow-minded, ignorant bore

the man was, and what hypocritical young humbugs he made of us! He employed, one at a time, a series of assistant masters, poor sycophantic wretches no one of whom ever remained in his employment for a longer period than a term. These youths were expected to profess the doctor's own stern religious sentiments, and I have a vivid recollection of the utterance of one of these disciples on the occasion of a meeting of our boys' 'Mutual Improvement Society'. The evening had been devoted to the reading of a 'paper' dealing with the destruction of Pompeii in which the wholesale wiping-out of the city and its inhabitants was described; the destruction, we were given to understand, was salutary and engineered by a Deity displeased by persistent 'idolatry'. 'But afterwards,' explained our young preceptor, 'God, in his goodness, sent a strong wind which blew away the clouds of ashes.' Even my young mind was unable to appreciate the evidence of God's goodness offered in this grotesque statement. That a Deity should blow the ashes from the remains of the several thousand people he had destroyed struck me as entirely unacceptable as evidence of benevolence. This seemingly trivial utterance remained in my memory chiefly, I think, because it marked the first occasion on which I seriously attempted to grapple with the logic of the religious stream constantly flowing over me.

This Mutual Improvement Society to which I have
alluded, and of which membership was more or less
enforced, met at the school on one evening in each
week for the purpose of listening to the reading of
a 'paper' by a member. Choice of subject was left to
the individual reader — though subject to censor by
the presiding power. Following the reading the
audience were permitted, and, in fact, expected, to
offer criticism of the essay, and as the members'
standard of criticism was universally regarded by
them as the degree of ingenuity with which
offensive and derogatory statements regarding the
lecturer and his subject matter could be made
within the limits imposed by the president, many
enmities were conceived at the meetings. Almost
invariably a meeting of the Mutual Improvement
Society was followed on the succeeding day by a
fight furtively conducted in a cul-de-sac
conveniently situated near the school. This, in its
turn, usually led to wholesale and impartial
canings of both the participants and the lookers-on
by our seemingly omniscient principal.

Mutual Improvement Society! By Jove, yes.

Occasionally Dr Styles was able to induce
returned missionaries to lecture to us; these events
were regarded as welcome breaks in the school
curriculum though the lecturers seldom dwelt
sufficiently upon the more romantic attributes of

the natives amongst whom they had been working. We were less interested in the conduct of the natives after conversion than in the technique of torture and cannibalism.

My life at that school passes through my mind in flashes, fading or superimposing themselves like the jig-saws of a modern German film. The faces of individual school-fellows — Sanders, the big ginger-headed Scot; another whose name I have forgotten, the son of a local publican and a fearsome fighter; the prig Humphreys with his curious backward-jutting skull; the lean, dark Wellcome continuously afflicted with a snuffling cold. And a seemingly endless, ghostly procession of assistant masters like the nun's lovers in Reinhardt's production of 'The Miracle'. Young or in broken middle-age, smug, shabby, bad-tempered, nervous or hopelessly resigned. But in place of the Spielmann's piping I hear, as an obbligato, references to, and hymns about, blood. Emanuel's blood; the blood of the Lamb; shedding blood; washing in blood. Blood.

But I fear my inexperience as a writer is betraying me; I have said nothing about the physical aspect of this school where I spent such a large proportion of my waking hours. And yet perhaps I am not so far wrong in trying to convey at first the general atmosphere which assisted the budding of my youthful mind.

The school was a private house situated about a mile from my home; and as the house still exists and may, for aught I know, be occupied by members of my late principal's family, I will refrain from specifying the exact address. A large back room on the ground floor of the house had been converted into a school-room. It was panelled to a height of about three feet with deal match-boarding stained a horrible yellowish-brown. Above this woodwork the walls were whitewashed. I think a portion of this room must have been a built-out extension of the original house, for a large skylight had been let into one end of the ceiling and the rear wall of the room consisted almost entirely of glass-work.

The school-room was warmed by an iron stove standing upon a stone slab, and beside this was an earthenware water-filter with a mug hanging from it by a piece of cord. Upon the wall near the stove hung a baize-covered notice-board which usually bore announcements of forthcoming missionary lectures, lists of positions and marks gained in class, a syllabus of the Mutual Improvement Society, and so forth. A door at one end of the room led into the private part of the house and by this were a series of book-shelves untidily stacked and, on the opposing side, the wooden dais of the

principal, bearing a black-board and a large desk
finished to the same offensive colour as that of the
wall panelling. Running across the room, and
facing this dais, were rows of desks and forms,
while further desks ran along the right-hand side
of the room.

We boys, numbering about forty, had entry to the
school-room by a rear door leading from a 'cloak-
room', which, in its turn, communicated with the
playground. To provide this playground Dr Styles
had sacrificed the greater part of what had been a
fairly large garden. It was covered with knee-
biting gravel (for most of the 'play' indulged in was
of a rough and tumble violence) and enclosed by
high brick walls. At one end the gravel ceased,
giving place to the surviving remnant of the
original garden. This, so far as we could judge,
consisted almost entirely of masses of raspberry
canes and gooseberry bushes, and was protected
from our intrusion by a light wooden railing. Our
principal appeared to be passionately fond of
gooseberries, and during the mid-morning play-
times of summer he could always be discerned,
wearing a pseudo-clerical hat, moving in a
crouching posture amongst his bushes like an
Indian brave patiently tracking the foot-prints of
an enemy. So great was our respect for this holy
piece of ground, and so dreadful did the penalty for

intrusion appear to our imaginations (though never actually specified by our principal), that never once during my school career do I recall that any spirit was bold enough to overstep the wooden rail. Yet that rail was more a symbol than a protection, for a child of five could have surmounted it.

Although the temptation to trespass upon the doctor's private patch and gorge upon his fruit was always withstood — or perhaps it would be more correct to say that the yielding to temptation seemed as unthinkable to us as would the flouting of a religious taboo to a South Sea Islander — another temptation lay at hand to offset it. On the western side of the playground lay, beyond the brick wall, another garden which, by the number of fruit-trees it contained, might almost be called an orchard. The penalty for climbing, or even peering, over this wall was distinctly and repeatedly specified and, moreover, frequently exacted to the uttermost tear; for infringements of the regulation were common.

Many were the raids carried out by the more lawless of my school-fellows upon this inviting domain and this despite the fact that detection was the usual rule. The owner of the orchard was an elderly man not physically unlike our Dr Styles, but with a large, black beard. He was referred to amongst ourselves as Bap — short for John the

Baptist – but his real name I never heard. However, we credited him with an almost uncanny perception in the matter of missing fruit. The saying arose in our midst that the pears of his orchard were, like the hairs of his head, all numbered; it was remarkable that the jump-and-grab extraction of even a single pear would be followed within the hour by a visit from Bap to our principal, and a dreadful Nemesis.

In discussing the unpopular Bap amongst ourselves we usually supplemented the nick-name by the term 'worldling'. That old worldling Bap; or the old wordling next door. In explanation of this apparently quite innocent pleasantry I should say that the word 'worldling' was one constantly in the mouth of Dr Styles, by whom it was meant to signify a person unduly interested in this earthly life as opposed to the promised joys of the hereafter. But the word caught our fancy and was used by us in exactly the way that a more objectionable word was, and is, used in a lower stratum of society. Just as the latter term, while literally to be interpreted as a vulgar allusion to sexual perversion, is yet applied with no real regard to its meaning as an epithet of contempt (or, perhaps, genial endearment), so was the term 'worldling' used by us. We meant exactly what the navvy meant when he used the (to us) analogous expression – no more and no

29

less. And our term was less likely to cause us trouble if overheard.

Incidentally when, by long usage, we had adapted the word 'worldling' to our own peculiar needs, it became to us a source of great joy to hear it continually cropping up in our principal's religious discourses. It was like listening to a clergyman preaching a sermon interlarded with the obscene colloquialisms of the tap-room.

My attendance at this school is distinguished in my mind, as I look back upon it, for two things. The first of these was that I suddenly evinced a talent for drawing. It blossomed under the sympathetic encouragement of one of that long stream of under-masters to which I have previously referred; the only one of those masters of whom I retain a clear recollection.

We learned in some roundabout way that this man, whose name was Pearson, had been an artist before his reduction to the lower dregs of schoolmastering. Other than that an artist was a man who painted pictures we had but a shadowy conception of the term, but a lad named Sanders, whose father was connected with the Press in some obscure capacity, was able to enlighten us. We learned from him that an artist is a man who paints pictures of girls with nothing on; that he lives in a

state of guilty splendour in one of certain
districts given over to debauchery — such as St
John's Wood and Chelsea — and that he can be found
in his lair at most times of the day with a naked
girl on his knee and a pot of beer beside him. This
ideal life postulates, of course, the satisfactory
earning power of the artist based, presumably, upon
the obvious market value of pictures of girls with
nothing on; and we could not reconcile it with Mr
Pearson's descent to schoolmastering. Speculation
and romance grew up around him, but I need not
retail the several suppositious stories which one or
two of my imaginative school-fellows brought
forward to account for it.

I question whether Dr Styles was aware of his
usher's previous occupation, for he would
undoubtedly have classed the artist with the actor
in the lowest category of worldlings. Strange as it
may seem, the turpitude of the artist was almost
universally assumed amongst the middle-classes in
my younger days, though the belief in his earning
capacity was entirely contrary to that advanced by
the lad Sanders. I am not at all sure that the old
popular conception is dead even now.

Drawing was one of the subjects included in the
curriculum of the school, and it was 'taken' by Mr
Pearson; not because Dr Styles assumed any
particular ability in drawing on the part of the

new-comer (for it is highly improbable that he suspected such ability), but simply for the reason that the subject always had been taken by the assistant master. The teaching consisted in the handing out of lithographed sheets representing various objects from tea-cups (Elementary) to horses (Advanced). These pictures we laboriously copied in pencil, and when our efforts reached sufficient accuracy to satisfy the master in charge we finished our drawings by cleaning them up with stale bread and 'lining them in' with hard, wiry outlines made by a sharp pencil. This method of 'teaching' drawing had always prevailed at the school and Mr Pearson was not encouraged to amend it. Nor did he show any inclination to do so; possibly because he felt no desire to advertise his own artistic attainments, but more probably from sheer apathy.

In common with several of my school-fellows I was in the habit of relieving the tedium of these useless drawing lessons by executing crude sketches of a fanciful nature on spare sheets of paper which could be slipped under the legal drawing on the approach of our master. But on one occasion the quickness of my hand was insufficient to deceive the eye of Mr Pearson.

'What have you got there, Carnac?' a voice asked at my elbow.

Reluctantly I drew out a sheet of paper and handed it to him, watching his examination of my unlawful sketch in considerable apprehension. After studying the sketch for some moments in silence, Mr Pearson folded it and placed it in his pocket. 'Come to me after school,' he said; and passed on to the next boy.

I assumed, not unreasonably, that at the forthcoming interview the principal would be invited to act as co-critic with Mr Pearson in the matter of my drawing, and there was no hope that it would be viewed with an indulgent eye. For it represented Dr Styles and the treatment was, to say the least, unflattering. It was therefore a pleasant relief when, remaining behind after school, I found that Mr Pearson was preparing to treat the matter as one between ourselves. He greeted my hang-dog approach in a manner which I can best describe as one of cheery severity.

'You know, you mustn't do this sort of thing, Carnac,' he said, fishing out the drawing and examining it afresh.

'No, sir,' I agreed.

'Making drawings of Dr Styles. It's not the thing at all.'

My forlorn hope that the subject portrayed had not been identified vanished. 'No, sir,' I said again.

He grinned. 'It's not at all bad, though. Not at all bad.'

Relieved, I allowed my expression of penitence to relax.

'Have you done much of this?' he asked, holding up the sketch.

'Oh no, sir!' I assured him hastily. Habitually to make libellous drawings of Dr Styles! Unthinkable!

'I mean, have you done much drawing,' Mr Pearson explained.

'Oh yes, sir,' I replied.

'Well, if I were you I should stick to it,' he said. 'I should like to see some more; I might be able to give you a few hints. Only you mustn't caricature the Head you know. I tell you what: make a drawing of me and let me see it. I think we had better burn this.' And as he walked to the stove and thrust my drawing between the bars I realized that Mr Pearson was not only willing to overlook the enormity but was actually making himself an accessory after the fact.

Although my chief feeling, as I left him, was that I had been dealing with a mild-mannered lunatic, that conversation bore fruit. I see now that had Pearson been of the usual narrow and sycophantic breed of assistant master to which I was accustomed, and had he, in the conventional manner, punished me in the interests of discipline, he would probably have set back the development of my latent talent (if talent is not too strong a word). But he had the knowledge to perceive signs of an ability which I did not suspect myself, and the wit to encourage it in direct opposition to the narrow discipline of the school, and that despite the fact that he was not normally lax on points of order.

I shall always feel grateful to Mr Pearson, for that interview initiated a course of striving and suddenly developed interest on my part, and criticism and help on his, which, if it did not teach me to draw, at least set me on the path I was later able to pursue. Unfortunately I was soon to be deprived of his encouragement, for at the school prize-giving he volunteered to assist in the concert. He was so ill advised as to entertain the audience of pupils and parents with a humorous imitation of a lady at her dressing-table, and the ability shown damned him quite definitely in the eyes of our principal as a worldling. The actor was, by the nature of his calling, beyond the pale in Dr Styles' estimation, and Mr Pearson's histrionic competence approached so closely to proficiency in that unholy craft that he was obviously unfitted to preside over innocent, budding youth. He was dismissed.

*　*　*

Years afterwards I saw Pearson again. He was
sitting on a pavement in the West End of London, his
back against some railings and a selection of
pictures chalked upon boards on either side of him.
He was thinner and his hair was white, but I
recognized him, though he showed no recollection
of me. I was with a − er − lady and had to content
myself with depositing in his cap as much money as I
could spare in the particular circumstances of the
evening. When I sought the same spot on the
following day he had gone; nor did I ever see him
again.

Chapter 3.

The second outstanding event which I associate with
Dr Styles' school deserves, I feel, the beginning of
a new chapter.

I have already referred to the constant
references to blood which occurred in the course of
our religious teaching. These were, of course,
purely symbolic and made by our principal they
were, I think, no more than expressions of zest for
the vindictive form of religion which he favoured.
Nevertheless I became accustomed to the familiar
usage of the noun and I believe my thoughts turned
almost sub-consciously to the attributes of blood.

This seems a suitable place for me to set forth my
own feelings on this matter of blood. Most people, I
have found, harbour a strange dislike for blood, a
dislike so strong that the sight and smell of it as it
wells from a wound or a nose is sufficient to
engender in them faintness or nausea. Even amongst
my school-fellows I had observed this curious

phenomenon. Such feelings puzzled me then and always have puzzled me. The colour of blood is very far from unpleasant; it is a fine, rich tint which is viewed without qualms in other objects. A person who shrinks from the sight of blood does not, for example, avoid looking at a bright red shawl. Nor can the smell be held responsible for the feeling of nausea, for the smell is not only rather pleasant than otherwise, but is so faint that only in the presence of large quantities of blood is it perceptible at all. I can only assume that the dislike of blood is really due to some sub-conscious association of blood with the ideas of suffering and death. And on the matter of death I shall expound my views later.

Not only did I not share this popular aversion to blood, but, on the contrary, the sight of it held, for me, a fascination. And I only refer to this feeling for the reason that, I judge from observation, it is not generally shared. In the same way I should only need to mention the satisfaction afforded me by sight if all other persons were blind; and just as, in that case, I should regard the blind as abnormal and not myself, so I do not regard myself as a curiosity for differing from other people in this matter of blood.

I have alluded to the frequent fights which took place after school hours; although not often an active participant, I was always in the forefront of the spectators. It was not so much the 'sport' (i.e. exciting brutality) of these encounters which interested me as the prospect — usually fulfilled — of a blood-letting. When one of the antagonists had retired from the encounter with blood streaming from his nostrils, I would stand beside him on the kerb watching with satisfaction the rich red drops splashing into the gutter.

One of the few school-mates who appeared to share my interest was a boy named Johnson whose father, as I soon discovered, kept a pork shop in the neighbourhood. It was one of those shops to which a poor person could repair with a basin for the purchase of hot boiled pork and pease-pudding. This latter delicacy now appears to be almost unprocurable, for shops of the class referred to have disappeared nowadays so far as my observation goes, and the secret of the pudding's preparation with them — a secret held exclusively, I judge, by professional pork-butchers. At the shop of Johnson's father one could also purchase hot saveloys and things called faggots, obscurely compounded comestibles of the rissole type.

Dr Styles, who occasionally manifested flashes of allusive humour, sometimes addressed the boy Johnson as 'doctor'. At this witticism we would all dutifully laugh, but our merriment was akin to

that of the courtier at the jests of a touchy
potentate behind whose throne lurk the shadows of
the boiling-vat and the gibbet. We had but the
vaguest notion as to who the historical Dr Johnson
had been, though the boy Johnson supposed him to
have been a friend of Shakespeare who used to get
drunk at the Cock Tavern — wherever that was.

Johnson showed a marked friendliness towards me
and as my way home from school led past his father's
shop he would occasionally draw me inside where
his jolly-looking red-faced father would dig a
tit-bit from one of the steaming trays over which
he presided and offer it to me on a slip of
newspaper. Had my mother ever met me returning
home munching a piece of faggot or sucking a dob of
pease-pudding from a paper, I know she would have
been horrified at my 'low' behaviour; but she never
did and I enjoyed these illicit snacks in peace.

One day Johnson approached me in the
playground. 'I say, Carnac,' he said; 'like to come to
tea at my place this afternoon? My father's killing
a pig this evening. Ever seen a pig killed?'

'No,' I replied, with interest.

'It's rare fun. You should hear it squeal. Don't
they bleed too! Like to come along?'

'I'll ask at dinner-time if I may,' I told him; for
this was during morning play.

When I returned home I put the matter to my

mother who was just bringing in the dinner.
'Mother, can I go to tea with Johnson after school?'

'Who is Johnson?' she asked. 'What is his father?'

'I think he's a butcher.'

She placed her tray on the table and looked steadily at me for a few moments. 'And is the son of a butcher the only boy you can find to make a friend of?' she enquired. At that moment my father entered the room.

'James wants to go to tea with a butcher's boy,' she told him.

'Do you mean a butcher's son or the boy who delivers the meat?' he asked.

'His son. It's a pity he can't find some respectable boys to associate with at that school.'

'Well, when I can afford to set up in Harley Street we'll talk about sending him to Rugby,' said my father.

'If you ever can he'll be too old for Rugby,' observed my mother, who always took my father's remarks quite literally.

'As for this boy being the son of a butcher,' my father continued, 'he may be none the worse for that.'

'But a butcher!' said my mother.

'Well, what of it?' exclaimed my father irritably. 'Let Jim go to tea with his friend. I've no patience with this silly snobbery.'

'No, and it's no wonder you can't keep your practice together,' complained my mother. 'What with —'

I shut my ears to the further conversation and applied myself to my meal. The only point which affected me seemed to have been settled.

'Be sure you get home by eight,' my mother admonished me as I left for afternoon school.

The pig-sticking which I was privileged to see that evening I can recall to this day. As a preliminary I partook of a substantial tea in the company of Johnson, his father, mother and a small sister. I have little recollection of the characteristics of these people; nor can I remember the composition of the meal beyond the fact that it included water-cress, a herb which never appeared on our tea-table at home.

At the conclusion of the meal Mr Johnson rose briskly from the table and, with a twinkling eye, stated that he would 'just fetch the knife', and left the room. Immediately Johnson's small sister retired to a sofa at the side of the room and, stuffing up her ears with both hands, buried her face in the cushions.

'She don't like to hear the pigs being killed,' Johnson remarked indulgently, jerking a thumb towards her as he led the way from the room.

I followed my friend to a yard at the back of the

building where we found Mr Johnson arrayed in a long overall, the front of which was stained and encrusted with dried blood. He was toying with a long, thin knife of the kind used to carve ham, and looking into an enclosure at the end of the yard from which proceeded a mixture of grunts and squeals.

'Which one are you going to kill, father?' Johnson enquired, ranging himself beside the man.

'Reginald,' replied Mr Johnson.

'I'm glad it's to be one of the pink ones,' said his son. 'Come and look at them, Carnac.'

I walked to his side and looked into the pen.

'You won't see pigs like them every day, Carnac,' observed Mr Johnson.

'No,' I agreed. 'They look fine pigs.' In point of fact I had hardly ever before seen a live pig except at a distance. There were some half dozen there and I was surprised to notice that instead of the small, prick ears with which pigs are represented in pictures, these had long, drooping ears like those of a dachshund. But I was too excited to observe any details.

The pigs were moving about the pen, grubbing in the straw, and Mr Johnson was apparently alert for the approach of the particular animal he had marked out. Suddenly he opened the small gate which he had stealthily unlatched and swiftly

grabbed a small pink pig by an ear as it was passing.
He dragged it squealing from the pen, kicking-to
the gate behind him. The pig twisted its head and
beat a kind of scratching tattoo with its legs on the
paving of the yard. But with a dexterous movement
and a shout of 'Stand clear!', Mr Johnson jerked its
head upwards and drove the knife into the front of
its throat. There was a spurt of blood almost as
though a bladder full had been slit and the animal,
uttering a squealing gurgle, collapsed on to the
pavement where it lay feebly twitching its legs.

'Next time you meet him he'll be with a lump of
pease-pudding,' said Mr Johnson jocularly, wiping
his knife on his filthy overall.

'Come on,' said Johnson to me, leading the way
into the house. 'You don't want to see him cleaned
out.'

As a matter of fact I did, but politeness to my
host prompted me to follow him. As we passed into
the parlour I caught sight of his face. His eyes were
bright and feverish, but he had gone rather white
round the mouth. I began to wonder whether his
stomach was as strong as his enthusiasm.

That night I dreamed I was in class. Brought out
before Dr Styles was Hawkins — a fat, white,
unhealthy-looking boy, far from popular with his
school-fellows. He was naked and his tight, fat

abdomen glistened. Before him Dr Styles crouched on his toes, a long, gleaming knife in his hand. He closed one eye and pointed with his knife. Then he retreated a few yards, took a short run but pulled up half-way to his victim and returned to the spot he had left. Then, poising himself on his toes, he leapt forward again. The knife went into Hawkins' stomach as though into butter. With a dexterous flick of the wrist Dr Styles ripped the white, bladder-like substance up to the chin. There was a gush of blood and Dr Styles, wiping the knife on the seat of his trousers, cried: 'I'll teach you to steal my gooseberries!' Then I awoke. It was a curious dream but I am not sure I would have called it a nightmare.

And if you, O reader, are one of those gentle-stomached persons who dislike even reading about blood, I advise you to go no further with this book. Exchange it for a cheery detective story.

Chapter 4.

Soon after my fifteenth birthday my father
inherited a considerable sum of money. An aunt of
his, whom I had never seen, died leaving him the
bulk of her property.

A letter advised him of the death but contained
no intimation of his good fortune, and my father at
first hesitated to take a journey across London for
the purpose of attending the funeral. Also he did
not possess a pair of black trousers, apart from his
dress clothes, and was reluctant to buy a pair in
which to assist in the burying of an old lady he had
not seen for twenty years.

However, my mother pointed out that since he was
one of the sole surviving relatives it would 'look
very bad' for my father to be absent on the occasion
in question. After some discussion he grudgingly
agreed to go subject to the difficulty of the
trousers being overcome without too great an
expense. Whereupon my mother fetched the dress

trousers, and when she had shown by ocular demonstration that the black of these was almost indistinguishable from the black of his frock coat he gave in. On the morning of the funeral he departed in a thoroughly bad temper. The weather was cold and wet and he would have to walk to Seven Sisters Station. He had refused to buy a pair of black gloves and went out of the house smoking a pipe which, my mother thought, was indecent in the circumstances. Apparently it had not occurred to either of my parents that he might benefit financially by the death.

The mourner returned in a very different mood. It was quite evident that he had been drinking; I was as well able to identify the symptoms in the flushed face and the glazed eye as my mother was by that time. My mother began to weep when she saw him.

'Where's your umbrella?' she asked from behind her handkerchief.

'Left it in the train,' said my father. 'Damn the umbrella!' I laughed.

'John!' cried my mother. 'Before the boy too!'

'Damn the boy!' cried my father jovially, slapping me on the back.

'John!' wailed my mother again. 'And you've been drinking!'

'Drinking?' said my father. 'Me? Nonsense. A drop

of grocers' port at the wedding-breakfast – I mean funeral-breakfast. Nothing more.'

'I don't believe you,' cried my mother. 'And I only hope none of your patients met you on your way home.'

'Cheer up, Mrs Gummidge,' my father said. 'And guess what I have to tell you.'

I think my mother must have had a flash of intuition. She paused and stared at him, her crumpled handkerchief held half-way to her face.

'Aunt Madeleine has left me most of her money!' cried my father.

My mother sat motionless. But her woebegone expression gradually changed to one of delight and satisfaction. Forgotten were my father's tippling and low behaviour; so powerful is even the mention of the word 'money'. 'How much?' asked my mother, breathlessly.

My father admitted ignorance of the exact sum, but mentioned a probable amount which took my breath away. Then he removed his silk hat, threw it up to the ceiling and endeavoured to kick it as it fell; but he was unequal to the dexterity demanded and reeled against the table, knocking over a jug of water and clutching the table-cloth. My mother began to giggle, and that unusual manifestation on her part was not the least surprising event of the evening. I had never before heard her giggle like that, and stared at her open-mouthed.

Then my father raised himself from the edge of the table and, throwing his arms round my mother, dragged her from her chair and began to caper around the room with her. This boisterous behaviour brought my mother back to a sense of reality; she disengaged herself and stood patting her hair and smoothing her crumpled dress, while my father swayed in the centre of the carpet.

Later on, after a somewhat sketchy meal, my father left the house despite the earnest pleas of my mother, and as he had not returned by nine o'clock I was then sent up to bed. It must have been past mid-night when he was brought home speechlessly drunk by a patient. I was awakened by the disturbance and, creeping from my room, viewed over the banisters the (to me) entertaining sight of my father being hauled upstairs by my mother and the neighbourly Samaritan.

In this way my father entered into his inheritance.

It was some time before my father was able to handle his fortune. His first state of excitement and geniality gradually faded into one of irritation as the weeks and months went by and nothing was heard from the executors. I gathered that a thing called 'probate' was responsible for the delay, and that

this probate was some piece of legal machinery
designed for the convenience of lawyers who, being
by nature dilatory, if not actually dishonest, were
glad to avail themselves of it as a means of keeping
an inheritor out of his just rights for as long as
possible. Finally my father in a sudden fit of
exasperation took his hat and dashed off to Town
'to see what they meant by it'. He succeeded in
wringing from the executors (or someone involved
in the business of clearing up the estate) the sum
of five hundred pounds on account of his legacy; to
me this sounded an enormous sum.

At once my father began spending with a casual
prodigality which delighted and excited me but
which filled my mother with alarm. He entirely re-
furnished our drawing-room, bought several
appliances for the surgery — including a new set of
glistening dissecting scalpels in a leather case —
half a dozen suits for himself and as many dresses
for my mother, a new suit and two pairs of boots for
myself and a number of cases of whiskey and wine. I
had never before seen cases of wine — in the past
drink had been more or less smuggled into the house
— and I assisted with enthusiasm in unpacking the
bottles from their straw coverings and arranging
them according to my father's directions in a
cupboard under the stairs.

Next I was removed from Dr Styles' academy and

sent to the grammar school as a kind of provisional step until a better school could be decided upon. Lastly the small, slatternly day-girl, who had up till then assisted my mother in the house, was dismissed and a general servant to 'sleep in' was engaged. My mother, poor woman, was gratified at this step; she had always felt keenly the social inferiority entailed by her inability to keep a 'regular servant', and her realization of a modest ambition was doubtless untinctured by any prescience of the sinister events to come. For it is one of the alleviations of this earthly existence that we are none of us able to foresee what the future holds for us.

The name of the new-comer to our household was Mary; I cannot recall her second name. She was about twenty years of age I should imagine, and was of the type usually referred to as 'buxom', being a well-developed young woman of rosy complexion and by no means ill-looking. It is very difficult for an old man of sixty-nine to recall and describe accurately his feelings and reactions as a youth to another person, particularly when those early feelings have been, at a later stage, strongly influenced by a particular series of events. When a certain thing has come to pass, it is easy to recall the series of events and manifestations of character which led up to it as a logical

conclusion; to blame ourselves for the lack of
insight which would have allowed us to perceive the
trend of things. In the same way I can, in the light
of after events, form a fairly accurate idea of the
character of this girl Mary, but it is difficult to
separate from it my first estimate of her.

I know that I took a sort of furtive interest in
the girl from the start, mainly, I think, because
she was the first personable young woman with whom
I had come into any sort of close contact, and to
have her living in the house with us was something
of a novelty. She was a country girl with none of the
fresh innocence fallaciously ascribed to the
average country girl, but on the contrary all the
coarse, dirty knowingness which is far more common
in the country girl than in her town-bred sister.
Her attitude towards me, after the first few days,
was a blend of what I might call lip-serving respect
and a sort of knowing familiarity as though we
shared in common a somewhat salacious secret. Both
to my parents, and to myself in their presence, her
manner was reserved and respectful, and I have no
reason to suppose that my mother had any doubts as
to the wisdom of employing Mary in a household
which contained an adolescent son and a husband
whose habits were open to criticism.

As for myself I found Mary a source of slight
embarrassment for I was afflicted by the shyness

common to my age; not only was I fully aware of
that shyness but I felt that it afforded Mary a
certain amount of amusement. I avoided her as much
as possible and it was, perhaps, as well that my mind
at that time was fully occupied by the interests of
my new school and with my hobby of drawing with
which I was making considerable progress.

Before dealing with the climax of this period of
my life I must try to convey, so far as my lack of
practice as a writer will allow, a general picture
of myself and my environment. For myself I was then
a youth of sixteen, on the whole fairly quiet and
well-behaved, considerably exercised by brooding
thoughts on half-understood matters and of a type
of mind tending distinctly towards the morbid. My
taste in literature was for the unhealthy and
bizarre and found ample food in my father's
extensive collection of books, of which he was
unwise or irresponsible enough to allow me the free
run. Many of these books were of the kind referred
to in booksellers' catalogues as 'curious'; amongst
them I recall two volumes: Roberts' 'Treatise of
Witchcraft' and John Cotta's 'Triall of Witchcraft',
both of which, published in the seventeenth
century, must have been fairly valuable and the
contents of which fascinated me extremely. He also
possessed a large tome whose name I have forgotten
which contained many plates portraying the

administration of various ingenious forms of torture. The only books in connection with which a half-hearted and ineffectual censorship was exercised were my father's medical works; and, on the whole, my favourite author was Edgar Allan Poe of whose works my father had the complete edition, published in 1875. Over these volumes I would pore for hours.

Apart from reading and 'home-work', practically my whole spare time was given up to drawing, though I must admit that in the home circle this occupation obtained very little encouragement. My mother was quite incompetent as a critic and my father was frankly indifferent. On one occasion when, during the course of a Sunday morning walk, my father asked me suddenly whether I knew what I would like to be when I left school and I replied, without hesitation, 'An artist,' his only comment was, 'Oh my God!' He did not then pursue the conversation and to this day I have no idea what his plans for me were or if, indeed, he had any.

My father's accession to comparative wealth (though since he had not yet handled the bulk of his legacy it was only potential wealth), had certainly effected no improvement in his character. He was fast becoming a confirmed drunkard and had lost all interest in his professional practice. This practice had fallen steadily away since the evening on which one of his patients had assisted him home following the celebration of his inheritance; and the advent of a patient at the surgery was rather an event and, to him, a boring event. He drifted through his days in a casual, indifferent manner varying between a hectic geniality and a petulance which, on occasion, flared into a ferocity in which he would actually smash furniture. In one of these fits I recall that he deliberately swept from the mantelpiece in the sitting-room the whole of the useless jumble of knick-knacks with which it was garnished, and then passed out of the house leaving my weeping mother to gather up the fragments in a dust-pan — for she was too proud to allow 'the girl' to do this for her in the circumstances. On a more serious occasion my father, returning home drunk after my mother had retired to bed and being presumably incensed by her remonstrances as to his condition, flung open a bed-room window and pushed out as much of the furniture as would go through it. Most of the bed-room crockery was smashed to atoms in the front garden below, together with the dressing-table mirror which my father succeeded in tearing from its fastenings. When my mother, dressing herself hastily and summoning me, passed down to the front garden in a pathetic attempt to salvage the goods before daylight revealed her

shame to the neighbours, the entire grass-plot was
littered with splintered furniture and fragments
of china. Unfortunately for my mother's remaining
shreds of pride the disturbance had not passed
unheard by our neighbours, and two of them kindly
came out in a half-dressed state and assisted us to
carry in the wreckage. I think that in all my
mother's shame of the night's work her greatest
embarrassment was caused by the fact that a
chamber had lodged on the top of a small tree in the
garden where, by a miracle of equipoise, it hung
jauntily in full view. The helpful neighbours were
tactful enough to ignore the shameful object, but
after they had retired to their respective houses
my mother again crept into the front garden and,
with great difficulty, dislodged the article and
carried it indoors.

The next day my father went out and bought a
complete suite of bed-room furniture, which was
delivered the same evening.

It may be assumed that my mother failed to
maintain even a semblance of happiness in the
circumstances which now obtained in the
household. The few little luxuries which resulted
to her from my father's legacy were more than
offset by the state of harassment in which she
lived. She degenerated into a shabby, weeping,
almost slinking figure, seldom leaving the house

except to attend church meetings in the evenings, and leaving all shopping expeditions to the care of the girl Mary who, in that connection, showed herself to be honest and capable. Had my mother been of stronger character she might have fought my father's habits and averted the tragedy which followed, but evidently she lacked the force to do so. Her self-pity was stronger than her desire to save something from the ruins, and she sought refuge in 'the consolations of religion'. She became a regular attendant at the local church and a rabid participant in the several vapid activities of that body; and so by her frequent absences from home in the evenings she unconsciously collaborated in the series of events which I am now about to relate.

Chapter 5.

My first intimation of something unusual going on
in our house — unusual, I mean, apart from the
state of affairs I have outlined — came to me on one
evening near my seventeenth birthday. My mother
was absent at one of her church meetings and I was
alone in the sitting-room. I had completed my home-
work and was engrossed in my drawing when Mary
entered the room with my light supper. I looked at
the clock and saw that it was nine; it was hardly
likely my mother would return before ten or ten-
thirty and I usually retired to bed before that
time. Mary set down her tray, and laid my meal on
one end of the table at which I was working; as she
finished I glanced up and caught a sly smile and a
curious sidelong glance as she left the room. A few
minutes later I heard the creaking of the stairs;
apparently she had gone up to bed.

As I was eating my supper I heard my father's
steps in the hall and then the loud slam of the

street door. I was paying no particular attention, as I was eating and drawing at the same time; I merely registered the impression that my father had gone out and it was only later that I recalled I had not heard his steps continuing down the front garden path. At about nine-thirty, feeling tired, I went up to bed.

My parents occupied a front bed-room on the first floor. My room was immediately above this and next to that occupied by Mary. As I undressed I heard a sudden giggle from this adjoining room and, a few moments later, a few words spoken in a low tone. And, in the silence of the evening, the dividing wall was not thick enough to prevent the character of the voice filtering through. I knew instantly that it was not Mary's voice; it was that of a man and in the light of probability could be no other than my father's. I think I felt surprise more than any other emotion; I remember standing there with my collar in my hand, staring at the dividing wall and straining my ears for further sounds. It occurred to me then that on other occasions recently I had, as I thought, overheard Mary talking to herself at about this time. Pondering, I finished undressing and slipped into bed which creaked loudly, as usual, under my weight.

In a few minutes I heard the door of the next room softly opened and the sound of footsteps on the stairs; hardly footsteps, in fact, but simply one or two creaks. The sounds were almost imperceptible and I am sure I should never have heard them had I not been listening intently. Then came the rattling of a key in the lock of the street door, followed by an ostentatious scraping of feet on the door-mat and a loud slam. I was not deceived by these noises; I knew now with certainty that my father had never left the house. He had pretended to do so and was now pretending to return. I lay thinking hard for some twenty minutes after which I heard the return to the house of my mother.

Now I could write pages on the subject of my thoughts and feelings following this nocturnal incident, but I shall not do so. Can I be expected to enter into a long self-analysis, or even remember with sufficient clearness the exact trend of my thoughts as a lad of seventeen? Such a procedure may be right and proper enough in the popular novelist; but I am not a novelist. I am an old man working more or less against time to set down a series of events, and already experiencing distaste for the physical labour involved in writing. I must concentrate on events — at least for the early part of this history.

Shortly after the revelation above alluded to (for it certainly was a revelation of my father's turpitude), the Providence which is said to shape our ends took on the aspect of a malicious demon — an aspect from which I have never been able to disassociate it in my mind. It arranged that my mother should be absent from the house for several relatively long periods. Religious piety had drawn her from the house on several evenings in each week and so allowed ample scope for the sowing of the seed. And now that the dreadful harvest was ripe, Sisterly Piety was the card played. In short her sister fell seriously ill and my mother was called away to nurse her. Had that illness not occurred exactly when it did I believe that the thing that turned out a tragedy would have ended in no more than a vulgar scandal.

My mother's sister visited us only on rare occasions, for she had disgraced herself in my mother's eyes by marrying a bookmaker. This man, whose name was Evans, had called at our house in my aunt's company, and although he was received by my mother with cold politeness I had taken to him at once; and I know that my father thought him excellent company. I shall have more to say later about this excellent man, and need not therefore enter into a description of him at this stage.

Now my aunt lay ill at her bookmaker-husband's house at Peckham and my mother felt it incumbent upon her to go there and take charge. I think she experienced some doubts as to the propriety of

leaving my father and me alone in the house with a
young female, for I overheard scraps of an argument
in which the phrases 'doesn't seem the thing', 'what
may people think!', 'silly convention', 'won't the
boy be here' and so forth, led me to gather that this
subject of propriety was under discussion.
Ultimately my mother presumably decided that I
might be regarded as a sufficient chaperon for my
father (or he for me) and she departed for Peckham.

Within a day of her departure things began to
happen. I found myself on several occasions
interrupting discussions between my father and
Mary, discussions which almost bore the appearance
of arguments and which dropped to whispers upon my
approach. On one occasion Mary was weeping noisily
and unrestrainedly while my father appeared to be
bullying her. On another he took her boldly into
the surgery and was closeted with her for half an
hour. And always Mary went about her household
duties white-faced, red-eyed and with a look of what
I could only analyse as 'funk'. And yet, despite the
scraps of sexual knowledge I had garnered from the
dirty hints of school-fellows and my catholic
reading, I was not sufficiently experienced to
realize at that time what was actually the matter.

After a fortnight's absence my mother returned
suddenly to the house, gave a hasty account of her
sister's illness (which account she had already

conveyed in a series of letters) deposited in Mary's charge a bundle of soiled linen and, packing a fresh supply, set off again for Peckham. She was too distressed by her sister's condition (I learned that the illness was cancer) to exercise much discernment, and she appeared to miss anything unusual in the appearance of Mary or of my father.

On the day following this fleeting visit I returned from school to find my father looking rather more harassed than he had appeared even of late, and a strange and particularly offensive old woman in charge of the household. Mary was not to be seen, and my father told me abruptly that she was in bed seriously ill.

The next two days seemed to be a kind of blur. I could not gather what was going on, but it seemed that the old woman was acting as a nurse to Mary; both the old woman and my father appeared to be labouring under extreme excitement, and in my father's case an additional emotion which I analysed as fear. Was he afraid that Mary might die? Such a theory hardly seemed to meet the case, for I knew that many of his previous patients had died and he had never before manifested any particular distress at the occurrences.

To this strange, sinister atmosphere I returned from school at mid-day and in the evening, to partake of a wretchedly cooked meal hastily served

to me by the old woman, spending my evenings alone
in the sitting-room in futile attempts to grapple
with home-work while my ears were strained to
catch the sounds occasionally filtering down from
the upper floor. Sometimes I could hear muffled
cries; once I was aware of a continuous gabbling.
Was Mary in a fever? Then would come an outburst
from my father muffled by the dividing walls but
sounding to me like the declaiming of a tipsy man.
And whispered colloquies between my father and the
old woman outside the surgery door.

At last, on the evening of the second day, I
returned from school to find a new-comer in the
hall. I recognized him as another doctor, a Dr Sims
who practised in our district. He was standing with
my father by the surgery door and the two seemed to
be engaged in a furious argument. My father looked
horribly pale and I thought, at the first glance,
that he had been drinking. When he caught sight of
me he drew Dr Sims into the surgery and slammed the
door; and the argument seemed to break out afresh.
As I passed into the sitting-room I heard Dr Sims
say: 'What do you expect me to do, eh? What can I
do?' And a muttered reply from my father. Then
something else from Dr Sims which I could not
catch, something about 'professional reputation to
consider'.

I left the sitting-room door ajar and sat down at

the table, trying to catch some more. But in a few
minutes the door was pushed open and the old woman
came in carrying a tray; giving me a quick, furtive
look, she hastily set out my meal and left the room,
closing the door behind her. But as she passed out I
heard the surgery door open and my father and Dr
Sims come into the hall. '— if she does,' I heard the
latter say, 'you'll be finished. And not only
finished —' The rest of the sentence was cut off by
the closing of the sitting-room door. A few moments
later the hall door slammed and then, quite loudly,
came my father's voice: 'Oh my God! Oh my God!' The
surgery door banged.

After gobbling down my tea I tried to fix my mind
on my home-work, but I do not know how I managed to
get through the evening. At about nine when I was
beginning to wonder whether I had not better go up
to bed, I heard the crunching of wheels outside the
house: I went to the window and peered through the
blinds. At that season of the year it was still light
enough for me to make out a kind of van standing
outside the house. The driver alighted and, coming
up our path, knocked at the door while another man
opened the back of the van and appeared to be
pulling something out.

I heard the old woman open the door and the
murmur of voices. Then my father's voice. The man
who had knocked returned to the van and assisted

the other in what he was doing. Then they both came up the garden path and I saw they were carrying a stretcher. Both men were wearing uniforms and peaked caps.

With a loud trampling everyone passed upstairs and there was an interval of silence. Then I caught the sound of the men's return, more slowly this time. One of them said: 'Mind the corner.' And then: 'Your end a bit higher. Steady. Steady. That's it.' By this time I had the sitting-room door ajar and was peering into the hall. I saw the uniformed men walk along the hall bearing the stretcher on which was a muffled figure I knew was Mary. My father and the old woman brought up the rear. As my father passed me he caught my eye, and I hastily retreated and closed the door.

Some time after the van had moved off the old woman came into the room and began to clear away the remains of my meal which had lain upon the table all through the evening.

'Ain't it time you went up to bed?' she said, curtly.

'Have they taken Mary to the hospital?' I asked.

'Yes, she's been took away,' the old woman replied.

'What's the matter with her?' I persisted.

'Nothin' you'd understand,' she said. 'You get up to bed.'

Although I was of an age to resent this old

woman's orders I saw no point in remaining up.
After a decent interval to show I was not to be
ordered about, I went to bed. And in spite of the
abnormal events of the evening and my general
bewilderment I fell asleep very quickly.

On the following morning I had no sight of my
father before leaving for school, and the only
evidence of his presence in the house at mid-day
when I came home for dinner was a low, continuous
muttering proceeding from the surgery as though he
were talking to himself. As I left the house to
return to school I saw Dr Sims coming down the road
and evidently making for our house and, acting upon
a sudden impulse, I stopped and raised my cap.

'If you please, how is Mary?' I asked him. 'I'm Dr
Carnac's son,' I added in case he should not know me
— though he evidently did.

He hesitated for a few moments, eyeing me
curiously. 'She's dead,' he said. And without another
word continued on his way.

I was so taken aback by this intelligence —
although I think I must have sub-consciously
expected it — that I hesitated as to whether I
should go to school or return home. Ultimately I
continued to school, for obviously there was
nothing I could do at home. I hardly think I felt
shocked at learning of Mary's death; my feeling was
more one of morbid excitement, for this was the

first time death had come within my personal
circle. And even that feeling was overlapped by
puzzlement regarding my father's position in the
affair. I had gathered enough during the past two
days to realize that the matter meant trouble of
some kind for him. His distress and the attitude of
the other doctor were, alone, enough to convey
that. But how could the death of a patient cause him
trouble? Other of his patients had died and nothing
had happened. Had he 'violated professional
etiquette', a term which, in the past, I had heard
him use and which I understood to mean taking
insufficient care of patients? Or had he made some
mistake in treating Mary? Given her poison by
mistake, or something like that?

The latter theory seemed the only one to meet the
case and, knowing my father as I did, it seemed not
improbable. Supposing my father had been drunk
when making up Mary's medicine, for example. And
had mixed poison with it. In that case would he be
'struck off the medical register' (another term I
had heard used) or would even worse befall? Would
he get sent to prison? What, exactly, did happen to
doctors who poisoned their patients by mistake – or
carelessness? (Incidentally, who would know if he
had been drunk when he mixed the medicine?)

And then my thoughts reverted to that other
matter which I had rather overlooked in the stress

of more recent events. I was not sufficiently innocent to be unable to realize pretty clearly how matters had stood between Mary and my father. And I now perceived that I had been sub-consciously feeling some sinister connection between that presumed relationship and Mary's death. Did I then get some faint glimmer of what that connection might be? After all these years it is difficult to say.

And then I displayed my first piece of initiative in this affair. I went into a post-office near the school and made out a telegram to my mother: 'Come home at once.' I knew the address at Peckham and fortunately had some money in my pocket.

Not only was I late for afternoon school, but I was kept in for inattention during the lessons.

Chapter 6.

My mother returned home on the following day soon after noon, the cab in which she had driven from the station arriving at the house just as I reached it after morning school. Hastily paying the cabman my mother, carrying a bag, followed me up the path to the street door. 'What's the matter, James?' she asked, fumbling for her latch-key. 'Why did your father send that telegram?'

'I sent it,' I replied. My mother paused with the latch-key in her hand. 'Is anything the matter with your father?' she asked breathlessly. At that moment we both caught sight of my father's white face peering out of the surgery window and, simultaneously, the street door was opened by the old woman. My mother stared at her in surprise. 'Who are you?' she enquired.

'Mrs Mahon's me name, mum,' said the old woman.

'And what are you doing here?'

'Come inside, mother,' I cried, before the old woman could reply. 'I'll tell you all about it.'

Reluctantly she followed me into the sitting-room; the old woman hovered on the threshold.

'Mother, Mary's dead,' I blurted out.

'Mary dead!' cried my mother, incredulously. 'Dead? When did she die?'

'Yesterday, I think,' I faltered, uncertainly.

'But — but I don't understand,' said my mother. 'Dead? What did she die of?'

'I don't know,' I admitted, glancing towards the old woman upon whose face I observed a sly smile.

'What did she die of?' my mother demanded of the woman.

'Better ask the doctor,' said the woman, jerking her head towards the surgery door. And with that she shuffled off down the passage. My mother made a move towards the surgery.

'Wait a minute, mother,' I stayed her. She turned and looked at me. 'Mother —' I hesitated, 'there's something awful been going on. Father's in some awful trouble. It's been — awful.' I could not think of another adjective.

Before my mother could reply to this the surgery door opened and my father came out. We both stared at him aghast as he stood on the threshold. His face was a horrible pasty white and behind his spectacles his eyes were red and bloodshot as though he had been either drinking or crying. He had not shaved and his chin was covered by a glistening stubble, while his clothes were all creased and untidy.

'John!' my mother cried. 'What's all this? What is the matter?'

My father licked his lips in a curious way and I saw the Adam's apple in his throat jerking up and down.

'That girl Mary's been getting into trouble,' he said.

'Trouble?' my mother murmured. 'What sort of trouble? James here says she's dead.'

'The usual sort of trouble,' my father replied. 'Some man —' He moved back into the surgery and, with a quick glance at me, my mother followed him into the room. The door closed.

For some time I heard the murmur of voices. I looked at the clock; no one seemed to realize that I wanted my dinner.

The rumble of voices went on and on until, finding it was nearly time for me to return to school, I foraged in the sideboard and found some cake and biscuits. I sat at the table munching, with the door open, and presently Mrs Mahon appeared in the passage, dressed for the street in a mantle and grotesque bonnet, and carrying under her arm a bundle wrapped in newspaper.

'I'm off,' she said to me. 'Tell the doctor I want my wages.'

'Tell him yourself,' I replied rudely.

She glowered at me and then turned to knock on the surgery door, which I could see from my position; but on the instant of knocking the door was flung open and my mother came out. One glance at her face showed me that she was more bewildered than anything else. She ignored the old woman and came to me in the sitting-room.

'There's something I don't understand about all this, James,' she said in a low voice. 'I can't get anything out of your father; he's been drinking again. I'm going along to the hospital. You had better get back to school. Have you had anything to eat?'

I reassured her on that point, wondering what lies my father had told her. Could she be so stupid as to have no suspicions regarding him? It seemed inconceivable; and yet I could not see suspicion or alarm in her face, but only perplexity. For I knew now — or thought I knew — what had happened to Mary. The phrase about 'trouble' uttered by my father had enlightened me. I knew what a girl being 'in trouble' meant. I also knew that in such circumstances things sometimes 'went wrong'; and I had read in newspapers of girls in trouble throwing themselves in the river or taking poison. I felt

quite grown up and manly beside my helpless-
looking mother.

I accompanied her out of the house, and as I
closed the street door I heard Mrs Mahon's voice
from the surgery: 'Yes, that's my wages all right.
And is that all I gets?' My mother caught the words
too, and made a half movement to return. But
yielding to the pressure of my arm she passed on
down the path and into the road.

'Why don't you go and see Dr Sims?' I asked her.
'He's nearest.'

While she pondered this suggestion I caught sight
of a policeman slowly pacing the street on the side
opposite our house. I knew the policeman well, for a
few weeks earlier he had chased me over the fields
for some distance for helping myself to a piece of
wood from one of the building plots. But it was not
that fact which made me look at him so closely now,
but the realization that he had been walking up and
down our street ever since I returned from school. I
had noticed him when I came home, and again from
the sitting-room window. The sight filled me with
disquiet. Could he be watching the house in case my
father tried to escape? My theory that my father
had in some way put himself on the wrong side of the
law returned in full force.

'I think I will see Dr Sims,' I heard my mother
saying. 'As your father called him in to a

74

consultation he may be able to tell me something.'

She left me a few minutes later and I saw her walking in the direction of Clyde Circus. But instead of continuing down Philip Lane towards the High Road, as I should have done, I paused at the corner to take another look at the constable. He had proceeded some distance past our house, and as I watched him he turned and began to return. Then I saw old Mrs Mahon coming out of our gate, and as she came in my direction I turned the corner and hurried away to school.

I left school as usual at four and hurried home at full speed in my anxiety – or excitement – to learn what had happened during my absence. And when I reached our house I saw immediately that something had happened, for the door stood ajar and a policeman was standing on the doorstep as though on guard. I hesitated at the gate and then hurried up the path towards him.

'What's the matter?' I asked, breathlessly.

'Who are you?' he countered.

'I'm Carnac; Dr Carnac's son,' I told him.

His manner changed on the instant. He gave me a curious look and then slipped into the house, leaving me on the step, for I felt too apprehensive to follow him. He was back in a few moments with another policeman – a sergeant. 'You're Master

Carnac, are you, sir?' said the latter. I nodded. He pushed up his helmet and thoughtfully scratched his head. 'Well, sir,' he went on, after a pause. 'I'm very sorry to have to tell you there's been an accident.'

'An accident?' I stammered.

'Yes, an accident. Now don't take on, sir —'

At that moment the door was again pushed open and an inspector stepped out. I vaguely wondered how many more policemen there were in the house.

'The son, sir,' I heard the sergeant whisper behind his hand.

'Well, my boy, I'm afraid we've got a shock for you,' said the inspector. 'I suppose you've just come back from school? Well, I'm sorry to say your father's had an accident while you've been away. And your mother too.'

'What sort of accident?' I faltered. Though I knew instinctively what he meant.

'Now take it easy, my boy. How old are you?'

'Nearly eighteen,' I replied. Adding in a burst of irritation: 'I'm not a kid.'

The inspector hesitated for a moment or two and then said kindly: 'Well, sir, I suppose I had better tell you at once: they're both dead. Your father and your mother.'

Without more ado I moved towards the door and began to push by him. 'Here, wait a minute, my boy,' he said, laying a detaining hand on my arm. 'I don't know whether we ought to let you in. It's — well, it's not a nice sight.'

I do not think that I then felt any particular grief at the news I had heard, but I was consumed by an overpowering curiosity to see whatever was to be seen inside the house. At the same time I felt dazed in the sense that I seemed to be moving in a dreamlike state, and I was filled by an unreasoning resentment at the kindly intervention of the police inspector. 'I'm going in,' I said bluntly. 'I live there, don't I?'

At that moment the street door was again opened and another man looked out; a civilian this time. He was a stranger to me, but I gathered later that he was a doctor — presumably the police surgeon. He had evidently overheard my conversation with the inspector for in response to an enquiring glance from the latter he muttered: 'Better let him in,' and something about 'identification'. So they flung the door wide and led the way inside, the doctor in front and the inspector walking beside me and holding my arm as though he feared I might collapse. On the threshold of the surgery we halted.

On the floor lay what appeared to be two wax-work figures bearing a curious resemblance to my father and mother. That suggestion of a wax-work

was the first impression conveyed to me, the figures
were so motionless and their faces had taken on the
colour and texture of yellowish wax. Round the
front of each throat was a gaping red cut and the
front of my mother's dress and my father's collar
and shirt-front were soaked in blood. The figures
lay close together and between them and,
apparently beneath them, was a lake of blood. I had
never seen so much blood before and gazed
fascinated at the dark red mass on the yellow
oilcloth. By the side of my father lay an instrument
which I recognized immediately — one of his large
scalpels.

I do not know how long I should have remained
there staring had not the inspector jerked my arm
and drawn me back into the hall. I looked at him
and saw that he had gone quite pale; I felt a mild
surprise. A police inspector to go white at the sight
of blood! He led me into the sitting-room and pushed
me into an arm-chair (he seemed to have the idea
that I was an invalid) and then, turning to a
decanter of brandy on the sideboard, poured some
into a tumbler and offered it to me. I was surprised,
for I felt no need of brandy; still I took the glass
and sipped the contents. The brandy burned my
throat and my eyes filled with tears. The
inspector evidently misread this latter occurrence
for he leant down and patted my arm in a

fatherly way. 'You'd better have some too,' I said.

He grinned in a sickly way and helped himself to a drink. With the glass in his hand he sat in a chair facing me and, after taking one or two sips and contemplating me for a short time, said: 'Now, my boy, do you feel like answering a question or two? I suppose that was your father and mother?'

'Yes,' I agreed. And took another sip of the burning fluid.

'And when did you see them last — before this, I mean?'

'About a quarter to two,' I told him.

'What were they doing? Having a quarrel or anything like that?'

'No, not exactly. At least —' I hesitated, 'I don't think so. They may have had one. My father was in the surgery — had been in the surgery with my mother — Oh, I don't know. He was there when I left. My mother came out with me; she was going to see Dr Sims.'

'Oh, going to see Dr Sims? You didn't leave them together then?' He thought for a few moments. 'Got any relations?' he asked.

'I've got an uncle and aunt living at Peckham,' I told him. 'At least — my aunt's ill with cancer; but there's my uncle —'

Just then the door burst open and in came our next-door neighbour, a Mr Everett. He was, in fact,

one of the neighbours who had lent his assistance
on the night of the furniture smashing to which I
have alluded.

'My poor boy!' he cried. 'This is terrible!
Terrible! I am sorry! He'd better come in with us,
Inspector. He can't stop here.'

'No, sir, he can't stop here,' the inspector agreed,
looking somewhat relieved. 'If you wouldn't mind
taking charge of him for the time – He tells me he
has an uncle over the other side of London. I'm
going to send for him at once.'

'Come along, lad, come along,' said Mr Everett.
'It's a terrible thing to happen. You must try to
bear up. We are sorry.' And to an undertone of
sympathetic exclamations he led me next door where
his wife was waiting, white-faced, in the hall.

And then under the sympathetic demonstrations
of these kindly people I suddenly broke out into
loud blubberings.

On the following morning a constable arrived and,
telling me he was the coroner's officer, drew out of
me by kindly but persistent questioning the whole
story of the curious doings preceding the tragedy.
He wrote it all down in a large note-book and then
made out a slip of paper which he handed to me
explaining that it was a subpoena for the inquest.
Mrs Everett, who was present at the interview,

promised to accompany me on that occasion.

'There is nothing to be nervous about,' the officer told me as he left. 'All you'll have to do will be to tell the coroner just what you've told me. He's a very nice gentleman; he won't worry you at all.'

Later in the day my uncle arrived from Peckham.

Chapter 7.

My uncle, Mr Charlie Evans, was a man well over
fifty years of age, short, inclined to stoutness, and
with a red, jolly-looking face framed in grey chin-
whiskers. His clothes were of a 'sporting cut', light
in colour and completed by a red and yellow check
waistcoat across which was slung a heavy gold
watch-chain. A diamond ring glittered on his left
hand and as he entered Mr Everett's sitting-room he
carried in his hand a light grey billicock hat.
Leaving home in a fluster on the receipt of the
police message, he had overlooked the unsuitability
of his dress for the occasion; but realizing his
negligence on reaching Town he had partly remedied
it by purchasing a large black silk cravat which he
now wore hastily tied and embellished by a gold
horse-shoe-shaped tie-pin set slightly askew.

He was excited and grieved by the tragedy, and
kept shaking my hand and patting my shoulder the
while he fired a long series of questions at Mrs

Everett, her replies to which he punctuated by deep sighs and head-shakings. 'Poor things!' he would say, every few minutes. 'Poor things!'

When I ventured to enquire after my aunt's illness he told me she seemed a trifle better 'in herself' but that there was a nurse in charge; and in the meantime I was not to worry because he was going to see me through this terrible business. As we sat down to tea Mr Everett returned home and was introduced to my uncle; and after a repetition of the manifestations of sympathy, Mrs Everett kindly suggested that Mr Evans might care to stay there until after the inquest. To which he gratefully agreed. And since he had come away from home quite unprovided with necessities, he took me along to the High Road that evening and made various purchases. These included, I remember, a black overcoat (which fitted him very badly), in order partly to conceal his light clothing at the inquest, and a black hat. He also bought me a ready-made black suit and black tie; these things, he thought, 'would do until after the inquest'.

The inquest was fixed for the following morning, and my uncle and I set out immediately after breakfast accompanied by Mrs Everett who, although relieved of her responsibility towards myself by the presence of my uncle, desired to

attend the proceedings. The news of the double
tragedy had evidently become known for a small
crowd of sightseers had gathered in the road, and a
youngish man with a note-book pushed forward and
accosted us as we left the house; but my uncle
elbowed him aside and led me quickly out of the
road. I cannot recall exactly where the inquest
took place for I was slightly dazed by the whole
affair; but I think it must have been in the
neighbourhood of the High Road for I recollect
my uncle stopping at the juncture of Philip Lane
and the High Road and commenting upon the
old pump which stands there. However, I know
it was a large, white-washed room having the
appearance of a school-room; I remember it seemed
full of people and that several policemen without
their helmets were loitering about near the
door.

I cannot pretend to give full details of the
inquest; I can remember only isolated details. I
know I felt slightly disappointed at the lack of
that formality and dignity which I had expected. I
had anticipated that the coroner would be wearing
a white wig like a judge, but he was quite an
ordinary-looking man in everyday clothes while
the jury, instead of being packed in a jury box, were
seated on two rows of wooden chairs behind a long
table. They looked very awkward and embarrassed

and seemed hardly to know what to do with their arms; most of them ultimately settled down with their arms folded.

We were given chairs near the same table, at the head of which sat the coroner, and I recognized near us old Mrs Mahon and Dr Sims. Between them and ourselves was an old couple of a countrified appearance clothed in mourning who, I discovered later, were the parents of our girl Mary.

I was not allowed to remain in the room during the whole of the proceedings. I was called to the table, given a small, black book to hold in my hand and asked to read aloud the words of the oath which were printed on a card pinned to the table before me. Then the coroner asked me a few questions. He seemed to have before him the whole of the story which I had already told to his officer, for he went through this bit by bit following with his finger the lines of what I took to be a written statement of my information upon sheets of paper. Every time he looked up at me I would agree to what he had said with a timid 'Yes'. It was not a bit like the giving of evidence as I had anticipated it. After the coroner had finished with me and Dr Sims had been called, my uncle tip-toed up to the coroner and whispered with him for a few minutes; I suppose the subject of the conversation was the propriety of my remaining to hear all the evidence, for presently my uncle

returned and told me we would go out for a bit and
return later.

I resented this strongly, but had no option but to
get up and follow him out. We went for a walk down
the High Road past my school and the old alms
houses, and round by Bruce Castle. My uncle
chattered all the time; he was trying to keep my
mind off a subject which my mind simply would not
keep off. Useless for him to talk about my school,
and the new steam trams, and John Gilpin and King
Bruce, when my mind was entirely occupied by the
visual impression of two wax-work figures with red
ribbons round their throats and a pool of blood
between them. I had thought about those figures all
night, tossing from side to side, with hot eyes and a
dry throat, in the strange bed provided for me by
Mrs Everett. 'Thought' is, perhaps, hardly the
correct word; the scene had been actually before
me, sometimes as I had observed it, sometimes, when
I sank into a doze, hideously distorted, the faces
twisting and mouthing, the blood spreading, rising
and whirling, and half-recognized figures groping
and pawing.

My uncle consulted a large, gold watch at
intervals and finally, thinking sufficient time
had elapsed, escorted me back to the place of the
inquest. We did not return to our original seats,
but stood in the doorway, for the coroner was

speaking, evidently framing in legal form the
verdict upon which the jury had just decided. I
gathered that Mary had 'died as a result of an
illegal operation performed by John Carnac' and
that this amounted to manslaughter against 'the
said John Carnac'; I learned also that my father had
been a murderer. He had murdered my mother and
then committed suicide 'while of unsound mind'.

Dr Sims came up to us after the proceedings had
closed and introduced himself to my uncle. He
seemed greatly shocked by the whole affair and
muttered with my uncle for some time. Then the
coroner's officer came to us and drew my uncle away
to the coroner's table where I saw that some kind of
paper was being prepared; this was handed to my
uncle who, after some further conversation with
the coroner, returned to me, took my arm and led me
from the building.

'Why did they say that Father was of unsound
mind?' I asked him, when we arrived at the street.
'Did they mean he was mad?'

My uncle explained that if there was any doubt a
jury always added that clause 'of unsound mind'.
'Then the poor chap can be buried in consecrated
ground,' he added. And went on to tell me that in
olden times a suicide was buried at the cross-roads
with a stake through his chest. I wondered whether,
had that saving clause not been inserted, they

would have so buried my father. And which cross-
roads would have been chosen. And who would have
driven the stake in; and whether they would have
left the end sticking up through the ground so that
people should know a suicide was buried there.

Some instinct deterred me from asking my uncle
exactly what an 'illegal operation' was; I knew it
was something shameful, not to be talked about. It
was a long time before I understood fully what the
term meant.

My parents were buried on the day following the
inquest, and in the evening my uncle took me home
with him to Peckham.

Chapter 8.

I now entered what I may call the second period of my life and I embark upon a description of it with extreme diffidence for I am called upon to deal not with a series of events so much as the development of a state of mind. No; I will be modern, I will call it a complex. And in writing about this period I am very conscious of my literary inefficiency. I am no Bennett or Dreiser to do justice to this time so barren of physical event and yet so fruitful in its purely psychic trend.

As I have said, immediately after the tragic end of my parents I went to live with my uncle at Peckham. His wife, my mother's sister, was then extremely ill; she was confined to her bed-room and a nurse was in constant attendance. It says much for my uncle's kindliness that in spite of the anxiety and distress occasioned him by his wife's painful illness he did everything possible to settle me comfortably in this new home, and to palliate what he supposed to be despondency over the loss of my parents.

In point of fact he not unnaturally misinterpreted my mood. I had received a shock, but I was not 'shocked' in the sense that term is usually meant to imply; that is to say I was not over-whelmed with grief at my loss. I missed my parents, just as I should have missed the sudden withdrawal of anything — animate or inanimate — with which I had always been familiar, but I do not believe I was suffering actual sorrow. Was I a callous young beast, or had I never cherished any real affection for my parents? I prefer to think that contemplation of the peculiar circumstances of their death swamped in my mind the feeling of sorrow at their death. And when I sat silent over the fire in my uncle's parlour, an unregarded book upon my knees, I was not thinking 'I shall never see them again' but 'What did my father feel like when he cut my mother's throat?' I was wondering whether the scalpel went in easily; whether human flesh cuts like cooked meat under the carving-knife or whether it is softer in its yielding. Whether the blood spurts out violently when a throat is cut, or whether it wells and trickles. And in the midst of these and similar thoughts I would be suddenly conscious of my uncle's hand patting my knee, and would make a show of returning to my book.

My uncle spent most of his evenings sitting opposite me beside the fireplace, puffing steadily at a meerschaum pipe, with an eye on me and an ear cocked for any sounds filtering down from his wife's room overhead. He read nothing but the newspaper although he possessed quite a number of books. I often wondered in what frame of mind he acquired them; probably he regarded books as dressings or embellishments to the furniture.

At the time of which I write my uncle was an elderly man on the verge of retirement, and he seemed content with little companionship other than my own. This may seem strange in a man of my uncle's trade, for the 'sporting man' is usually supposed to enjoy a large circle of acquaintances by the very nature of his interests. My uncle may, or may not, have had such a circle, but during my residence with him very few business friends were invited to the house. He kept his business interests and his private life distinct and separate. It is possible and, I think, probable that I was, to some extent at least, responsible for this. From the first he made it quite clear that he did not wish me to have anything to do with his business or to take any interest in it. 'I've not done so badly out of racing,' he told me, 'but it's a mug's game and I want you to steer clear of betting and gambling. You see, Jim, I know something about it.' He never allowed me to accompany him to race-meetings, and only on rare occasions had I been to the little office in which he employed a wizened man who acted as his clerk and, I gathered, went with him to meetings.

My first month with my uncle was a sombre and slightly nightmarish time. I was brooding, thinking and dreaming: I do not mean day-dreaming, but dreaming in my sleep. I cannot profess to recall the details, I only know that they oppressed me with a repetition and development of my thoughts of the day. And a benevolent and all-seeing Providence was seeing fit to torture my aunt to death with cancer while my uncle could do nothing but sit hopelessly by.

He and I took occasional walks to Greenwich and Blackheath, I glum and silent, he chatty with a spurious and pathetic cheerfulness. Then one day he asked me, with some diffidence, whether I would care to go to the theatre; I think he felt it was a trifle soon after my parents' deaths. But I assented readily to the suggestion. We went to Town and saw William Terriss in a dramatization of 'The Vicar of Wakefield'. (It was, I think, that actor's first big part and, as it happened, I was also present many years later on the occasion of his last performance, in 'Secret Service', at the conclusion of which he was stabbed on leaving the stage-door of the

Adelphi Theatre in Maiden Lane.)

My uncle, it appeared, was passionately fond of
the theatre, but this, alas, was his last treat for
some time to come. For on our return to Peckham
after the performance we learned that his wife had
died during our absence. The poor old chap bitterly
reproached himself for not having been with her at
the end.

I am becoming more and more sensible that this is
going to be a tragic book. In all great tragedies
like 'Hamlet' and 'Punch and Judy', most of the
characters are killed off before the fall of the
curtain. But I have already killed off most of my
characters before getting to the events which
justify the narrative. I am left only with my uncle,
and I must make the most of him and my thoughts and
emotions in an effort to bridge the passage of time
from my nineteenth birthday to that time when his
turn-down collar — no, I must not prematurely
refer to that collar — when I fled from his house.

After my aunt's death we moved to a smaller house
at New Cross. My uncle felt he could no longer bear
to remain on the scene of his wife's sufferings, and
he bought a squarish, stuccoed house which
appealed to his fancy not far from New Cross
Station. It had, I remember, a square portico
flanked by two round pillars of dubious

composition and approached by a short flight of
steps. Although a double-fronted house it was
deceptive as regards size; the two living-rooms were
of moderate dimensions, but the other rooms were
quite small. The portico to which I have alluded
formed a kind of miniature verandah which could be
approached from the window of either of the two
front bed-rooms − approached, that is, by anyone
with a mentality curious enough to prompt him to go
there; for it was dirty and offered no advantages
when attained. I hardly think anyone can ever have
sat there to take the air for it would have been
difficult to get a chair there, and the good-sized
garden at the rear of the house was a far pleasanter
resting place. But I mention this verandah because
I found a use for it − on one occasion.

Of the two bed-rooms referred to I occupied one,
my uncle the other. There were two other bed-rooms
in the house; one was given to the housekeeper whom
my uncle engaged, the other was used for the storage
of trunks, boxes and the miscellaneous rubbish
which every householder contrives to accumulate.

My bed-room was well and solidly furnished by my
uncle from the effects which he had removed from
Peckham, and to this furnishing I added the large
selection of books which had once belonged to my
father. I also had his microscope and his set of
scalpels − including the scalpel, which had been

politely returned, cleaned, after the inquest on my parents. My uncle was averse to my keeping this thing; he wished me to break the set by disposing of the instrument of tragedy.

Looking back on that time I realize that my uncle was, in his way, an excellent old fellow; he had many good qualities. This reference may seem lacking in the extreme cordiality on my part which may be expected, for he was kindness itself to me and I have every reason to feel grateful to him. But he had one bad fault, a fault which in him and in other people had been — and always will be — a source of almost excruciating irritation to me. He was a dirty feeder. He made a god of his stomach and the rites with which he carried out his worship were of the beastliest description.

Every meal was, to me, an ordeal and I marvel that I managed to conceal my irritation. At breakfast-time he devoured large quantities of toast. He was passionately fond of toast, but not the toast of the ordinary Christian feeder. He liked his toast very thick (it always looked to me nearly two inches thick), the crust toasted to the consistency of hard stone, and the whole soaked in and dripping with butter. This toast he would attack in the manner characteristic of his attack upon most food; taking up his knife he would raise his elbow to the

level of his shoulder and force his knife-blade into
the toast with, apparently, all the effort of which
he was capable. Meat he divided in the same way with
evidence of extreme force, so that the gratings and
squeakings which his knife made upon his plate kept
my teeth perpetually on edge throughout a meal.
The toast, suitably divided, he conveyed in dripping
lumps to his mouth and, when that organ had been
adequately packed, he would commence to talk. He
always filled his mouth before opening up a
conversation, and in talking he had a habit of
leaning over the table towards me, one fist holding
a knife in a vertical position, and dribbles of fluid
butter falling over his chin.

Whenever I hear a reference to a person 'enjoying
his food' my mind leaps back instantly to the
thought of my uncle eating toast.

Dinner was an even worse ordeal than breakfast
for it lasted longer. My uncle attacked each course
vigorously and with the entire abandon of an
animal, guzzling, grinding away at his plate,
slapping his lips and talking throughout with his
mouth full. And, a meal finished, it would linger
in his memory for hours. Quite late in the
afternoon (we dined at mid-day at that period),
when he and I were sitting over the fire, or walking
together if the weather happened to be fine, he
would suddenly say, apropos of nothing at all: 'That

was a lovely bit of pork we had, lad!' And he would smack his lips reminiscently.

It may be thought strange that I should dwell upon this relatively trivial matter of my uncle's gluttonous table habits; but to me the matter was not trivial. I am one of those people who cannot tolerate the sounds and sights attendant upon careless eating; to this day I have become no more tolerant in that connection. I am not alone in that prejudice; was it not Byron who stated that he could not bear to see food pass the lips of the most beautiful woman? And, generally speaking, I have decided that the table manners prevalent amongst the lower-middle-classes in this country are extremely objectionable. Carelessness in eating is, I think, even more general to-day than it was at the time of my youth; or does it seem so on account of the more general habit of eating in public? I do not mean only the legitimate eating in 'popular' restaurants, but the constant mastication of sweets in which women indulge everywhere. Nowadays one of my pet amusements, the cinema, in the artistic and technical side of which I take great interest, is impaired by the inseparable sweet-eating of the female portion of the audience. I cannot enjoy a good German film without being incessantly annoyed by the noisy chewing of adjacent women.

But I am falling into a weakness of old age; I am wandering. Let me return to my life with my gross-feeding uncle.

Chapter 9.

When I had been living with my uncle for some time
he suddenly decided, after scrutinizing me one
morning, that it was about time I began to shave.
And I was forced to agree with him. My hair was
dark, and a noticeable fluffy down was appearing
on my jaws.

My uncle said he would buy me a razor. 'Do you
think you can use it without cutting your throat?'
he asked, jocularly; and then pulled his face
straight with a jerk. The old chap evidently
remembered the tactlessness of referring to throat-
cutting. I thought I could manage the operation of
shaving without accident, but in order to 'see how it
was done' it was decided that my first shave should
be conducted by a professional, and I paid a visit to
a neighbouring barber.

I think it was on first handling the razor
presented to me by my uncle that I realized the
existence of a curious feeling which had been

growing upon me for some time in connection with knives. How can I possibly explain that feeling? It was not a fear of knives; it was more nearly an attraction. I had a special sensitiveness to knives which I had not for any other inanimate objects. Let me put it in the form of an analogy. I believe that a man in the early stages of locomotor ataxia is conscious to an exaggerated extent of the effort necessary in walking. I do not mean simply that he finds it difficult to use his legs, but simply that he is conscious of using them. The normal person walks with sub-conscious action; the man suffering from a disease such as I have mentioned exercises, and knows that he is exercising, definite mental effort in using his legs. He is conscious of them.

So, although I laced my boots, used a pen, combed my hair without any but a sub-conscious regard for the laces, the pen or the comb, as soon as I took a knife into my hand I became definitely aware of the properties and uses of a knife. It was something special, something with the attributes of novelty without being novel, something distinct from anything else which I handled. I fear I cannot hope to make this feeling clear; the person oppressed by some special fear — such as a fear of cats or thunder-storms — may possibly comprehend me, the person with normal reactions probably will not.

When I handled my new razor and commenced, with

some hesitation, to shave myself, I realized that the feeling, which I have tried to indicate, had been steadily growing in me, and the discovery set me thinking. I tried to analyse it. I decided, at once, that I was not afraid of knives in the sense that I feared I might cut myself; I applied my razor to my cheek without any sense of apprehension whatever. Nevertheless it was the cutting properties of the razor which gave it distinction, and it was the fact that the razor possessed greater efficiency in its cutting properties than a table-knife or a pen-knife which had suddenly brought home to me the appreciation of my special 'sense' for cutting edges generally.

Once I had perceived this curious 'sense' for knives – or, perhaps, 'fascination' will more clearly express my sensations – I began to watch it. I became increasingly aware of my feeling whenever I picked up my knife at the table; I handled it as I might have handled some rare and precious object; I fondled the handle and looked (I may say almost lovingly) at the sleek shininess of the blade and the thread of special brightness running along the edge. (Though our table-knives were usually deficient in sharpness owing to my uncle's plate-sawing habit.) And then came my second realization. For in watching with disgust my uncle's feeding I became aware that what appealed to me about knives

was not only that they would cut, but what they
would cut. And the association of that cutting —
the flowing of blood. Whenever my uncle introduced
a portion of food into his mouth on the tip of his
knife, I paused in my own eating, furtively
watching for the slitting of his mouth. When, using
his knife as a squeejee, he scraped up a mass of
thick gravy and tossed it into his mouth, I waited
expectantly for the sudden cry and the gushing of
blood. But it never came; long practice had made my
uncle dexterous. He always succeeded in
withdrawing the knife without accident.

I think it was this fascination of knives which
clinched my decision to embrace my father's
profession. I had no desire to doctor mumps or
measles nor, I will admit, any wish to alleviate
human suffering. But I wanted to dissect. I wanted
to cut flesh, not cooked meat but human flesh. How
ghoulish it must seem, set down in black and white.

Soon after we moved into the New Cross house I
learned from my uncle that the sum of money which
my father had inherited from his aunt — but the
bulk of which he had never handled — would descend
to me. My uncle took up my financial affairs
energetically, and he and I had several interviews
with a firm of solicitors who were dealing with the
estate. My uncle, upon the information he received,

estimated that I could rely on an income of about
two-hundred and fifty pounds a year and his
estimate subsequently proved to be fairly accurate.
My uncle, by the way, had been nominated by my
father as the sole executor of his will.

I have forgotten exactly what arrangement was
come to in the matter of my inheritance; whether my
uncle was appointed my trustee either by the terms
of my father's will or by the courts, or whether he
simply 'minded' my money. I do remember that he
allowed me very lavish pocket money and that it was
an understood thing that when occasion arose for
my use of any larger sum the money was available
for me.

After my parents' deaths I did not return to
school; my uncle was no believer in 'book-learning'
and in those days a high degree of education was not
considered so essential as it is to-day. But my uncle
held very strongly the opinion that, in spite of the
fact that I had an independent income, I should
embrace some calling. He had a great contempt for
what he called 'idle young loafers' and suggested to
me that as the means were available I should
qualify in some 'respectable profession'. He was
aware of my passion for drawing, but he viewed it
indulgently as a rather childish pastime and could
not be made to accept it as a definite occupation. He
was of the opinion that I could not do better than

enter my father's profession, and as I could not think of anything else and was, as I have previously indicated, biased by certain feelings, I agreed that my uncle might make enquiries as to the procedure of learning to be a doctor. I was somewhat dismayed to learn, as a result of the enquiries, that I should have to commit myself to a course of study covering five years before I could qualify; but still, that study promised to be interesting. I fell in with my uncle's scheme if not with absolute enthusiasm, at least with a certain pleasurable anticipation, and so the thing was settled. I succeeded in passing the preliminary examination required, and was duly entered at a London medical school which there is no need for me to specifically mention.

I continued to live with my uncle, but in view of the fact that my new life of studentship would necessarily be accompanied by a freedom to which, up to that time, I had been unaccustomed, my uncle took an opportunity on the eve of the commencement of my studies to favour me with a few words of advice. Even after the lapse of time I can almost recall his exact words. 'Now, Jim, my boy,' he said, 'I know a youngster don't take no notice of an old man's advice, but I'm going to say it for all that. I reckon you'll have your fling like every other lad, and by all I hear medical students are a pretty wild lot. But go easy on the cards and the women. Playing cards for money is about the silliest way of wasting time I know of; as for women, well you're old enough now to know what's what and if you don't you soon will know it. But be careful and don't make a damned fool of yourself. For one thing don't begin to think of getting tied up to some young woman by marrying her. A young man married is a young man marred. And above all, my boy — while we're on the subject — do be careful. Many a youngster's been ruined for life by catching something; you'll soon learn all about that as you're going to be a doctor. But remember, Jim, if you do get into any sort of trouble you've got an old uncle to come to; and that old uncle ain't a canting saint.'

I have thought that fathers might do worse than give similar advice to their sons. And shall I be thought unduly cynical in saying that it has afforded me a certain amount of satisfaction to know that I have always observed my uncle's advice on the matter of cards?

It would be unprofitable, and would occupy too much time, for me to set down here the details of my daily life in London at that period; that life was the life of the average medical student and can have but little interest for the reader in comparison with the details of my later activities, an account of which is, after all, the main justification for this book.

I could write much on the subject of the dissecting-room, that rather uncanny, vault-like room where the 'subjects' were raised out of 'pickle' by means of a kind of ship's tackle; of old Henry, the red-headed demonstrator with his wart-covered hands. Of the Hunterian museum with its pickled specimens in their large jars of spirit — a museum which, being unavailable to the ordinary sightseer, might form the subject of quite an interesting description. That museum I know well, and I recall that after my first visit to it my stomach experienced certain qualms on perceiving the nature of the meal prepared for me upon my return home. It consisted of pork-chops; white meat. Perhaps only a person who has visited the museum will appreciate the niceties of this point.

Practical anatomy which I took up in due course was, of all my studies, the branch which interested me the most. There is something fascinating to me in the very feel of the flesh under the razor-like edge of the scalpel; it cuts almost like cold ham. And the process of methodically taking to bits a human member, such as an arm, I found extraordinarily engrossing. Of course, we students were not given each an entire carcass on which to operate; 'subjects' could not be purchased by the score. We had to content ourselves with an arm, a leg or, in partnership, a trunk. And a certain drawback, to my mind, lay in the absence of blood.

When, later on in my course, I attended the operating theatre to see my first operation, I was one of the few younger students who was not, judging by observation, afflicted with nausea.

Chapter 10.

In reading what I have so far written I am appalled
by the relatively small amount of ground I have
covered; I am becoming increasingly aware of my
insufficiency as a writer. When I began this
autobiography I had no intention of involving
myself in the compilation of several volumes of
reminiscences, and it is evident that unless I can
curb my tendency to dwell in detail upon what I
regard as the more interesting events of my early
career — which is probably a manifestation of the
tendency to verbosity usual in a person of my years
— I shall never maintain the energy to complete
this record. I must therefore refrain from a
detailed account of my life at the medical school
and the few friends I made there — which would be,
after all, irrelevant — and press on with my
story.

  I did not qualify as a doctor, for I did not
complete my course of studies. Circumstances (I

cannot think of a better word) conspired against me; and when I say circumstances I am thinking of one particular event which, in itself, was almost laughingly trivial. My uncle suddenly decided to shave off his whiskers.

As I have already mentioned, my uncle's red and jolly-looking face was framed in a fringe of grey chin-whiskers of the kind vulgarly known as 'nitties' or, to make it plainer to the present generation, the kind of whiskers with which Dan'l Peggotty is represented in illustrations to 'David Copperfield'. When my uncle removed his whiskers he revealed an expanse of smooth, shining throat. It was not the kind of throat usually seen in the elderly, when the flesh, having lost its elasticity, exhibits sagging folds; it was like a roll of stretched fat, bladder-like or resembling in its sleek surface a large, flat goitre.

I was curiously disturbed when I first saw this exposed throat and without offering any exposition of self-analysis I may say at once that it fascinated me to such an extent that I experienced a sudden desire to cut it.

Now I am not so foolish as to suppose that my reaction in this matter was normal; I am quite prepared to admit that in certain ways my mentality is abnormal. But the difference between the person who, say, holds an unreasoning aversion

to cats, and the person with an inclination to pass
a razor across a temptingly bladder-like throat is
a difference only of degree. The first is not
regarded as insane even by the most narrow-minded;
why then should the second? The incipient throat-
cutter may be homicidal, but he is not necessarily a
maniac for on all other matters of daily
comportment he may be rigidly conventional. The
fact of the matter is that the popular conception of
insanity is graded according to the danger involved
to the community. The abnormal person who is
unable to resist the temptation to possess himself
or herself of another person's property is not
called a lunatic but a kleptomaniac — a sort of
half-way to lunacy. When apprehended the
kleptomaniac is accommodated with a seat in the
dock and fined a trifling amount, but is not sent to
an asylum. But the person labouring under an
apparently unreasonable urge to cut throats is, in
the popular view, a maniac; for a human life is held
to be of more value to the possessor than his watch.
But note well, you writers of encyclopaedias, that
the difference is one only of degree.

When I first became conscious of my feelings in
the matter of my uncle's throat they had not grown
beyond a vague curiosity and itch as to the
sensations to be derived — perhaps I should say the
satisfaction to be derived — from such an

enterprise. I did not feel immediately that I must cut his throat; my mind merely toyed with the idea. But even if I made any serious endeavour to dismiss the idea I did not succeed, for that fascinating throat was always before me. Particularly at meal-times was my attention directed to the object of my thoughts, for in the process of gobbling and guzzling my uncle contrived, in some indescribable way, to exhibit his throat. I could not avoid looking at it. And mixed up with my vague inclinations was my intense feeling of irritation at his table-manners, which developed into the realization that if I should actually cut his throat that irritation would cease.

At the same time I do not wish to convey the idea that my inclination was tinged with resentment towards my uncle. On the contrary, when the inclination grew into an urgent desire with which I had seriously to cope, I mastered it for some time by opposing the thought of my uncle's excellence of character. I knew, and I told myself over and over again, and thoroughly realized, that I had no grievance against my uncle — apart from his table-habits. I had a great regard for him; he had been kind and generous; we were great friends. No; there was no question of my wishing to kill my uncle for motives of dislike or revenge. I merely felt that keen desire to cut his throat as a fascinating experiment because his throat was of a kind to affect me in that way.

Students of Edgar Allan Poe will be familiar with the tale 'The Tell Tale Heart' in which a somewhat similar urge is portrayed. In that case it was an old man's eye of a peculiar character which led to a development of homicidal tendency in the imaginary narrator. But there the parallel ends, for Poe's 'subject' was, on his own showing, a lunatic. For, quite apart from his desire to kill the old man, he was unbalanced in every respect and, as shown in his behaviour towards the investigators, quite incompetent to conduct his own affairs. I never stood for hours during the night on the threshold of my uncle's room focusing a single ray from a dark lantern upon my uncle's throat; I never lost sight of the fact that in the event of my succumbing to the temptation which assailed me I should be placing myself within the vengeance of the law. I knew, and did not shirk the fact, that throat-cutting is not a permissible enterprise; that if I did actually cut my uncle's throat one night as he lay in bed I should, if caught, be undoubtedly hanged.

I admit that for a time I toyed with the idea that it was possible for me to cut that throat and escape detection, but common sense convinced me that even were the police not so omniscient as they were generally supposed to be, the fact that I was the person in closest contact with my uncle would arouse a certain suspicion in the dullest mind.

I remember very vividly how I wrestled with my strange inclination. Night after night I would lie sleepless upon my bed, tossing about in a hot, feverish condition, to fall asleep in the small hours of the morning into dreams in which the principal object of my oppression was a large, sleek, shining throat which gaped redly — like two other throats which I had seen.

The crisis came at last on one night after weeks of troubled thought. I arose from my bed at about two in the morning unreasoningly intent upon carrying out my project. The desire to cut that throat had suddenly become so over-whelming as to swamp entirely all thoughts of risk to myself and all recollections of kindness received from the old chap sleeping in the adjoining room. In a kind of unthinking deliberation I lit a candle and exchanged my night-shirt for my day-clothes. Although I say I was unthinking, I was obsessed by an adventurous expectation; a rather pleasant sensation of anticipation which was accompanied by a definite physical feeling, which it is almost impossible to describe, in the region of the solar plexus. I was in no hurry; I prolonged this sensation deliberately by dressing fully, even to my tie. But I finally drew around my neck a dark muffler, and put on my felt slippers.

Then I went to the chest of drawers and brought from beneath a pile of clothing where it had lain my father's large scalpel. It glistened in the candle-light and I examined the edge; my desire received a fresh impetus as I realized (from memories of my hospital dissection) the feeling of satisfaction which would accrue as that keen edge sunk into the fat, shiny roll of my sleeping uncle's throat. I blew out the candle and opened my window.

As I have previously mentioned, the verandah-like portico outside the house was approachable from my own as well as from my uncle's room. I stepped out on to it and crept softly to my uncle's window which, as I had supposed, was slightly open, for the time was midsummer. I made haste, for already there was a slight lightness in the sky and, in spite of my dark clothes, I feared that I might be seen if a policeman happened to be passing near. Softly raising the window sash I dropped into my uncle's room.

For some minutes I stood in darkness, but as my eyes became accustomed to the light, I was able to make out my uncle's bed and his form upon it. He was grossly snoring with a blowing, rattling sound. I stood beside him and looked down in the gloom.

But I could not see him clearly; the night was too

dark. And I felt my deed would lack satisfaction unless I could see as well as feel my scalpel penetrating the goitre-like surface. A candle stood beside my uncle's bed and, feeling around this, my hand encountered a box of matches; I resolved to light the candle for even if this awoke him I needed but a fraction of time for one slash of my blade. Very cautiously I fumbled the match-box open and, striking a light, applied it to the wick of the candle. In the instant during which the wax around the wick melted and the light of the candle grew bright, the snoring abruptly ceased and, turning again to my uncle, I perceived that his eyes were wide open.

I think that the ensuing moment was the most dramatic I have experienced, not excluding, even, the phases of my later exploits. I stood looking down at my uncle, the scalpel poised at the level of my breast; he gazed fixedly up into my face. Our faces were hardly a yard apart. His first expression was one of extraordinary amazement, and this changed briefly into horror as he evidently read my purpose in my eyes; for my face, as well as his own, was in the full light of the bed-side candle. He uttered no sound, but lay and stared up at my face.

Had that expression of horror lingered, or had it changed to definite fear, I think I should have

thrust my scalpel into the fat throat which lay
exposed above the bed-clothes; but it was gone in an
instant giving place to another which strangely
stayed my hand. I can describe it no more clearly
than by saying it resembled that of an affectionate
dog who has suddenly received an unexpected and
undeserved kick from his master. It was surprised,
pleading, altogether pathetic. Beneath that gaze
the hand holding my blade slowly sank; and then I
took a stumbling step backwards. My uncle's
unblinking eyes were still fixed upon my own and,
unable to bear that reproachful scrutiny, I
suddenly bent forward and blew out the candle, and
stumbled towards the window. As I climbed through
it I heard a low, shuddering sigh from the direction
of the bed.

When I regained my own room I was trembling and
covered in a cold perspiration. I leant against the
chest of drawers and, allowing the scalpel to slip
from my grasp, wiped my clammy hands on the sides
of my coat. I stood there for an appreciable
interval, gathering together my scattered wits and
listening intently. But not a sound came to me from
the room I had left. From the death-like silence I
might have supposed that the deed had been
actually done, my failure and retreat no more than
a dream. The thought flashed across my muddled
mind that the whole thing might have been a dream.

Had I really crept into that room with the deliberate intent of cutting my benefactor's throat?

But, standing there with an unaccustomed icy feeling at the back of my skull, I knew it was not a dream. My obsession had at last mastered me, and I perceived clearly that but one course was open to me — instant flight. Whether that course was dictated by my realized inability to face my uncle again, or whether I felt I was fleeing from my obsession, I do not know. But hastily and feverishly I lit my candle and began to thrust a few belongings into a leather bag which I dragged from beneath my bed. And as I fumbled I still strained my ears for any sound proceeding from my uncle's room. I expected a sudden outcry, a hammering upon my door; was my uncle too amazed, too overcome by the revelation to move? Was he supposing he had dreamed? I did not know.

Within a space of a few minutes I had packed my bag, thrust within it the scalpel which I perceived lying upon the floor, and again climbed through the window. In what must have been almost a panic I slid and scrambled down the pillar of the portico, letting the bag drop before me. And then, with one glance towards my uncle's dark window, I began to run.

The streets were quite deserted, and the eastern sky was flushing red with the promise of dawn.

Chapter 11.

I had walked, I suppose, over a mile before I began to
think coherently; I say 'walked' but my progress must
have been more in the nature of a blind rush
unconscious of direction. I had no thought but to get
away from the vicinity of my uncle's house.

I have a dim recollection that the aching of my arm
as a result of the bag I carried was the thing which
ultimately dragged me back to reality. I know that I
stayed my footsteps and leant against some railings.
And then I gave way to uncontrollable laughter; I had
suddenly seen the funny side of my adventure.

The remembrance of my uncle's face no longer
struck me as pathetic, but as grotesque. He must have
had the surprise of his life. And he was probably
still lying in bed waiting for morning in a state of
funk, watching the window and wondering whether my
head would suddenly appear round it. (Unless, of
course, he had heard the sounds of my departure.) And
all the time he was lying there sweating, afraid to

move, I was a mile or more away. I was still chuckling over this when I perceived in the distance a figure approaching and, picking up my bag, I resumed my journey. The figure was that of an early workman, and he gave me and my bag a curious glance as he passed.

I was now sufficiently controlled to observe my surroundings and to think sensibly. I saw I had been walking towards London, and as this seemed as good a place to make for as any other I had no reason to alter my direction. But as I went I pondered my future movements, and it occurred to me to examine my financial resources. Placing my bag on the pavement I examined the pocket book which, luckily, I had left in my coat pocket over-night. I knew there was a five-pound note there, but I wanted to confirm this. My trouser-pockets yielded nothing, for it had been my habit to fold my trousers each night upon retiring and to hang them over a chair-back; and this necessitated emptying the pockets. But a waistcoat-pocket contained, I found, half a sovereign.

I was not dismayed by my shortage of ready cash, for I had a banking account at a Town branch of my uncle's bank – more convenient to me by reason of my days spent in Town than a suburban branch would have been – and I knew that over fifty pounds lay to my credit. I had left my cheque-book behind, but I could easily obtain a fresh one and there seemed no reason why I should be unable to draw against my account. I felt quite confident that my uncle would take no steps against me, and, after all, what had I done which could not be explained as a joke?

It then occurred to me that I might very well return home, but on thinking this over I perceived that such a course would be impossible. Primarily it would be difficult for my uncle and myself to live comfortably together in the future; he would almost certainly regard me with a feeling of suspicion. Such a feeling is unavoidable between two persons, one of whom has betrayed a desire to cut the throat of the other. And it was highly probable that my uncle would suspect an outbreak of insanity on my part and insist on having me 'seen to' by doctors. But the factor which finally decided me against a return home was the realization that were I to do so I should, sooner or later, cut my uncle's throat. I knew instinctively that I could no longer live with that sleek, goitre-like throat. In this particular matter I could no longer rely upon my strength to withstand temptation.

And, on the whole, I was not sorry to enter upon a period of absolute freedom. I was tired of my medical studies, which had lost their first novelty, and although nothing more than a merely conventional restraint had ever been exercised over me by my uncle I had not, in the past, experienced the sense of absolute freedom which I now did — the knowledge that I could do absolutely whatever I pleased without question from any person.

That afternoon I deposited my bag at a small London hotel, but I did not spend the night there. I slept in the bed of a young person I encountered in Shaftesbury Avenue.

Having definitely decided not to return to my uncle's house, or to my medical studies, I took two rooms in a street off Tottenham Court Road. The district was then a sordid one, but my particular street consisted largely of houses which had not long since been in the occupation of 'gentlefolks' and had not yet fallen into actual degradation. Most of them were tenanted by women who let rooms to young men of the student class; my landlady's name was Mrs Brooks and my two rooms were on the first floor of her house. Mrs Brooks was a kindly and rather casual old soul with a tippling husband who was employed in some minor capacity at the Olympic Theatre in Wych Street.

Within a week of settling in these rooms I received, through my bankers, a letter from my uncle. He begged me to return home and he wrote in terms of sorrow but with no word of reproach. 'I found this,' he wrote, 'with your poor father's papers. I was not going to let you see it, but as things are I think you had better know. I am afraid it is in your blood, my poor boy, but do come and talk things over.' He concluded with a

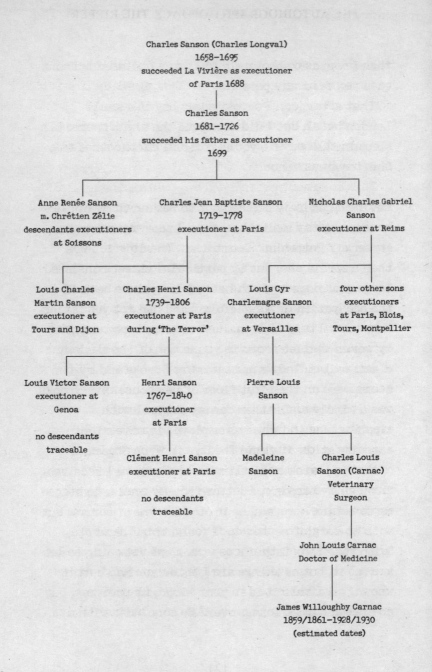

Charles Sanson (Charles Longval)
1658–1695
succeeded La Vivière as executioner
of Paris 1688

Charles Sanson
1681–1726
succeeded his father as executioner
1699

Anne Renée Sanson
m. Chrétien Zélie
descendants executioners
at Soissons

Charles Jean Baptiste Sanson
1719–1778
executioner at Paris

Nicholas Charles Gabriel
Sanson
executioner at Reims

Louis Charles
Martin Sanson
executioner at
Tours and Dijon

Charles Henri Sanson
1739–1806
executioner at Paris
during 'The Terror'

Louis Cyr
Charlemagne Sanson
executioner
at Versailles

four other sons
executioners
at Paris, Blois,
Tours, Montpellier

Louis Victor Sanson
executioner at
Genoa

no descendants
traceable

Henri Sanson
1767–1840
executioner
at Paris

Clément Henri Sanson
executioner at Paris

no descendants
traceable

Pierre Louis
Sanson

Madeleine
Sanson

Charles Louis
Sanson (Carnac)
Veterinary
Surgeon

John Louis Carnac
Doctor of Medicine

James Willoughby Carnac
1859/1861–1928/1930
(estimated dates)

vague hope as to the possibility of a doctor being able to 'do something' and with a further pleading to me to come home.

'This' was a document in my father's handwriting in the form of a genealogical tree and I reproduce it here as it was set out.

This document astonished me, containing as it did information at which my father had never even hinted. I was also rather pleasantly excited to learn of my descent from such a famous – or should I say infamous? – family; but at the same time I experienced a vague uneasiness. I perceived the drift of my uncle's remarks; he supposed I had an hereditary taint. Ever since he had discovered the document he had doubtless suspected the possibility of such a taint and he must have regarded the homicidal outbreak of my father as tending to confirm his suspicion. Had the poor old chap been even waiting in dread for some similar manifestation of abnormality on my part? I felt pretty certain that he had. In a flash of imaginative insight I experienced a real sympathy for my uncle.

In the light of this document I could fully understand what my uncle's point of view may have been, but I resisted the lurking suspicion that he was right. I tried to laugh it away as being too grotesque for serious consideration. Within limits I was prepared to admit that my reactions to certain phenomena, such as the shedding of blood, were peculiar; that there might be a connection between those peculiarities and the fact that I came of a long line of executioners and torturers I perceived as a possibility. But I was not prepared to subscribe to the doctrine of heredity beyond a certain point. Never, I told myself, would I believe that I, the master of my own actions, the author of my individual feelings and emotions, was a mere puppet manipulated by the dead hands of my ancestors. The idea, I rammed into myself, was preposterous. I refused to entertain it. Why, the alleged genealogical tree might even be a work of imagination on the part of my father.

I may say that in later years I made the half-hearted attempt to confirm that tree. Owing to the difficulty of conducting my researches, which involved reference to documents lodged in a foreign country, I did not get very far; but I must confess I was unable to discover any discrepancies in my father's document. Up to a point, at least, it seemed perfectly correct.

After some hesitation I replied to my uncle's letter, for it seemed callous to ignore it entirely. I was fully conscious of his past kindness to me, but I realized with absolute conviction the unwisdom of attempting to live again within the very circle of temptation. So my reply was evasive and concerned mainly with thanks to him for his care and kindness.

I never saw him again and he died two years later.

Part 11

Chapter 12.

In the summer of the year 1888 I was living in rooms
in Henrietta Street, Covent Garden. I shall not
mention the number of the house, but it is one on
the right-hand side as one walks towards the
Market. My landlady was an elderly widow, rather
stout, very talkative, but a kindly and motherly
soul. She kept my rooms spotlessly clean; mainly by
her personal efforts, for although a young maid-of-
all-work lurked somewhere in the lower recesses of
the building her contact with the 'gentlemen' (i.e. I
and my fellow lodger) was limited to the carrying
of coals, water-jugs and heavy trays, and the
cleaning and returning of boots. Mrs D., my
landlady, dusted, made my bed and carried in and
arranged my meals.

Of her two lodgers I was, I think, regarded by Mrs
D. with the most consideration, for I was
financially independent; and the moneyed drone is
always, in this world, treated with more respect

than the worker. In the popular view the possession
of money would seem to postulate intrinsic merit in
the possessor. I had inherited my uncle's savings
in addition to my father's money, and the combined
capital was, and is, sufficient to provide me with a
comfortable income.

Technically I was, I suppose, a drone, but my time
was fully occupied. I did not live the life of the
'young man about town'; I was neither dissipated nor
extravagant. Although a comparatively young man I
took little pleasure in the flippancies of youth; my
disposition was that of the student, and reading and
drawing were my principal interests.

I kept up my drawing. I have never had occasion
to practise as a professional artist and am quite
aware that such proficiency as I now possess is no
more than that of the average industrious amateur.
I am not even sure that the drawings I have made for
this book reach the standard of merit expected by a
publisher.

In pursuit of my hobby of drawing I explored
many parts of London and particularly the East
End. I was attracted by the grotesque and the
macabre, but never by the 'pretty-pretty'. I take
more pleasure in drawing a leprous, tumble-down
building enveloped in the sinister shadows of a
London slum than I do in depicting a sun-lit
haystack with cows in the foreground. Owing to the

impracticality of setting up an easel in a crowded East End street I had to learn to rely upon my memory assisted by rapid, rough jottings made on the spot, and to work out my actual drawings at home.

I grew thoroughly familiar with the East End of London; the grimy, dilapidated houses packed with grotesque caricatures of humanity seemed to hold a message for me and yet I could not interpret that message. Fantastic stirrings of what seemed a remote memory moved me as I loafed about brooding over these mucoid and decaying tenements; they recalled a vague familiarity as though in a remote and nearly forgotten past I had lived and wandered among them. Yet I seemed to recall that the houses had once been taller, more angular; leaning outwards and precariously balanced one against the other; fantastically lit by sharp, angular patches of bluish moonlight and yellow splashes from drunken-looking lamps suspended from the walls. And as I stood in a street letting my imagination – or memory – range about the scene before me, there would come to my ears the sound of muttering, gnomish voices with snatches of guttural song. Not the cockney and Yiddish intonations with which the street really resounded, but something stranger and even more foreign than those mixed dialects. And in the course of time one voice slowly developed and separated itself from the muttered unintelligibility until I began to recognize it above the undertones of my imagination and even above the actual, existing chatter and uproar of the Whitechapel streets.

Am I unwise in mentioning these curious imaginings of mine, and especially the Voice? Am I perhaps giving another fillip to the popular assumption of my lunacy? That the hearing of imaginary voices as a symptom of insanity is pretty generally recognized I am fully aware. But was Joan of Ark insane? Were the other saints insane? Confidence in my own sanity is strong enough to permit me to ignore popular conceptions of insanity and its symptoms.

I heard the Voice. But was it an actual voice speaking to me from outside the borders of this earthly life, or was it a phenomenon of a too-active imagination? After all these years I cannot say, for the Voice has long been silent and memories fade.

My taste in reading was 'morbid' by popular standards. I have always been interested in what is loosely called the occult, in which term I include witchcraft, sorcery, certain aspects of priestcraft, hypnotism and modern spiritualism. These things are usually regarded as trivially fantastic by the conventional stolid citizen, but as one who, in all modesty, can claim to be something of an authority I say that they are worthy of careful consideration if only as exemplifying that pitiful striving of humanity towards the favour of an assumed Power, which striving still goes on to-day in the unreasoning faith of dogmatic religionists.

During the period between my flight from the house of my uncle, and the time of which I now write, my strange obsession in the matter of knives had slumbered. Fitfully and uneasily, it is true; but still it had slumbered. By this I mean that although I was still conscious of an eager interest in knives, I had experienced no return of the over-whelming desire to demonstrate their properties; I began to regard the unfortunate affair which had terminated my connection with my uncle as an isolated manifestation of nervous instability following upon the shock and continued morbid brooding on the deaths of my parents. Nervous debility was not so well understood at that time as it is to-day and in the popular view 'nerves' was merely a synonym for hysterical cussedness. But my own medical knowledge and reading had shown me that nervous outbreaks may take strange forms. That I had been the victim of such an outburst I preferred to believe.

Yet there was no blinking the fact that knives were still to me something more than mere utensils for everyday use. They still fascinated me and occasional incidents would arise when I would become intensely aware of the fascination. On one morning, for example, I found two brand-new table-knives by my plate; my landlady had bought a new set to replace the old worn ones. I picked up those new knives and examined them critically; they were wretched-looking things, clean and bright, it is true, and with handles of ivory whiteness. But they were mere imitations beside the old friends to which I had become accustomed. The blades of the latter had been worn to thinness, with sharp, pointed tips and blades of razor-like keenness; what if the handles were yellow and stained, the blades gaping from the hafts and exposing parts of the tangs? I resented these new knives, and fumbled with my breakfast in a fit of irritation.

I did not care to complain to Mrs D. − or to ask for my old favourites; but I surreptitiously sharpened the new table-knives on a bone which I kept in my bed-room, and in the course of a few weeks I had all the blades of the good lady's new set in a fair state of keenness. Whether she noticed it or not I do not know.

But in spite of this, and other incidents pointing to my interest in knives I had not, since leaving my

uncle's house, experienced an impulse towards
throat-cutting; I had not experienced it, yet I am
not justified in saying that I had not, deep down, a
lurking suspicion that I might again experience it.
I think I had such a suspicion or at least an uneasy
feeling that under stress of excitement or shock my
reactions might take an abnormal course. I can
perceive now that, having that vague suspicion, I
should never have allowed full play to my feelings
for Julia Norcote; I should have known at least that
in some respects my temperament was – shall I say –
peculiar. But I look back at the affair with the
dispassionate eyes of an old man, while at the time
I was of an age when inclination is not readily
controlled by reason.

I met Julia Norcote in the early part of the year
1888. She was the sister of an old fellow-student of
my hospital days whom I re-encountered one night
at a London music hall. This meeting, trivial as it
seemed at the time, I place as a definite step
towards that which I was ultimately to become; in
the latter contemplation of these seemingly
purposeless and yet significant steps on life's
highway I am led into a sneaking sympathy with the
conviction of the professed fatalist. 'The fate of
every man have we hung about his neck,' says the
Koran; was my fate hung about my neck in earliest

135

childhood or even, perchance, years before my
conception – on the steps of the blood-stained
scaffolding of the Place de la Revolution or in some
gloomy vault beneath the Palais de Justice?

And if my course was mapped for me by 'Fate', who,
or what, is that Fate? Can it be anything but a
malevolent demon? And the Voice, to which I have
already lightly alluded but of which I shall
presently say more: was that the voice of an
attendant devil, the Kah, maybe, of one of my blood-
weary ancestors deputed to watch and guide me
along my appointed path? I am not, as the reader
may have already surmised, a religious man; I pay
no service to a benevolent Deity because I can
perceive nothing to justify a belief in the
benevolent supervision of mankind. But I can
perceive much which may be regarded as evidence of
the existence of an inimical power. The question is
one which must ever remain open, nor will I attempt
to pursue it at the moment.

Let me return to my meeting with John Norcote.
The music hall was, of course, of the type now
extinct. It boasted a chairman whom it was
considered an honour to ply with drink, and
members of the audience sat at marble-topped tables
moist and sometimes sloppy with spilt beer.
Perspiring waiters threaded their ways with
difficulty amongst the tables, balancing upon

upraised hands trays precariously laden with glasses. The table at which I seated myself on this evening had one other occupant, and we recognized each other simultaneously.

Norcote told me, after our first exchange of reminiscences, that he had taken his degree and was then in partnership with his father. He wanted to know why I had so suddenly dropped my studies and to satisfy his curiosity I told him of my accession to comfortable financial circumstances following the deaths of my father and my uncle. He was, of course, ignorant of the events which had led to my father's death, for of these I had never spoken to any of my associates; nor did I tell him anything of the circumstances now.

We left the music hall at an early hour, for Norcote, upon whom the dignity of his new profession seemed to weigh heavily, mentioned that he had only 'looked in for half an hour'. In deference also to his professional standing, we refrained from celebrating our meeting except with one modest glass of beer each, and we parted at the door of the theatre after an invitation on his part for me to visit the Norcote household.

I availed myself of the invitation and so met old Dr Norcote and Julia.

Of Dr Norcote I need say little; he was a big, red-faced man with a nearly bald head, and a pompous

manner which sometimes broke down into a rather
irritating facetiousness. I carried away from that
first visit only a vague picture of the doctor for
my attention had been too wholly taken up by his
daughter.

Julia struck me as an extraordinarily beautiful
girl; she was tall, well formed, and possessed a
mass of golden hair. I was, I think, slightly
embarrassed at first by this radiant vision, while
she was reserved and shy with me, having the
bashful unsophistication of the period; for there
was then none of the frank camaraderie which
prevails between the sexes to-day. Yet, disguise
and muffle it as you will, sex has always been sex
and always will be. In spite of our mutual
awkwardness there flashed between us a hint of a
telepathic message; she sensed my interest, I knew,
and she did not resent it. It seemed almost that
she reciprocated it; yet I was by no means an Adonis,
for I was short, sallow-skinned and distinctly
fattish of face. Nor could she have been attracted
by any mental brilliance on my part for I was not
in a state to adequately display such wits as I
possessed.

When I left the Norcotes' house that evening I
knew I had fallen in love.

To the average reader there will doubtless appear
an element of horrid humour in the idea of 'Jack the

Ripper' being in love; for, as I have previously
hinted, there is some difficulty, no doubt, in
associating an unknown and rather fearful being
such as J.R. with the common reactions of ordinary
humanity. While admitting that J.R. was a man, the
average person cannot perceive (or so I judge from
reading and conversation) that the particular
activity which brought him under public notice was
a manifestation of but one unit in his mentality.
Love! What can a man who could cut up women know
of love!

Let me tell you, O reader, that as a younger man I
was quite as capable of love as you are; and possibly
more so. You may be, and probably are, one of those
conventional and 'respectable' individuals who, in
the mass, comprise the back-bone of the nation. It
is even possible that you are (pardon me if I am
wrong) one of the rabbit class: one of those smug
little clerks, creeping fussily to Town each
morning; plodding through your boring and
monotonous clerking, one eye on the clock and the
other on your superior officer; oppressed by fear —
fear of being late, fear of making mistakes, fear of
offending the chief your master; fear of losing
your job. Scurrying home to your rabbit-hutch of a
suburban house; pottering over your rotten little
'garden'. A product of fears, anxieties and
repressions. What can you know of love or, indeed,

of any human passion? Again I ask your pardon if I have misjudged you.

But I have known life. Even before I became a man I had known life. And I have known real fear; not the fear of a testy employer; not the 'fear of God' as you unctuously term it in your churches. But the fear of the intangible Unknown; the dreadful, hovering Something moulding my destiny, muttering at my elbow, malevolently distorting the trivial chances of my life. And I have known thrills such as you will never know.

My love affair progressed upon the lines which are usual, I presume, in most love affairs, and it is needless for me to tell of my courtship in detail even were I willing to do so; for it was only in its dreadful conclusion that it became remarkable.

After my introduction to the Norcote household I paid other visits at intervals of a fortnight or so; and then, encouraged by the increasing cordiality of my reception by Dr Norcote, who, I soon perceived, realized in which direction the wind lay, I began to call more frequently.

Discreetly, and in the most casual manner, old Dr Norcote drew from me particulars of my financial standing and since his friendliness to me showed no signs of abatement I gathered that he found my position satisfactory. He asked after my parents and

140

I told him simply that they had died when I was eighteen; naturally I made no mention of the manner of their passing.

Of Julia herself I will say little; I do not care to recall the little mannerisms, the tricks of speech and gesture, the trivial incidents which endeared her to me. Even after the passage of so many years the memory of them is tinged with bitterness. Is it better to have loved and lost than never to have loved at all? No; I dispute that old adage. A thousand times better had I never met my love.

Poor Julia! Did you mourn your sallow, black-haired James for long? Did you, through the years, sometimes wonder regretfully what had become of him; whether he still lived? Were you ever told why the happiness you expected was so suddenly wrenched from you? That you no longer live, I know, but did you die a wife or a grandmother perhaps, the palimpsest of your first love affair almost obliterated by later joys? That you did love me I know; I hope you loved again; I hope my 'poor Julia!' is needless.

My courtship reached its crisis in the later days of July, 1888. I had arranged to take my Julia to the theatre, with the tacit approval of her father and, after a careful examination of the bills of fare offered by the various houses, had booked two stalls for an entertainment which, I thought, would contain nothing likely to offend the susceptibilities of a lady. To the modern mind such delicacy on my part will doubtless seem grotesque.

I dressed myself that evening with the greatest care; I examined myself from several angles in my inadequate bed-room mirror. I split my gloves in pulling them on to my perspiring hands and tingled with anxiety in case I should be late while my good landlady hastily stitched the tears. For the prospect before me that evening was not only a visit to the theatre, but a proposal; and though I had little doubt of the outcome I could not wholly restrain my nervousness.

I have no recollection of the play I witnessed that evening.

After the theatre I took Julia home in a hansom, my declaration not yet made. I might have proposed in the hansom, but by the time I had made up my mind to do so we had arrived at Julia's house. I asked permission to come in as I had 'something to say', and Julia, with an air of being entirely unsuspicious of what that something might be, allowed me to do so.

I left the house just before mid-night an engaged man.

Chapter 13.

I should prefer not to write this chapter; its composition recalls too vividly that which I would rather forget. But it is essential to my narrative and I cannot omit it.

De Quincey remarks, in one of his essays, upon the difficulty of a man's assignment of any particular day as the happiest in his life; and goes on to point out that if any such day could be specified the event which distinguished it must necessarily be of such an outstanding character as to illuminate many ensuing years. Of my own experience I can say that a day which contains such terror or misfortune that it may be set aside and distinguished as the most unhappy, the most horrible day of a man's life must, of equal necessity, cast a shadow upon many years to follow. The day after my acceptance to Julia was such a day.

It would be more correct to say the evening following, for the day itself opened well enough. I

143

had had an uneasy night, for having retired in a condition of nervous excitement I was unable to sleep until about four in the morning. I lay turning over in my mind the events of the evening; pondering the best form of words to employ when approaching Julia's father next day. And from these two sets of thoughts which alternated in my mind like two recurring units of a roundabout I suddenly took to a side track. I began to envisage my future; to speculate upon that life which lay before me. I pictured the house I would like to occupy with Julia; how we would furnish it; I deliberately projected my mind into a future which I desired. And then some detail which I pictured would, by an association of ideas, recall to me some event of my past. My mind would be wrenched out of the delightful future where it had been dwelling to something dull and forbidding which I would strive to dismiss.

But those thoughts could not be wholly dismissed; my wandering and now somewhat feverish thoughts took another turn; I commenced to toy with certain doubts which I had, in the sanity of day-time, thrust from me but which now, in the soul-searching darkness of night, could not be so readily ignored. A certain Voice gradually grew into my consciousness, insistent and disturbing. It spoke colloquially and in a logical manner of things which I did not wish to discuss; it broke in upon my thoughts like the voice of a garrulous travelling companion upon the thread of a book which one is trying to read. I told myself the Voice was purely imaginative; that my mind was too active; but I listened and then tried to ignore what it had said.

When, eventually, I fell asleep I was visited by dreams of an extremely unpleasant character.

In the morning the sun was shining and I felt like a man who, having been constrained to spend the night in some foul den, cleanses himself by plunging into a cool, gleaming river. I put behind me all recollection of the vile night I had spent and passed into my sitting-room singing. (The term is a courtesy one for I am not far from being tone-deaf.) The sound brought an arch smile to the fat face of my good landlady as she entered with my breakfast. It was not a critical smile; rather one of indulgence and understanding. Had she not practically sped me on my wooing the evening before; and could she doubt now, from my caterwauling, that my enterprise had been successful?

At about mid-day the sun disappeared and it began to rain as it had rained almost incessantly for weeks. For that summer of 1888 was, I remember, a loathsome one. But even the rain could not

dissipate my feeling of gladness. I sat at my
sitting-room window and watched the downpour; and
thought. I did not leave the house until the
evening, when I set out for the house of Julia's
father.

I was nervous, I admit; for I could not avoid a
slight anxiety as to whether the Doctor would
consent to my formal engagement to his daughter. I
felt reasonably certain, from his past attitude to
me, that he would raise no objection, but I could
not fail to perceive the remote possibility for,
after all, my acquaintance with Julia had been
short. I had no suspicion of the blow that was to
fall upon me, no foreboding of the ghastly jest
which Destiny had prepared for me. I hurried along
the streaming streets humming cheerfully under my
breath, sheltering myself and a bouquet of roses
under my umbrella. I was contented with the world,
rain-sodden as it was. 'Happy' is purely a relative
term I know; but on that particular evening I was
happy as I had never been before; happier,
certainly, than I have ever been since.

It is from such elevated heights as these that
Destiny loves to dislodge us; our fall is so much
harder.

A smirking parlour-maid admitted me to Dr
Norcote's house and, in a few moments, I was

greeting Julia in a manner proper to the occasion.
Her father and brother were at a medical dinner I
learned; but I was quite content to await their
return. Julia and I sat together on a sofa in the
drawing-room.

I possess, to a high degree, the faculty of visual
recollection. My memories frequently take the form
of actual pictures in which I and my fellow-actors
move silently like the performers on a cinema
sheet. More especially is this the case when the
events have been of an outstanding character; I
then seem to have forgotten most of the
conversation; the auditory side of the memory seems
to have been ousted by the visual. So, on this
occasion, I can picture, quite clearly, the Norcotes'
drawing-room; I can recall little of what was said
between Julia and myself. The room was papered, I
remember, with a kind of silvery buff and much of
the wall-space was concealed by oils, water-
colours, photos and those little black silhouettes
which were once so common; all framed in gilt.
There was a certain amount of gilt, also, about the
furniture, but no definite style prevailed. There
were two fine Jacobean chairs; an ormolu cabinet
containing china and silver; an upright piano and a
harp (Julia had some skill with the latter
instrument); an inlaid satinwood side-table. And on
one wall was one of those round, gilt-framed convex

mirrors which reflected Julia and me as we sat upon a pale-blue upholstered settee. Our every movement was re-enacted there, our figures diminished to microscopic proportions and slightly distorted by the curvature of the glass. That bright-lit circle of glass was like a miniature marionette show. It fascinated me then, but now I can never see one of those convex mirrors without experiencing a shudder.

I was looking into that little mirror. I could see two doll-like forms, close together. Julia was, in fact, reclining against me, her head upon my shoulder. I could see in the glass the white gleam of her shoulders, for she was in evening dress. Then, as I gazed, the circle of glass suddenly darkened with a swirling movement as though its face had been obscured by a wreath of moving vapour. This smoke-like effect gradually coalesced and from it the wraith of a face appeared; it was like the gradual development of a photographic image on a modern 'negative'. In a moment the face had gone; almost before I had had time to analyse the sense of vague familiarity which the face engendered. It had gone, and the glass cleared, though only partially; through the vagueness one surface only gleamed with almost startling distinctness – the white of Julia's neck and shoulders. Then I felt myself go rigid, for I had perceived that round the white column of that neck ran a line of vivid scarlet, and that drops oozed and dripped from it to the white bosom beneath. And, in an instant, I was not horrified; I felt a wave of excitement, a sudden thirst. I turned from the miniature picture before me; moving my head slowly and almost furtively until my eyes rested upon the real neck beside me.

There was no thread of scarlet there, of course; but in my suddenly awaked imagination I saw it. That softly rounded mass was no longer the neck of my beloved, but a pillar of flesh pulsating with blood, an object of fascinating possibility. My hands trembled; I could feel the sensation of piercing and slitting that smooth surface with the razor-like edge of a scalpel; I could anticipate, with horrible relish, the gush of blood which would ensue.

Something wrenched my eyes from that tempting neck back to the mirror. It was now swirling and twisting again, but this time with a reddish tinge. The image of the neck could still be perceived, but the thread of red had now become a gushing fountain; it flooded the surface of the mirror as though it had been a horizontal object charged to overflowing with blood. Then drops began to creep over the frame and to drip steadily down the wall.

I stiffened and must, I think, have uttered a gasp. I seemed to hear a hoarse guttural sound, and the figure beside me straightened and Julia's face peered into mine. The lips moved but I do not know what she said. I saw a pair of large, dark eyes gazing into my own; they widened until a circle of white surrounded the irises. That expression of horror fanned my overmastering excitement; I cast a swift look around the room in search of a weapon – anything with a blade, a paper-knife, a curio. And, sub-consciously, one of my hands rose, the fingers crooked and twitching, towards Julia's throat.

At that moment the spell was broken. A sharp sound penetrated my consciousness; the slam of the street door. With a return to partial sanity I rose abruptly to my feet and took one or two staggering steps backwards, my face towards Julia. She was huddled back on the settee, staring at me, the back of one hand pressed against her mouth.

At the back of the settee was another mirror – a large, flat one; and in this was reflected the round convex glass with its miniature marionette show. I could see in this tiny circle the black-clad back of a standing figure, curiously humped and distorted by the curvature of the glass; as I retreated from the settee I was conscious, though my eyes were upon Julia's face, that the little black figure was growing into a bloated, fantastic shape until it filled the entire circle of the mirror.

Then I turned abruptly and rushed from the room.
I collided with Dr Norcote who had just reached the
threshold. He gripped me firmly by the shoulders
and stared down into my face which, owing to my
shorter stature, was considerably lower than his
own. Without speaking he held me for some moments
and in that brief time I was conscious of a vague
surprise that this face which looked into my own
was not the face of Dr Norcote to which I had been
accustomed. The rather stupidly pompous expression
had given way to one hard and forbidding.

He suddenly relaxed his hold and, as I staggered
back against the lintel of the door, I realized that
his hands had been almost supporting me. He stepped
into the drawing-room and looked fixedly towards
where I knew Julia still sat on the settee. Still he
said no word, and the only sound to be heard was the
grave tick, tick, of a grandfather clock which stood
near the street door.

Dr Norcote returned to the hall and closed the
door of the drawing-room behind him. He took his
stand directly before me, his legs slightly apart
and his thumbs resting in the pockets of his
waistcoat. 'I met an old colleague of your father's
this evening, young man,' he said. He spoke kindly,
but his face was still stern and cold. That brief
sentence and the manner in which it was uttered
told me that he had discovered who my father had

been and the whole hideous tragedy of my parents'
deaths. I had no need to hear more, for whatever he
was preparing to add to his remark had no
significance for me now. Something far more potent
than Dr Norcote's objections had stepped in to
render my marriage to Julia impossible.

I attempted to speak and found, to my surprise,
that my mouth and tongue were stiff and dry. I
raised a hand and made stabbing motions with my
finger towards the drawing-room and Julia. I do not
know what, exactly, I was trying to say, but I
desisted on seeing the strange expression upon the
doctor's face. It was a look of curiosity, of
scientific appraisal, like that of a man who is
examining for the first time some strange curiosity
of nature in which he is interested. That look
filled me with shame, but also with indignation. I
stepped backwards until my head bumped against the
edge of a heavy picture-frame. The jolt must have
imparted a slight motion to the picture, for Dr
Norcote momentarily turned his eyes from my face
to the wall behind me. That released a kind of spell
and I burst into a croaking laugh. Then, without
more ado, I turned to the hat-stand where hung my
hat, umbrella and light overcoat and, seizing these
articles, unlatched the street door. I turned for a
last look, and saw that the doctor still stood in the
same position regarding me; I stepped out of the

house and slammed the door loudly behind me. I was
met by a perfect hurricane of rain.

I can recollect standing on that step fumbling
with my coat and swearing at my own clumsiness. I
did not stop to button the coat, nor did I raise my
umbrella. I just staggered off into the rain, my
coat-tails flapping behind me.

It all sounds like a scene from a 'Surrey'
melodrama, I know.

The tiger had been sleeping. The tiger had only
been sleeping. I could never marry Julia; never
marry any woman. The tiger which lurked within me,
setting me apart from my fellows, would not allow
it. Fool, to suppose that I was like my fellows. The
affair of my uncle, my reaction to knives, many of
my thoughts and feelings should have shown me the
difference! 'The tiger awakes!' The phrase struck me
as absolutely fitting and appropriate. I culled it
over and over again, trying to fit it into the
rhythm of my splashing footsteps. The — tiger —
awakes — splash splash. The — splash — tiger —
splash — awakes — splash. No; that was too slow.
The tiger —

Plodding through the puddles I was still only
sub-consciously aware of the rain. I knew it was
raining, but no glimmer of common-sense prompted
me to guard against it by closing my coat or

unfurling my umbrella. In a few minutes my
trousers were soaked to the knees. A passing hansom
spattered my shirt-front with mud; I only cursed. I
had no thought of where I was going; what did it
matter now? I walked on, with long strides, my head
down, my coat flapping like the ragged feathers of
some black bird of prey. I passed a policeman in a
glistening cape, standing beneath an archway. He
stared at me owlishly as I swept by. On I went. Then
I gradually became aware of a woman's voice at my
elbow; some painted creature of the night, evidently
misinterpreting my condition as one of
drunkenness, had fastened upon me considering me
an easy prey. I caught a few words: 'Come on, dearie
– give me something, dearie – come along home with
me, dearie –' as she tried to suit her gait to my
swinging progress. At last her importunity annoyed
me; it did not fit in with my rhythmic phrase; it was
discordant. I turned on her with a snarl. 'If I come
home with you, dearie,' I muttered, 'I shall cut your
throat. Cut your throat. The tiger awakes; I shall
cut your throat.' I thrust my face into hers and saw,
in the uncertain light, how the rain had streaked
and raddled her paint. Her hat was a sodden mass,
and wisps of damp hair hung over her eyebrows. Her
sooty-rimmed eyes widened with fear as she caught
the gist of my muttering, and she stepped away from
me with a gasp. 'Cut your throat. Cut your throat.'

154

That phrase fitted in as well as the other. I repeated it to myself as I strode on.

I must have walked miles that night. What route I took I do not know, but after an interval of time which I cannot estimate, something familiar in my surroundings caught my attention. It was in the High Road, Tottenham. There was the old pump at the corner of Philip Lane. And somewhere about here the inquest had been held. The inquest on my parents. I stood on the kerb and looked around me. The rain-swept streets were empty of life except for a black cat which peered at me from beneath a litter of wooden boards stacked beside a gate.

'Philip Lane,' I said to myself. 'I used to live somewhere near here.' I tried to recall the name of the road, but could not. I only knew I must pass down Philip Lane to reach it, and a desire arose to see the old house. Did it look the same, I wondered, or had tragedy set some indefinable mark upon it? I turned to my left and set off down the Lane.

The cumulative recollections kept me going; each building and trivial landmark leapt to my memory as I encountered it, though my memory could not anticipate it. I found myself, at last, standing in the road immediately opposite my old home.

The windows were in absolute darkness, but the brick-work seemed to glisten, not only with the rain beating upon it but with a kind of inherent

phosphorescence, a faint greenish grey just
sufficient to render visible the details of its crude
and clumsy architecture. As I stood aimlessly in
the beating rain my brain began to lose some of the
numbness which had, up 'til then, oppressed it; the
sight of a once so familiar object as this house
stirred all sorts of childish recollections.
Trivialities which had seemed long since forgotten
now came trooping back from some dusty and
cobwebbed attic of my brain where they had been
lurking. A wave of melancholy oppressed me. I stood
in the wet puddles gently savouring this rather
novel sensation; it was quite different to the
feeling of blind fury and despair which had, up
until then, been my driving power. My resentment of
the injustice which Destiny had meted out to me, of
the knowledge that I was a pariah, had, so far, been
untinged with self-pity; but now I suddenly felt
extremely sorry for myself.

I continued staring at the house and I perceived
something which, at first, I had not realized. Its
aspect differed from the house I had known; in this
half light, with its greenish tinge and its
glistening sweat of rain, it appeared obscene,
indecent. It was like some disease-ridden hag who,
usually seen in the tawdry trappings of everyday
life, suddenly appears in hideous and eye-offending
nakedness. And while I was turning this thought

over in my mind I became conscious of a curious
phenomenon; how can I describe it? I can best say
that it consisted of an entire cessation of those
undercurrents of sound which are evident in even
the stillest night. Even in what we call the silence
of night there is no absolute silence. The faint
movements of unseen animals, the distant rumblings
of traffic, the hundred tiny and almost
imperceptible sounds which serve to indicate that
this is a live, though a sleeping world; even the
suggestion of rustling in trees and grass, all
combine into a muted suggestion of sound which
never ceases. But now it had ceased. Nothing, simply
nothing, came to my ears but the slight hiss and
splash of the rain. I felt as though I and the house
stood together in a vast, enclosing cavern which
had grown around and enveloped us.

I had barely analysed this sensation when the
street door of the house began to open very, very
slowly.

For hours, it seemed, that door stealthily moved,
a fraction of an inch at a time. The space of dirty-
looking blistered wood decreased and beside it grew
an ever widening oblong of black. The blackness of
the house's interior; that house where murder had
been done. I do not think I was so frightened as
fascinated; I knew that something would, at some
remote time, emerge, something probably horrible

and devastating to the sight. I waited, motionless in the cavernous stillness, for what that something would be. And at last it came. A feeble blotch of grey in the blackness of the open door gradually evolved into the figure of a man.

Once this form had become recognizable as a human semblance, the ordinary standard of time in relation to familiar movement resumed sway. The man stepped briskly over the threshold and stood on the step regarding me. I then saw, but with no feeling of surprise, that he was clothed in a tight-fitting suit of black; round his thin waist was strapped a thick belt from which hung a large knife in a black sheath, and upon his arm dangled a coil of rope. His crown was covered by a curious head-dress the nature of which I could not at the moment discern, and from under this hung straggling locks of long, black hair.

He moved towards me and, for an instant, I had the extraordinary feeling that, in spite of the dark hair, this was my father. I cannot explain this feeling except by saying that his face held a curious, unnameable resemblance; not a resemblance of feature, but one of expression. It suggested that likeness which is sometimes encountered in two people who, although physically unlike, have yet lived together for so long that their thoughts and feelings have merged into the same groove.

158

The figure came directly up to me and I then saw that his head-dress consisted of a leathern mask which had been raised above his forehead.

Chapter 14.

The man grasped me by the elbow and began
muttering to me, his face near my own and his mouth
twisted into a knowing grin. His expression was
neither malevolent nor altogether repulsive; it was
strangely suggestive of a man who is telling a dirty
story in a tap-room. And, underlying and belying
the grin, was a sadness; the eyes did not smile, they
were sad, weary but yet with a spark of recklessness
in their depths. They were the eyes of a man who
knows there is no God to lighten the tedium of his
days and who, for all his knowledge, does not care.

But what caused me the greatest astonishment was
his voice; I recognized it instantly. It was the Voice
to which I have previously alluded; the Voice which
had broken in upon my thoughts on several
occasions, in the snugness of my sitting-room, in
the slums of Whitechapel. And with recognition
came the speculation: was this my guardian angel or
— more likely — my guardian demon?

I cannot say what the figure spoke to me; I do not
mean that I cannot remember, but that I must not
say. I must not put the substance of his speech into
actual words; there are some things which cannot
be written. But as I listened I experienced a thrill
beside which all the thrills of my early life were
as nothing. New thoughts rushed over me; I tasted
them doubtfully and fearfully, but I did not thrust
them from me. I listened eagerly and when the
figure half turned and commenced to guide me
towards the house I made no attempt to resist his
pressure upon my arm. I followed him, engrossed
with a fascinating curiosity.

The house had increased enormously in size. The
tint of the walls had changed to a dark, greenish
black and in the interstices of the large stones,
which had once been shoddy bricks, fungoid growths
sprouted. The blistered paint of the door had gone;
the woodwork was black and cracked with age and
the massive planks which composed it were bound
together with broad ribbons and rivets of rusty
iron. I stepped over the slimy threshold, my
whispering guide beside me. There was what had been
my father's surgery but was now a well of blackness
in which could be heard the stealthy rustling of
unseen figures — unseen, that is, except for their
eyes, which glowed cat-like in the darkness but
without the cat's yellow brilliance. They were like

the phosphorescent eyes of dead and decaying men.

The stillness of the outside world was broken by a furtive whispering as we passed the open door and turned towards the stairs which had — ages ago, it now seemed — led to the cellar. And while I hesitated at the gaping doorway, feeling cautiously with my foot for the first downward-leading step, I caught from the depths a sound which drowned the whispering. It was a low, guttural moaning, almost an animal sound, a sound which some wild beast may be expected to utter as its life slowly ebbs away in pain and solitude.

Obeying the touch upon my arm I began to descend the stairs. They no longer creaked as I remembered they had creaked in the time of my boyhood, for now the cheap wooden boards had given place to stone slabs. They were hard to the tread; I could even feel their hardness though my feet were almost deadened by long walking and standing in the rain. I could sense the hardness, and I knew they were slimy and slippery. Very slowly and cautiously I proceeded, down flight after flight, winding and twisting into a blackness which presently began to give place to a suggestion of redness.

We emerged at last in a large cellar, feebly lit by several braziers of glowing coals; the atmosphere was misty with smoke and insufferably hot. The confines of the apartment were lost in the murky

THE AUTOBIOGRAPHY OF JACK THE RIPPER

shadows, but in the centre was an oasis of reddish
light in which stood a singular apparatus which
necessarily riveted my attention immediately I
entered the chamber. It was a large, vertical wheel
of wood and iron; almost, I might say, a double wheel
for the rim was perhaps a foot wide and was supported
by two sets of spokes. It was held between a pair of
strong uprights and from the hub on either side
projected an iron handle. Upon the upper
circumference of the wheel and occupying roughly a
third of that circumference was a still, white
figure bound down with blackened cords.

Obeying as much my own feeling of curiosity as my
guide's pressure upon my elbow, I approached the
wheel and its burden. The figure was that of a
woman twisted and, apparently, unconscious.
Several gaping wounds upon her person slowly oozed
blood which ran and dropped down her sides on to
the framework of the wheel. And then I perceived
that upon the floor beneath was clamped a kind of
adjustable slide bearing upon its upper face a set of
blood-stained triangular spikes.

My guide went to the wheel and, grasping the
woman's hair, pulled the head sideways towards him;
I uttered a quick gasp as I caught sight of the
expression upon the face thus brought into view. The
man in black released the hair and, putting out a
finger, tentatively poked the flesh of the shoulder.

He turned away with a shrug and, following the direction of his eyes, I perceived another figure.

Upon a low stool just within the circle of light cast by a brazier, sat a man in a black gown, his head covered by a flat, black cap terminating in a long scarf-like appendage which was wrapped about his throat. Before him, upon a grotesquely low desk, was an ink-horn and several sheets of parchment, and he was slowly and deliberately sharpening a quill pen. He looked up at my companion and me, and his mouth stretched into a grin which revealed toothless gums. Almost instantly the grin faded and his face assumed an expression of sanctimonious solemnity. That rapid change suggested to my mind a man who has recalled a joke in church and then suddenly recollected his position.

Note. At that time I had never seen a representation of the wheel which I describe, though I had read a brief and incomplete reference to such an instrument in Reade's 'The Cloister and the Hearth'. Some twelve or fifteen years later, however, I saw a model almost identical in its main structure at an exhibition at Earl's Court. Some readers may possibly recall a newspaper account of an affair which happened at that time; it was reported that two men connected with the exhibition quarrelled. One of these stunned his companion, removed the wax figure from the wheel and placed the man on it. Fortunately for the victim the model was not a workable one.

Attracted by a repetition of the moaning sounds which had reached my ears when descending the stairs, I now looked around the vault, trying to penetrate the darkness with eyes rendered more susceptible to it. I could perceive dimly several contorted forms and curious appliances around which moved gnomish figures; but I had no time to examine these things further, for my guide took my elbow and led me back up the stairs.

We passed into the cold freshness of the night and I took a deep breath of the moist air. It was still raining heavily but, far off on an unfamiliar skyline, I could see a dim streak of light suggestive of a clearing dawn. My companion grasped me affectionately by the arm and led me, at a rapid pace, across muddy fields.

The sound of breathing at my other elbow drew my attention and, looking sideways, I perceived a second man. He too was clothed in black, but his dress was of a different fashion. He wore a black shirt with wide sleeves and a black waistcoat descending nearly to his knees. His head was close cropped and the face was that of the first man. I turned my eyes from one to the other, examining each attentively, and then I realized the cause of that sense of familiarity of which I had previously been conscious when approached by the first man. Both faces were my own. It is true that both were thinner and older, but the likeness was, when once observed, unmistakable.

I had barely remarked this phenomenon when a third figure joined our party and, a few seconds later, a fourth. Then a fifth materialized from the darkness and I found myself walking in the midst of a group; and all those nightmare figures bore my own countenance.

The fashion of each man's dress varied, but all were black with the exception of that of the last comer. He was clothed in dingy red. His coat was cut away sharply to long tails, and its collar was absurdly large and high. Round his neck was a high stock of dirty white, and upon his long, greasy hair was set rakishly a triangular hat bearing a filthy tricolour cockade. I fixed the period of his costume immediately from recollections of David's paintings which I had seen in the Louvre.

So, surrounded by these solid and yet ghost-like forms, I tramped on and on towards that brightening ragged cleft of light on the horizon. We encountered, and paused a few seconds to examine, in the course of that walk almost every device for inflicting mutilation and death which relatively modern mankind has had the ingenuity to construct. That which I first supposed to be a line of telegraph poles resolved itself, as I looked

upwards, into a row of almost incredibly tall
gibbets from which hung ragged forms which swayed
in the wind creakily. A loathsome smell was borne
to my nostrils, and vast, black flapping shapes rose
from the gallows' heads and vanished, croaking,
into the darkness above. At the foot of one of the
gibbets squatted and crooned a bundle of wet rags;
it raised its head as we passed and I saw the face of
my old acquaintance Mrs Mahon.

We passed wheels raised upon high poles from
which hung tatters of flesh and flapping rags;
bones projected from them and large birds wheeled
above or settled upon the remains, pecking with
quick digging jerks of their bills. Many other
things we saw and then came, at last, to a ghostly
square in which stood a tall erection painted or
stained a dirty red. It looked like the elongated
lintel of a door which has been separated from its
surrounding walls, and between the uprights a
triangular silhouette rose and fell with the
unfailing regularity of an engine's piston. To my
ears came an alternate swish, thump; swish, thump;
and underlying the rhythm the low, scarcely
perceptible sound of singing.

I was suddenly alone. The guillotine had vanished,
as well as my companions. It was growing light and I
stood, soaked and shivering, in the middle of a

field. In my ears still rang the echo of a low,
guttural chuckling.

I looked around me, and there, but a short
distance away, was evidence of a roadway —
telegraph-poles, lamp-posts and, further on, a
group of houses. But I did not immediately move
towards these signs of civilization; I was muzzily
revisualizing the things which I had seen, and
groping for their import. As my brain cleared to
something like its normal coherence I perceived, in
a flash of insight, who and what I was. I was not the
descendant of hang-men and torturers; I had been,
in my own person, each of those hang-men and
torturers. I knew now, for a certainty, that life —
as we call it — does not begin with birth and end
with death; it goes on endlessly. There is no heaven
and no hell; no cessation from a long sequence of
one existence after another, pre-ordained and
inexorably directed. The fate of every man has,
indeed, been hung about his neck, but in the dim
remoteness of a past beyond our reckoning. And as
this truth (as I then supposed it to be) came home to
me I understood fully for the first time that which
I had before dimly suspected. Mankind was, indeed,
in the grip of a Power, but not a benevolent one;
rather was it devilish and remorseless. The horrors
and sufferings of humanity were now made plain; it
was fathered not by a benevolent Deity susceptible

to prayers, praise, tips of shrines and candles, and the smell of incense; but by the Powers of Darkness, implacable and probably satyric.

I raised my fists to the grey sky and cursed the Powers with every foul expression I could call to mind. And in that moment my experience moved from the plane of grotesque horror and despair to the realms of pure pantomime.

"Ere, you mustn't use that sort of language 'ere, sir,' said a voice. A policeman was standing beside me, and near him was a lamp-post. How I had reached the road I do not know. The appearance of this solid harlequinade-like constable arrested my rhetoric and I burst into a peal of laughter.

'I should get along 'ome if I was you, sir,' the officer continued, eyeing me unemotionally.

I took his advice and got along home; at least I set about that enterprise, for I had no idea of my whereabouts and did not think it discreet to enquire. The constable had already misinterpreted my emotion, I had no doubt.

I reached my lodgings at five that morning to the surprise of my landlady who assisted my dripping and staggering form up to bed.

Chapter 15.

I am well aware that nowadays my associates at the
club regard me as a cynical old man with a perverse
and almost malevolent sense of humour; they are too
polite knowingly to betray this, but I am not
deceived. And I am equally aware that they
attribute my cynicism to my physical infirmity, and
tolerate it largely on that account — and because I
happen to play a good hand at bridge.

But although I was never of a sunny disposition,
I can date a definite change in my outlook on life
from that evening on which I realized that some
warp or kink in my nature set me apart from my
fellows or, if not entirely from my fellows, at least
from certain amenities of life. To say that I was
embittered would, perhaps, be hardly correct; for
embitterment, as I understand the term, implies a
certain misanthropy and possibly despondency.
Perhaps embitterment is as good a term as any, but it
was a cynical and devil-may-care bitterness, and

once I had overcome my first access of horror I was able to leaven my attitude of mind with a certain spice of grim humour.

However, I had to look this fact in the face: that for a reason presumably due to hereditary influence I felt, on occasion, an almost overpowering urge to cut human flesh and to shed blood. What a penny-dreadful phrase that seems and how contemptuously it would be regarded by the gentle reader if encountered in a work of fiction!

I looked the fact in the face, as I say, examining it with cold calculation, and I arrived at the following conclusions:

That sooner or later I should yield to my obsession and cut a throat. I had already had one narrow escape in connection with my uncle; the incident with my fiancée would have been a second had a knife been then available. I must make it clear, however, that the actual deed to which I was tempted was not, in itself, unpleasant to contemplate. It did not fill me with revulsion even when looked back upon after the temporary feeling had passed. Nor did the result which my yielding to temptation would entail to my protagonist appeal to me as the stronger motive for the effort of withstanding temptation. I was not thinking so much of the effect upon my victim as the effect upon myself. For if I yielded to my urge in ordinary

circumstances it was in the highest degree probable
that I should be taken and hanged.

The foregoing being admitted, the question arose:
could I overcome my craving by deliberately
yielding to it in circumstances which would insure
the minimum amount of risk to myself? Could I keep
it in abeyance by 'blowing off steam'? And would
one indulgence still my craving? Having once
experienced the sensation of cutting a throat,
would my craving be satisfied? In other words,
could I insure a higher degree of safety for myself
and, incidentally, for other reasonably useful
members of the community, by cutting the throat of
a person who could well be spared in carefully
arranged circumstances of secrecy?

This may seem a cold-blooded and callous
speculation, but it was a logical method of dealing
with a situation in which I had to think out things
for myself. And I rather pride myself on my ability
to grapple with personal problems uninfluenced by
feeling, as opposed to pure reason. I like to worry
out details, to exercise my foresight, to look at a
thing from all sides. But in dealing with this
particular problem I was conscious of, but tried to
keep down, the fact that I wanted to reach the
decision that the solution lay in yielding to my
urge in circumstances of secrecy. I craved for the
experience of cutting a throat.

Above: Alan Hicken outside the Montacute TV, Radio and Toy Museum.

Below: Sydney George Hulme Beaman.

Two images of Tottenham in the 1870s.

Above: Martha Tabram's body is discovered at George Yard Buildings by dock labourer John Reeves.

Above: Mortuary photo of Martha Tabram.

Below: George Yard Buildings in the 1960s. They were later demolished.

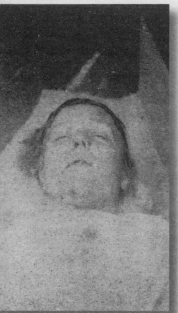

Above: Mortuary photo of Mary Ann Nichols.

Below: Durward Street in the 1960s.

Above: Police Constable John Neil discovers Mary Ann Nichols' body in Buck's Row (now Durward Street).

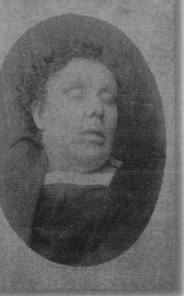

Above: Mortuary photo of Annie Chapman.

Above: A close-up of the murder scene.

THE REAR OF 29, HANBURY STREET.
(The + shows where the body was found.)

THE FRONT OF 29, HANBURY STREET.

The rear of 20 Hanbury Street where the body of Annie Chapman was found.

Mortuary photo of
Elizabeth Stride.

WHERE THE CORPSE WAS FOUND IN BERNERS STREET.

The court in Berner Street where the body of
Elizabeth Stride was discovered.

A police sketch of Mitre Square made shortly
after the discovery of Catherine Eddowes's body.

Mortuary photo of
Catherine Eddowes.

Above: The outside of 13 Miller's Court, Dorset Street, taken the day after the murder. It was through the broken window (arrowed) that the horrific discovery of Mary Jane Kelly's body was made.

Below: The mutilated body of Mary Jane Kelly.

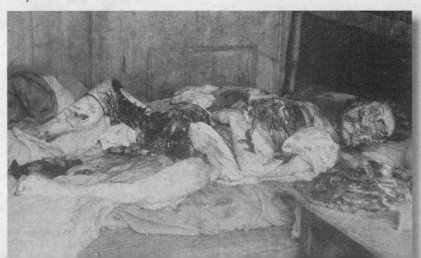

Above: An image of East End tenements in the 1870s taken from *London: A Pilgrimage* by Blanchard Jerrold and Gustave Doré.

Below: Dorset Street, Spitalfields, sometimes called 'The Worst Street in London', circa 1902.

When I speak of secrecy in connection with the enterprise which I contemplated I mean, of course, that the circumstances of time and place must be so planned as to render detection improbable. For I was not so abstracted as to be unaware that what I had in mind – no matter what the status of my 'subject' – amounted to the punishable offence of murder. For the community as a whole has for long professed to labour under the belief that all human life is sacred.

People refer occasionally to the sacredness of human life and appear to believe in it, but I see no reason to regard human life as any more sacred than animal life. A man is permitted to kill an amiable and inoffensive animal, such as a dog, because the dog's life is not 'sacred', but he may not kill a man who, by his disposition and habits, may be obviously far less fitted to live than is the dog. The life of the drunken, dissolute and dishonest scoundrel is 'sacred'.

Apropos of this matter of life-taking: I remember that, quite recently, a fellow-member of my club mentioned to me the fact that a man with whom he had some slight acquaintance had been killed by an elephant in the 'course' of the 'sport' of big-game hunting. He referred to the accident with sorrow. I agreed that it was unfortunate for his acquaintance, but pointed out that had the latter

succeeded in his enterprise of shooting the
elephant it would have been equally unfortunate
for the animal. (Not that an elephant is necessarily
amiable and inoffensive, nor hunters necessarily
scoundrels.) My fellow-member looked at me askance
and moved away. Being quite unable to think for
himself he was obsessed with that idea: the
sacredness of human life.

In order to demonstrate the hypocrisy and cant
behind this 'sacredness of human life' plea it is
only necessary to refer to one fact — the
persistence of war through the whole history of
civilization. It is true that at the time of writing
a genuine attempt to 'outlaw' war is being made in
enlightened circles; but that there is no real
belief in the wickedness of war is shown by the
continued respect in which the professional killer
is held. The army is still considered a respectable
career. And not only do we respect these warriors,
we also honour those ingenious fellows who add to
the killing efficiency of their active confreres.
Inventors of killing devices to be used in war are
not boiled in oil; they are rewarded with riches
(unless they are unbusinesslike enough to get
exploited by a capitalist, in which case the
exploiter is rewarded with riches).

Let it be understood that I am trying to indicate
the impossibility of squaring the existence of war

with a belief in the sanctity of human life; I am not stating that war is any sillier than the belief. For war, after all, is a result of the instinct to kill implanted by Nature in the human breast as a co-operator with pestilence, earthquake and so forth, for the limitation of the world's population.

Touching the 'sacredness of human life' idea, I will produce another fact, though this is not necessary — the development of the motor-car.

Nobody will deny (and if anybody does there are statistics to confute him) that the motor-car is a dangerous device. In the hands of the unskilled — and, to a lesser degree, in those of the skilled — driver, the motor-car is a menace to human life. Every motor-driver is a potential homicide. In a community which really believed in the sanctity of human life a man in a motor-car, driving at the speed at present permitted, would be regarded with as little favour as would a boy playing in Ludgate Circus with a loaded shot-gun.

I must admit to a strong prejudice against the automobile; not because it assists to thin the population, however, but because it has ruined our previously peaceful countryside. Where now in all England can I be free from this noisy, stinking and dust-raising contraption and from the horrible advertisements and petrol pumps which arise by its spoor?

* * *

However, I must not ramble from my point.

I was beginning to state, when my testiness led me afield, that I was under no misapprehension as to the lawlessness of the enterprise which I contemplated; I have no great respect for the lunatic laws of our civilization but I recognize that they exist. I knew that if I was convicted of killing even the most degraded outcast I should be hanged. This did not deter me from working out my plans; in fact, it added a sporting touch. Although I am no gambler in the accepted sense of the term — inasmuch as I never bet and am quite indifferent to the stakes when I am playing cards — I felt rather excited at the thought that I was contemplating an enterprise in which every man's hand would be against me, one in which my stake was the highest I could wager and an enterprise, therefore, which must be planned with every atom of foresight I could muster.

And in the early days of August 1888 I sat down and deliberately thought out the adventure to which I now felt practically committed.

Chapter 16.

In the days of which I write there was no supply of
popular 'detective' literature; the flood of studies
in criminology disguised as novels which now cover
our bookstalls had not then begun. Edgar Allan Poe
was the only writer of note — or, at least, the only
writer with whose work I was familiar — who had
dealt with crime and its detection in the form of
fiction. I do not include De Quincey with Poe
because his 'Murder as a Fine Art' has little
bearing on the detection of crime.

In common with my contemporaries, therefore, I
had received no priming in the technique of murder,
such as is nowadays automatically acquired in the
course of novel reading. In pitting my wits against
the professional crime detectors I had nothing but
my common sense to guide me; and being, as I have
said, unprimed in police procedure I could only
estimate the methods employed, though I had, of
course, assimilated a few hints from my reading of

criminal trials in the newspapers.

I could perceive, however, that the police not being gifted with supernatural powers could only arrest a criminal – let us say a murderer – in certain definite circumstances which could, I thought, be brought under three headings. First, they could catch their man red-handed; that is in the actual commission of the murder or in an environment closely connected with it. Secondly, they could establish his identity by following up a clue to that identity such as a personal article left on the scene of the murder. Thirdly, they could reach an assumption of identity by establishing the motive of the murder, ultimately confirming the assumption by ascertaining the movements of the suspect at the time of the murder and examining any apparently suspicious circumstances connected with him.

I could think of no method outside these three classes whereby a murder could be brought home to the person responsible.

In examining the three possible circumstances likely to lead to detection, it seemed to me that in all cases of murder the strongest card in the hand of the police was supplied by motive. From my subsequent reading in the extensive crime literature of to-day, I think I was correct in my belief. So far as class number three was concerned, therefore, I was at an advantage; the murder which I meditated would appear to be motiveless; or rather, any motive which appeared to underlie it — such as revenge — would be erroneous. I may say, in passing, that the various motives attributed to me by ingenious theorists have afforded me considerable entertainment.

Feeling certain that detection through the channel of motive could be absolutely disregarded, I concentrated my thoughts upon classes one and two.

I must not be caught in the act; the precaution here was self-evident, for I did not propose to operate in the middle of a crowd. I should naturally choose a secluded spot and need only satisfy myself that it was secluded and that it could be vacated at an instant's notice, preferably by one of several directions.

My principal danger seemed to lie in class number two. I must not drop any personal article near my 'subject' or allow him or her to clutch anything of mine — such as a handkerchief or button — during the throes of dissolution. Not that I imagined such a trivial article as a button or handkerchief (unless marked with my name) would afford any information, but the principle must be maintained consistently. Nothing whatever must be found on the scene except the remains of the subject. I could only guard against a mishap in this connection by keeping perfectly calm and free from nervousness and this, I had no doubt, I could do; for although my imagination is active enough I am able to keep my nerves under control by concentrating my thoughts entirely upon my actions. I am one of those fortunate persons whose 'nerves' do not betray them in emergency; I seldom get excited, in spite of my alleged Gallic ancestry.

Touching this matter of leaving traces: it should be noted that finger-print identification was not at that time in use by the police.

Having carefully turned over in my mind the matters outlined above, I then began to consider who would be the most suitable subject for my purpose. It must, or at least should, be a person who could well be spared by the community; a person who would not lose much in losing their life. The state to which it had pleased God to call them should be such that death would be a not unwelcome release. Who would fill this description?

I decided instantly that so far as my limited experience and observation went, the middle-aged prostitutes of the East End of London are the most pitiable and degraded of our fellow-beings. They have nearly all sunk to depths of almost unimaginable misery and degradation: most of them are drunken and probably many of them are diseased. They must be a misery to themselves and, in some respects, a menace to others. What can life possibly hold for these women that it should be worth their keeping?

If any reader should doubt my conclusions let him pay a visit to the East End of London and exercise his powers of observation and inference. Let him remember, also, that bad as are the conditions there to-day, they were even worse forty years ago.

Not only would a woman of the class alluded to be the most suitable from the point of view of economics, she would also be the most convenient. She would be readily approachable and would, of her own free will, conduct me to a spot sufficiently secluded for my purpose. For a place suitable for bawdry is a place eminently suitable for throat-cutting.

I am not certain that up to this point in my reflections I had definitely determined to put my project into execution, though I write as if my thoughts were prompted by actual intent. I toyed with the idea as a possibility or a probability but more, perhaps, in a purely academic spirit. But I do know that after several days' consideration of the proposition and of carefully weighing the difficulties and risks, I had finally determined to put my plan into immediate operation. This was on the 5th August 1888.

* * *

In the early evening of August Bank Holiday I
prepared to set out upon my enterprise. I had
decided that until late at night, or even early on
the following morning, the East End streets would
be too crowded for the execution of my purpose; in
that rabbit-warren of slums it would be difficult
for me to work with the minimum risk of
disturbance until such time as the bulk of the
inhabitants had settled down for the night. If the
woman I chose conducted me to some lodging of her
own I might be seen entering with her or leaving,
for so packed with humanity were all the buildings
of the Whitechapel area that a strong probability
existed of my being noticed unless I postponed
operations until few people were about.

But I had worked myself into such a state of
excited anticipation that I felt strongly the need
of some means of occupying my mind during the
evening. I determined to go to the theatre; the
first performance of Daniel Bandmann's 'Jekyll and
Hyde' was billed for that evening and this I would
attend.

I assumed a dark suit which, although not new,
was not shabby enough to excite notice in the
theatre – for I anticipated that I should be unable
to obtain other than one of the higher-priced seats
for a first-night on a Bank Holiday evening – but

over this suit I put on a very old, long, black overcoat. This I could remove on entering the theatre and when, later, I went to Whitechapel it would conceal the relatively decent quality of my suit and should render me inconspicuous. Fortunately the weather had been particularly cold and miserable for the time of year, and there had been a tendency towards rain. An overcoat would not, therefore, seem out of place.

In the breast-pocket of my suit I placed my father's large scalpel; in the side-pocket of my overcoat a thin, straight knife or dagger of Malay origin which I had inherited, with other curios, from my uncle and which usually hung on the wall of my sitting-room. But then I hesitated; the knife was of an awkward length for my overcoat-pocket, and I perceived that when I removed and folded my coat there was some risk that the knife would fall out. I removed it and placed it with the scalpel in my breast-pocket.

I stood for some moments dressed for the street and pondered; another idea occurred to me. I went through all my clothing and emptied the pockets of every article they contained apart from the knives, my handkerchief, my latch-key and some money. A pen-knife, a pencil-case and one or two other oddments I carried into my bed-room and laid in a drawer. I would reduce the risk of dropping

anything on the scene of my enterprise. Even a
pencil-case might prove a danger.

I looked at myself in my wardrobe mirror,
examining my person critically. Did I look shabby
enough in my long coat to pass unremarked in the
East End? I could not visualize a typical East
Ender for comparison, because there is no typical
East Ender. The types and nationalities to be
encountered in that district were so mixed that
almost any type of dress could be seen. The sole
distinguishing point was a universal shabbiness.
My long seedy coat, my rather short figure — for I
am slightly below the medium height — my sallow
complexion and my longish black hair gave a total
effect suggestive, in an indefinite way, of a Jewish
type. Certainly I could see nothing in my
appearance to attract notice.

My rooms were on the first floor and as I passed
downstairs I called over the banisters to my
landlady, whose presence below was indicated by a
rattling of crockery, telling her I was going to the
theatre and that I might be very late. I purposely
omitted to enlarge upon this statement, for I had
thought the point over with other details. If, I
argued, I told the good woman I was going to a
friend's house, or invented some other explanation
of my probable lateness, it might look suspicious. I
was not in the habit of giving any explanations,

and I had frequently been away from my rooms until the early hours of the morning. A gratuitous statement to-night <u>might</u> seem unusual, and I was unwilling to risk even such trifling possibilities as this. Let my landlady suppose I was engaged in the bawdy pleasures of a bachelor. When I came home with the milk my landlady would probably suspect me of wenching, but she would certainly not suspect me of that which I had really done. And for me to vouchsafe an unusual and uncalled-for statement would entail the <u>remote possibility</u> of speculation on the woman's part.

I let myself out into the street and took my way to the Opera Comique Theatre.

I had previously seen Richard Mansfield in 'Jekyll and Hyde' and was interested to be able to compare Bandmann's version with it. But the curtain had not been up for half-an-hour before I appreciated that here was no sinister drama of psychology, but something which soared almost into the regions of classic harlequinade. I gave myself up to pure enjoyment; when Mr Bandmann carried out his metamorphosis from Jekyll to Hyde by the simple expedients of turning up his collar and inserting a set of grotesque teeth while the footlights were conveniently lowered, I crowed with delight. When, in the character of the ogre-like Hyde, he hopped about the stage uttering hoarse

crooning sounds I momentarily lost sight of my
ultimate aim that evening in the entertainment
immediately provided.

I know the moralist would prefer to learn that
the play was a well-handled commentary upon my
own existence; that I recognized in myself the dual
personality of Stevenson's sinister puppets and
that, filled with self-loathing at the thought of
the thing I contemplated, I resolved to stifle the
evil Hyde in my own nature. That I left the theatre
a changed man, the tears streaming from my eyes.
Such a reaction would be so obviously the right and
proper treatment in a fictional account of such a
man as I that I almost feel I should apologize for
writing the truth. But I am sure that even a
moralist would have laughed at this
'dramatization' of 'Jekyll and Hyde'.

But sometimes my chuckles would be cut off short
as a wave of excitement swept over me induced by a
sudden recollection of what lay before me that
night. The scene on the stage would be blotted out
as my thoughts turned inwards to a predictive
tableau of a dark slum, with a slinking slattern
and a dark figure with his hand on that which lay
within his coat-pocket — and then the vision would
fade and the glare of the footlights would appear
again. I would continue my interrupted chuckle.

It may seem unkind for me to write so

disparagingly of Mr Bandmann's production, but that my personal opinions as to its demerits were also the opinions of others was clearly indicated by the tone of the critiques which I read on the following morning in the course of my search in the papers for news of a death in Whitechapel.

Towards the end of the play a choir of boys was introduced to sing, inconsequently, 'Rock-a-bye baby on the tree top', and this definitely recalled me to reality. For my wriggles of merriment were such that the point of the dagger which I carried in my pocket penetrated the lining, and I felt it pressed uncomfortably against my ribs. I stiffened, and cautiously inserted my hand to adjust the position of my weapon.

I remained in my seat until the apotheosis of Dr Jekyll concluded the performance in a kind of transformation scene and then, not waiting to hear Mr Bandmann's speech before the curtain, I left the theatre.

As I came out into the dark street and my mind leapt again upon that which faced me, as a dog leaps instantly upon a bone which has been for a time withheld from him, I realized that I had made one slip in my planning. A trivial, almost negligible slip, but in my circumstances was it possible to say that anything was quite negligible?

Suppose my landlady entered my sitting-room

during my absence and noticed that the Malay dagger was not hanging in its usual place! I paused in my walk and turned the matter over in my mind. But my mistake could not be remedied now, I decided. I could not return home at this time; I could not postpone my enterprise. To live through another day of anticipatory excitement was unthinkable. I must rely upon the extreme improbability of my landlady entering the sitting-room where she had normally nothing to do in the evening; and, even if she did enter it, on the unlikelihood of her noting the dagger's absence. Nevertheless I was annoyed; I, who had pondered details so carefully, had made a childish blunder. I should have taken the scalpel only!

I dismissed the matter from my mind, and set out, walking slowly, towards the east.

Chapter 17.

I walked along Fleet Street, Ludgate Hill, past St
Pauls to the Bank and then down Lombard Street,
Fenchurch Street and Aldgate to Whitechapel High
Street. I purposely loitered, but even then it was
barely mid-night as I turned into the last-
mentioned thoroughfare. The streets were still
teeming with people, and I stood at a corner and
looked about me. Very few of the passers-by gave me
so much as a glance, but one loafer stared hard at
my feet and then glanced up into my face as he went
by. I looked down and the cause of his interest was
evident. I had forgotten that a decent pair of boots
is as rare in a poverty-stricken area as a silk hat.
Mine were slightly mud-splashed, but they compared
more than favourably with other footwear around
me; they were neither broken nor ill-fitting, and
the laces were carefully tied.

I turned down Commercial Street and as I went I
deliberately soiled my boots by walking through

the mud, of which there was a plentiful supply. In a few minutes my boots were no longer in a state to excite remark.

I loafed about that district for what seemed hours, passing from one garbage-littered slum to another, watching the knots of people around the closing public houses and the roisterers, single or in groups, who staggered singing down the gloomy streets. There was a good deal of drunkenness, which accounted for the singing; no one sings in that part of London unless he is drunk. There is nothing but drink to make him sing.

Several women, mostly drunk, accosted me in the course of my perambulations, but it was too early yet for what I had to do. One of these creatures was persistent, following me along the street and hoarsely whispering Mephistophelian suggestions into my ear. Her diction was crude, but her intentions were by no means obscure. So suitable a 'subject' did she appear in her urgency to make my better acquaintance, that I hesitated; she misinterpreted this and, laying a dirty hand on my coat, stared into my face with bleary eyes. But no, I decided; the streets were still too far awake; I would take no risks. I roughly disengaged her hand and hurried away.

Gradually the streets cleared; by this time I felt tired and footsore, but the feeling of excitement

which had filled my mind during my walk had grown
rather than diminished. But it was a controlled
excitement and I enjoyed the sensation which
accompanied it; a sensation, I think, such as
hunters must experience when tracking a beast to
its lair. As the slums into which I entered became
more and more quiet until only occasional isolated
stragglers could be seen, I knew that the time of my
choice of subject was near at hand.

I was thrilled by the thought of my power. I was
Death stalking this jungle of slums; it was for me to
take or to spare. Should this slinking woman who
came towards me be the one to die, or should I pass
her by? And that bundle of rags lying in a doorway;
surely she was ready for my reaping?

And then I saw another woman at the end of a
street, staggering, obviously drunk. I followed her
with long, feline strides. If she turned on feeling
the black shadow at her elbow and met me with
importunity, she should be the one. If she ignored
me, she should be spared. Let hers be the choice.
She was too drunk to notice me and I brushed by
her.

At last, on turning a corner, I came face to face
with a woman who seemed relatively sober. We almost
collided.

'Hold up, dearie,' she said. Then she stepped back
and looked into my face.

'You look as if a bit 'o fun wouldn't do you no 'arm,' she said.

'Fun!' I muttered, for my mouth had suddenly become dry. I knew that here was my subject.

'Yus, fun,' she replied; and was more explicit. 'Come on, you've got some money, ain't yer?'

A spirit of impishness descended upon me, and I began to demur to her suggestion. Let her persuade me; let her plead for death!

The creature was insistent. 'Come on,' she said. 'Why shouldn't yer; Bank Holiday an' all? I ain't so bad. Come on; I know a quiet place.'

We argued for an appreciable time, and then she began to swear in a jocular way. At last I yielded. She led me through several lanes, now practically deserted, down Commercial Street, and suddenly dived into a doorway. 'Come on,' she whispered and, grasping my sleeve, drew me up a flight of dark stairs to a landing dimly lit by a gas-jet from above. 'We shall be all right 'ere,' she muttered; and flopped down on the landing.

'What 'ave yer got for me?' she asked. I stared down at the recumbent figure for a moment before replying; I could just distinguish her. Then I placed my hand in my inside pocket.

I hesitated, savouring to the full the excitation of the moment, and then slowly drew out the Malay dagger. As the dim light caught the blade I saw the

woman's eyes widen, and then her mouth open for a
scream. I pressed my hand over her mouth as I raised
my weapon. 'Oo my Gawd!' came in a sort of strangled
gasp from between my fingers; and then I struck
swiftly downwards. I felt her body give a quick jerk,
and her heels banged against the wooden flooring. I
struck again, and again. And then I pulled out my
scalpel . . .

The doctor stated at the subsequent inquest that the
body bore thirty-nine wounds. He had taken the
trouble to count them and probably knew. But I am
unable to confirm his statement.

I have no clear recollection of descending the
stairs, but I found myself outside the building, the
dagger and the scalpel in my hands. I think that for
a few moments I was almost dazed, but I suddenly saw
my hands and full consciousness returned to me.
They were red and glistening. Reason resumed its
sway, and I thrust the knives into my breast pocket
and buried my hands in the pockets of my overcoat.
I glanced up at the place I had left and observed an
iron tag bearing the name George-yard Buildings; I
looked up and down the street. Not a soul was in
sight. Without hurry I crossed the way, passed into
Commercial Street and down another narrow street
which was, I think, Dorset Street. Here I passed a

man, but he gave me but a glance. I walked through several lanes, all of the same slum type, and as I went I became conscious of an extraordinary lassitude. I wanted to sit down and rest; but I could not sit down and rest. I had to get well away from the district, for the remains of my subject might have been already discovered, and I could not afford to be seen and, possibly, remembered.

As I mechanically stumbled on I bethought me of the state of my hands; and, under the light of a street lamp I looked down at the front of my overcoat. It was sodden with moisture and when I touched it I found this to be blood. It would not be observed in the dim light of these streets, of course, but it was disquieting. Could I walk safely in my present condition all the way home to my lodging?

I had now come into Houndsditch and here I removed my overcoat, folded it with the lining outwards, and draped it over my left arm in such a way that my hand was concealed in a fold. My other hand I thrust into my jacket-pocket, and in this fashion I set off, walking rapidly in spite of my fatigue. I reached Henrietta Street as the sky was lightening, let myself quietly into the house where I lodged and crept softly up the stairs to my rooms.

I would willingly have tumbled into bed without more ado, but there could be no rest for me until I had done certain things. I washed my hands and, as I did so, perceived from my reflection in a mirror above my wash-hand stand a single large splash of blood on my chin. I went cold when I noticed it, for what if someone else — one of the few pedestrians I had passed — had noticed it too and should remember! Certainly this business of mine was fraught with more pit-falls than I had estimated; and what on earth was I to do about my overcoat?

I could not lock it away in its present state in case it should, by some accident, be discovered by my landlady. Its very presence was a menace, and I could not destroy it. I could only try to clean it, and this I did. I placed my hand-bowl on the floor and scrubbed the front of the coat with a nail brush. And the damned nail brush became reddened! At last I thought I had removed the blood from the coat, but I could not be sure until it had dried; I locked it away in my wardrobe.

After that I carefully cleaned the scalpel and dagger with moistened newspaper, and hung the dagger in its accustomed place on the wall. The scalpel I replaced in my drawer with its fellows.

At about six in the morning nothing remained, so far as I could observe, to bear witness to my activities but a wash-bowl of blood-stained water and a few scraps of reddened newspaper. With the paper and bowl in my hands I crept from my sitting-room to the landing and listened; no one was yet astir. I passed silently to the lavatory and disposed of the last of the evidence.

After that I went to bed and slept soundly until nearly mid-day.

Chapter 18.

The mental state of the conscience-stricken
homicide has been treated by many imaginative
writers according to their individual conceptions
of what that state must be; and those conceptions
show a great similarity. For it seems to be
universally assumed that the homicide must be
necessarily conscience-stricken. I question whether
this assumption is borne out by actual fact.

A distinction must be made between what is
called the 'working of conscience' which, in the
case of a homicide, I assume to be meant a species of
remorse; and the fear of being found out. It is
extremely probable that the latter acts as an
irritant or stimulus to the former. But in fiction,
in which I include the drama, remorse on the part
of the homicide is pictured as sufficient in itself
to cause acute discomfort to the sufferer, the main
symptom being a tendency to 'see' the spectre of his
victim.

I can well imagine the mental harassment caused to an ill-controlled person by the fear of being found out which, in the case such as I am discussing, would imply subsequent hanging. I can understand such a person, in a nervous effort to reduce the object of his worry to a minimum, doing this and that in an effort to hide his traces — real or imagined — and I have gathered that quite a number of homicides have drawn detection upon themselves entirely by their needless precautions.

But when I consider the matter of conscience as an active and independent agent of discomfort, I arrive at the conclusions first that these ideas of conscience are very much exaggerated, and secondly that when a homicide does become 'conscience-stricken' as a result of his act it can only be in those cases where the active party cannot justify that act to himself. In other words, he has gone against his own ingrained principles in killing another person at all.

The reader, being doubtless a respectable and conventional person, will at once say that the killing of another can never be justified; that it must always be contrary to the principles of the killer. But I do not agree. In certain circumstances the killing of another is justified; cases occur in which the killing should be regarded as justifiable by any person able to free his mind from cant. And, of course, there are circumstances in which the killing of another is held to be right even by the hide-bound — or, if not absolutely right, at least not to be condemned. The execution of a condemned criminal is not held to be murder and the public hang-man does not, probably, suffer the twinges of conscience. I have not met that gentleman, but in the unlikely event of my doing so I must ascertain whether this is correct. And as for killing in war — well, we all know how our youngsters were egged on to go out and kill a few years ago, particularly by members of the tender sex who went to the length of distributing white feathers to those young men who exhibited reluctance.

But apart from these recognized examples of justifiable homicide there are others, the recognition of which is shirked. As an example: had my uncle poisoned his cancer-stricken wife with the intention of saving her unnecessary suffering, his action would have been praise-worthy in the eyes of any reasonable person.

Where, you will ask, is all this leading? Are you, J.R., suggesting that your disposal of the Whitechapel woman was justifiable? Well, no; I am not suggesting exactly that; but I do claim that it was on the border-line of the justifiable. Primarily I killed the woman in the hope that by 'blowing off steam' I should be less likely to kill a

useful member of society. I will admit to the
inclination, but surely I should not be blamed too
much for an inclination implanted in me through
the medium of my ancestors? I did not ask for that
inclination and should have been unquestionably
happier without it. Yes, I know, O reader, that we
are 'intended' to fight against our temptations, and
I have no doubt you have fought against your own.
But I venture to think you have never had a
temptation like mine.

Whether or not the workings of conscience (if
any) vary in the homicidal class in proportion to
the degree of justification of the killing I do not
know; but I do know that in my own case my
conscience, such as it is, caused me no
inconvenience whatever. I felt perfectly certain
that a woman I had killed was no worse off after my
action than she had been before, it being difficult
for me to conceive any circumstances (leaving out
the 'fires of hell' theory, to which I was not
prepared to subscribe) in which she could be worse
off. At the best she had been reborn to a better and
happier life (see Church Service) and at the worst
she was dead in the materialistic sense and
therefore free from her past troubles. She had had
what is popularly called a 'happy release'. Feeling
this, why should I be troubled by conscience?

As regards the fear of detection: I will confess

to a certain slight uneasiness here, for I was not
then a practised and experienced homicide, and the
remote possibility that I might have left some trace
occasionally troubled me during the first few days
following the affair. But I soon overcame this,
being reassured when I read the newspaper reports
of the inquest.

The first sitting of the inquest (which I thought
it impolitic to attend) took place on the 9th August,
and was reported on the 10th. I read the account of
this, and of the adjourned inquest, with great
interest, and learned that the name of my subject
had been Martha Tabron or Turner, and that her
remains had been discovered by a labourer named
Reeves when he left George-yard Buildings for his
work at about 4.45 a.m. Previous to this, however,
another man had seen the woman lying on the
landing at 3, but had ignored it assuming, from his
experience of the district, that she was drunk. I
estimated, therefore, that I had had a good margin
of time in which to retire from the scene.

Dr Killeen, who had examined the body, gave a
list of the organs penetrated, and showed
remarkable acumen in estimating that two weapons
had been used.

It appeared in the course of the proceedings that
Mrs Turner had been seen during the evening of the
6th August in the company of two soldiers. Later on

the military were paraded at the Tower and also, I
believe, at Wellington Barracks, and two men were
picked out by the Witness concerned as being the
men in question. But both men were able to show
alibis which was, to me, a relief; for had an
innocent man been charged in connection with the
affair my own position would have been an awkward
one. I should not have known quite what to do.

Nothing appeared at the inquest which gave an
indication of a 'clue' to my identity, unless
information was being withheld from the public and
the police were at sea; and I saw no reason to feel
uneasy.

So far as I could judge, the case caused but little
excitement; my landlady, a garrulous woman, made
no reference to it in my hearing, although she
showed, as a rule, considerable interest in similar
items of news.

At this stage I should like to clear up a popular
misconception, and to state that Martha Turner was
the first person I disposed of. I desire to do so
because of the following facts:

In certain journalistic accounts of my exploits
it has been stated that I was responsible for the
death of a woman named Emma Smith on 3rd April
1888. In fact, during the 'Terror' of the autumn of
1888 this was assumed to have been one of my cases

even by responsible persons such as coroners.

In one newspaper article which I have observed it is stated that 'Emma Smith was found dead and horribly mutilated, lying in a small entry in Osborne Street'. The writer goes on to say that 'Dr Phillips declared at the inquest that the mutilations were the work of someone skilled in anatomical dismemberment'. And that it was something 'diabolical and uncanny', that 'Londoners were horrified' and so on and so forth.

Now this statement is not merely an exaggeration; most of it is absolutely untrue. Mrs Smith was set upon by a party of men who assaulted her and severely injured her by driving an iron stake, or some such instrument, into her body. Mrs Smith's body was not discovered anywhere; she was able to get home to her wretched lodgings where she gave an account of the assault. A woman friend assisted her to the hospital where Mrs Smith died of her injuries twenty-four hours later. As to the attainments of those responsible for the assault, Dr Phillips may or may not have made the statement attributed to him; but I cannot trace it, and it seems highly improbable that he regarded an ability to drive an iron stake into a woman's body as evidence of 'skill in anatomical dismemberment'. As for London being horrified; well, I question whether many persons knew or troubled anything about the case, for

murders in the East End of London were then by no
means uncommon.

But let it be noted that Mrs Smith's death was due
to a party of men according to her own statement.
She mentioned four, and said that one of them
appeared to be about nineteen years of age.

Later on, when my handiwork began to earn
recognition, it was almost universally assumed by
those without knowledge of the above facts that Mrs
Smith was one of my subjects. But there was never
the slightest evidence to bear out this assumption.

I may also touch upon the modern popular belief
that 'atrocities' by J.R. were of almost nightly
occurrence, and that they were very numerous. This
again is quite incorrect, as this record will show.
And any person who doubts my statement can
confirm it quite easily by reference to the
newspapers of the period.

Chapter 19.

I had hoped that my enterprise of the 7th August would dispose, once and for all, of my unfortunate craving; that, having allowed myself to experience a satisfaction, I should have permanently satiated that craving. But I soon discovered, with rather mixed feelings, that the assuagement was purely temporary.

Although in the past I had always been fascinated by blood and, during later years, by knives, the urge to shed blood had only occurred on isolated occasions and then suddenly and unexpectedly. But now my experience had resulted in actual knowledge of the satisfaction to be derived from blood-letting; from a slumbering beast, awakening only at rare intervals, my 'complex' had become an ever watchful thing awaiting an opportunity to glut itself.

And, in addition to the satisfaction of the act, I had discovered a new and unexpected source of

interest: the excitement of the attendant
circumstances. I began to realize the fascination
exercised by the sport of hunting when the prize is
the death of the quarry, and the forfeit that of the
hunter. And being a comparatively young man I was
not unaffected by conceit on realizing that I had
set myself against the forces of law and order and
come off best.

I had not then, and never have had, any feeling of
contempt for the police. Our police force is, I
should imagine, one of the most capable in the
world; with certain newspaper offices it shares,
probably, the honour of being the most efficient
organization in this country. But the police,
although able and industrious, are not omniscient.
They cannot find their man without some traces to
guide them.

Nevertheless I congratulated myself on having
avoided the attentions of the police; and I was
afflicted by the sin of pride.

Now the fact that I had baffled the police (if the
omission to leave clues may be regarded as a process
of baffling) was, in itself, an incentive to me to
try my luck again. The game of 'hare and hounds'
seemed to offer a fresh source of interest in
addition to that attached to the actual commission
of homicide. But I knew that every enterprise I
carried out would mean a fresh risk, and that the

risks would be cumulative. To make a hobby of the
thing would not be homicide but suicide.

So I curbed my desire — for a few weeks.

But towards the end of August my craving was
such that I decided to satisfy it once more. This
would entail another risk of detection which, in
conjunction with my former risk, might be
considered to give an arithmetic product equal, not
to two risks added, but risk squared; for it was
possible that the police already held some trifling
clue regarding the first case, useless in itself, but
possibly of value if combined with any
intrinsically trifling clue which I might leave in
the future. I must therefore look well to my
precautions, acting on the experience gained
during my first exploit.

I considered that first occasion: where I had
been right and what mistakes I had made.

I had been right in my choice of subject, locality
and time. The first had practically placed herself
at my disposal, and the locality had proved to be
most suitable. The time had been well chosen, being
late enough for the streets to be uncrowded, and yet
allowing me leisure in which to reach home before
the early risers at dawn.

As for my mistakes I had, so far as I could
estimate, made two. I had removed the Malay dagger
from its usual position and its absence might have

been observed by my landlady. There had been no need for me to take the dagger at all; the scalpel alone would have been sufficient. And by confining myself to one knife on this second occasion I should reduce the risk of dropping a weapon by half.

My second, and more serious mistake, had been in allowing myself to become blood-spattered. I should have remembered the admonition of my old school-fellow's pork-butcher father when killing his pig to 'stand clear'. Or I should have despatched my subject more carefully; instead of violently stabbing her I should have cut her throat. I need hardly enter into the technical reason for this alternative method.

On future occasions – for I now admitted the probability of several future occasions – I must endeavour to avoid getting my clothing stained. The obvious plan was to wear a protective garment, but as it was impracticable for me to assume an overall in which to work, my long black overcoat would appear to fill the bill; for I could remove and fold it as I had done before.

The refined reader will doubtless view these calculations of mine with distaste; but they were necessary. No one enters upon even such a relatively trifling affair as a summer holiday without some preliminary planning. How much more so, then, is planning necessary in such an enterprise as that of mine, where the smallest slip may lead to the most unfortunate consequences? And I record my schemings in order to show that the homicidal maniac theory, to which I have earlier alluded, cannot be regarded seriously. I question whether a lunatic, such as popular imagination pictures, would have been capable of such preliminary precautions. He would more probably have simply run amok without regard to consequences.

But I was careful; I held my anticipatory excitement in check the while I looked at my problem from all angles, examining it logically and critically. Surely no symptoms of lunacy here!

I fixed upon the 30th August as the date of my second adventure; but on the afternoon of that day I suddenly bethought me of another point.

On the first occasion I had not attempted to explain my lateness to my landlady, beyond the insufficient statement that I was visiting the theatre. My reason for not enlarging upon that I have already mentioned. But it now occurred to me that if several occasions arose – and this seemed extremely likely – it might flash across the mind of my landlady that at those times when certain 'atrocities' had taken place I, her lodger, had been absent from my rooms until an exceptionally late hour. I could guard myself against her possible suspicion by inventing someone in the nature of what Oscar Wilde calls a 'Bunbury' – a sick friend or relative whom I frequently visited; this idea I decided to ponder at my leisure. But pending some such invention, was it, I wondered, necessary for my landlady to know I was absent at all?

By leaving my rooms after mid-night I could easily reach the East End of London in time for my purpose. My landlady retired, as a rule, before eleven, and unless she knew that either I or her other lodger, who occupied rooms above my own, was out, she bolted the front door before going up to bed.

But the good woman slept at the top of the house, and it would be quite easy for me to descend unheard to the front door, unbolt it and slip into the street, releasing the catch afterwards by the aid of my latch-key. My only risk lay in the possibility that my fellow-lodger might hear me; but this, I thought, was negligible. And as to his being out until late on the same evening: if he were, the door would be left unbolted, and I should know by this that he was in his rooms. There was no possibility of his returning home after I had left and bolting me out.

My plan seemed a perfectly safe one, and I resolved to try it experimentally.

* * *

I left the house that night just before twelve. I had heard my landlady go up to bed, and was also aware of my fellow-lodger's presence in his room by his movements overhead. I crept softly down the stairs, unbolted the street door and let myself into the street without mishap. Henrietta Street was deserted, and it was not until I got into Covent Garden that I met anyone.

I walked through into the Strand, and made my way eastwards. I was wearing my long, black overcoat, and in the breast-pocket of my under-jacket reposed my scalpel.

Soon after twelve-thirty I entered Whitechapel High Street; I was keyed up by excitement, though by an effort of will I kept my brain cool and collected. I was inconvenienced on this and other occasions by certain purely physical symptoms which, since I do not wish to appear indelicate, I will not specify. My feelings, as a whole, were probably similar to those of my younger fellows of a few years since when waiting to 'go over the top'.

As I came into Whitechapel I paused and looked around me. The hunt was on!

The tale of my wanderings would be a mere repetition of the early part of my first adventure; but there was this difference: that this not being Bank Holiday night the streets appeared to be settling down at a slightly earlier hour.

I passed many women of the 'unfortunate' class before selecting my subject. In most cases the women were either walking in couples, or the streets in which I passed them were not absolutely deserted; or for some other reason I hesitated to address them. I actually spoke to one woman, but as I stood with her on the kerb I observed a light spring up in a neighbouring window and the shadow of a face – man's or woman's, I could not tell which – peering through the broken window-pane. I left the woman with a suitable excuse.

Finally I met a woman in what I think was Court Street who seemed to answer my requirements. The time must then, I think, have been nearly three o'clock in the morning; but as I had left my watch at home I am uncertain. The short street was otherwise deserted and the windows were in darkness.

I hesitated when this woman spoke to me, for she seemed to be slightly less degraded than the usual run of the sisterhood; but I feared to delay longer and, after a brief colloquy, I accompanied her down the street.

She led me into Bucks Row, a narrow slum of typical two-storied East End dwellings, deeply shadowed by some tall warehouses which arose on one side of the street.

The woman gave me no trouble whatever; she did

not even cry out. I made a better job of this than I had of my first subject and, with the exception of my hands, I was unstained when I had finished. I left her lying in the gutter and left Bucks Row by way of Bakers Row.

I reached home at about four-thirty and let myself in without mishap. The house was quite silent as I crept up stairs.

Compared with my later adventures this was a somewhat dull affair.

Chapter 20.

My first exploit had caused but slight interest, but my second aroused a certain mild excitement. It seemed to be recognized that the two affairs were the work of 'the same hand' and the death of Mrs Smith in April (to which I have alluded) was recalled and quite unwarrantably classed with the other two. Even at that stage the word 'lunatic' began to be whispered.

I write as if I had my hand on the pulse of public opinion, but of course my only knowledge of what was being thought and said was derived from the newspapers — and from my landlady, who was a newspaper in herself.

This good lady seemed to take as much interest in bloodshed as I did, though in her case I have no reason to suppose that her interest was other than purely academic and theoretical. The 'Whitechapel Murders', as they were now called, quickly gripped my landlady's imagination; she revelled in them and appeared to memorize all the details she read. I verily believe she could have repeated to me without an error a list of the 'organs penetrated' in each case according to the medical testimony; but, of course, she was too refined to do so.

Still she contrived, in the course of her household duties in my rooms, to discuss the affairs with me very freely, while skimming delicately over such details as she considered indelicate; in fact, she began to bore me. She was not an original thinker; her opinions were the conventional opinions of the cant-ridden populace. 'Poor creatures!' she would say, at frequent intervals. 'It does seem dreadful!'

'Why "poor creatures"?' I asked her on one of these occasions. 'Surely women of that kind are better out of it?'

'Oh, don't say that, sir!' she cried.

'But don't you think they are?' I persisted. 'You believe in Heaven, don't you, Mrs —?'

'I go to church regular,' she replied, with dignity. 'But going to Heaven when you die and having your inside cut up are two very different things!' (Being a woman, you see, she was quite unable to stick to the point.)

'How would you like having your stomach cut open?' she added, losing a trifle of her delicacy in the excitement of the moment.

'I don't think I should mind whether I had my
stomach cut open or whether I was hanged,' I replied
reflectively. 'I doubt whether it would make much
difference in the long run.'

'I do,' said my landlady, with a toss of the head.
'I want to die in my bed.'

'Well, if you really want to, Mrs –,' I said, 'I
expect you have a nice, comfortable bed handy.'

'Ah, it's all very well for you to laugh, sir,'
remarked the good lady. 'We never know what's
coming to none of us!' With which dark truism she
picked up the tray of breakfast-crockery and left
me.

I mention this conversation because it gives a
fair indication of the popular point of view; and
her voracious interest in the 'Whitechapel
Murders', which grew later, in common with the
interest of the public as a whole, to a state of
morbid hysteria, must be recorded because it led to
something which appealed to me as an exceedingly
good joke. The incident in question occurred after
my disposal of Annie Chapman in Hanbury Street.

On Friday 7th September, I allowed myself another
'night out'. I find it slightly difficult to explain
why I came to work again so soon after the Bucks
Row incident, but I rather think I allowed myself
to get worked up into an undue state of excitement

through the interest caused by that second exploit.

I believe that had my affairs passed with but little public notice I should have indulged my craving only at long intervals and only when that craving grew too strong to be withstood. I should have observed the procedure suggested by that Duke of Norfolk who used to say, according to De Quincey, 'Next Monday, wind and weather permitting, I purpose to be drunk.' I should have fixed definite periods between my indulgences, saying to myself: 'Next month, on the thirtieth, I propose to go out and kill another woman.' And I should have held myself rigidly in check until the date decided upon.

But I really believe — and, since I desire to be candid, I must admit — that at that stage my feelings were not so far removed from those of the modern cocaine addict. I had discovered and experienced a novel and exciting indulgence; but the craving for it grew by what it fed on. A 'vicious circle' was formed; every experience resulted in an increased desire for further experience.

And when my imagination pictured the increase in popular excitement which would be caused by another demonstration on my part, I was influenced. I fear there must be something of the mentality of the modern film-star in my make-up. An appetite for notoriety.

Be that as it may, I set out on the night of 7th

September deliberately intent upon another of my
indulgences.

I decided, as before, to avoid any suggestion that
I had been away from my lodgings on that evening
but, in a spirit of fantastic playfulness (as I must
admit), I developed this suggestion. In place of mere
non-suspicion, I would provide a definite idea that
I was at home. Something not far short of a real
alibi.

On Friday morning I told my landlady I had a bad
cold in the head.

The good lady was concerned for me and as, during
the day, my 'cold' got worse (one can do a lot with
pepper), she told me that 'a stitch in time saves
nine' and that she was going to take the matter in
hand. She told me I ought to be in bed, and I
reluctantly agreed. I consented to go to bed.

She brought up to my room a can of nearly boiling
water and a tin of mustard; she filled my wash-hand
basin with hot mustard and water and insisted that
I should sit for some time with my feet soaking in
this. I followed her instructions, wrapped in a
dressing-gown. Then she made me a basin of onion
gruel which, under her eye, I was forced to consume
(I detest onions) and while she removed the
mustard-bath I got into bed.

This was at seven in the evening.

I lay in bed during that evening reading 'Marie

Roget' and 'The Purloined Letter' first by daylight
and, later, by the light of my candle. At about
eleven my landlady knocked at my door and enquired
whether I was 'all right'. I reassured her in a
sleepy voice and then heard her pass up the stairs
to bed.

At mid-night I arose, dressed in my oldest suit,
put on my long overcoat, placed the scalpel in my
pocket and crept softly down the stairs. The front
door was bolted; I unfastened it and let myself into
the street.

Before one o'clock I was in Whitechapel.

It seemed to me that on this evening I passed more
policemen than I had been used to seeing in the
district. Whether or not an increased number had
been posted as a result of the recent 'atrocities' I
do not know, but I think I probably magnified the
number since my mind had been dwelling upon the
notoriety according to my exploits and I was
prepared to find a keener watchfulness. The police
were, as a rule, walking in couples; but this was not
uncommon for that period; for in this vice and
crime-ridden slumdom the officer of the law was
regarded, and sometimes treated, with marked
hostility. The 'bashing' of policemen not
infrequently took place.

The streets, and particularly the smaller lanes,

were very badly lit at that time, and I moved about in a semi-darkness which seemed, to my imagination, to be a hot darkness. It was not the ordinary warmth of a September night which I experienced, but a kind of feverish heat due, as I realized later, to my own pitch of excitement coupled with the fact that I was really developing a cold. For, you will remember, I had taken a hot mustard foot-bath and a basin of gruel which had given rise to a heated condition of the body; and I had arisen from my bed and gone out into the night air. A very foolish thing to do, alibi or no alibi, and I remembered having shivered as I passed along Henrietta Street.

I felt almost intoxicated on that night as I walked from street to street. The isolated patches of light cast on the pavements by the street lamps appeared to me like islands separated by seas of sinister shadows; shadows in which policemen, harlots and drunken men moved silently and furtively. When I stepped out of an island of yellowish light and waded towards another island I was passing through a macabre region peopled by ghost-like beings, some of whom were inimical to me, but one of whom I should catch and slay. And on entering on every belt of darkness I thought: 'Shall I catch her here? — Or in the next one? — Or in that swamp of shadows at the end of the street?'

This whimsical fancy kept me employed for some

time, but in spite of my feverish view of my
surroundings I did not lose sight of the fact that I
was in the streets. I was not labouring under
delusions, but only under slightly nightmarish
illusions to which I deliberately surrendered
myself. I kept my wits about me, and when I observed
policemen I avoided their strict scrutiny. I altered
my stride to one calculated to pass them in one of
the pools of shadow, and not under a street lamp. I
did not court their attention, but I did not
obviously avoid it by crossing the street or
retreating the way I had come. In any case few of
them gave me more than a passing glance.

I met the woman at the corner of New Street. She
looked over fifty years of age (though she was only
forty-seven, it appears), she was miserably dressed
and had on a grotesque bonnet which looked as if it
had been rescued from an ash-bin. She seemed
perfectly sober and accosted me in the usual terms.

This woman proved to be of a chatty type. She
ambled along beside me, occasionally touching my
arm with her scraggy hand. She told me she had been
out since before mid-night 'Lookin' for some
friend'. 'My landlord wouldn't let me 'ave no doss
cos I 'adn't the money,' she told me. 'So I bin
walkin' about since. I 'ad another try and wot d'yer
think the — 'ad the sauce to say? Said I bin eatin'
'ot spuds: and if I 'ad the money for 'ot spuds I

could pay for my doss. The dirty —. All right, I sez
to 'im, I'll show yer. 'Ot spuds indeed. Don't yer go
a-lettin' of my doss, I sez, 'coz I'll soon get the
money. Yus, you can larf, I sez; I ain't one o' them
smart young gals, I sez, but I ain't one o' them pore
old tear drops wot a blind sailor wouldn't look at.
I'll be back soon, I sez, what with this new bonnet
of mine an' all. And, I sez, if you wasn't a —' And so
on.

'Of course 'e ain't really my landlord,' she went
on. 'Wot I mean, 'e only keeps a doss-'ouse where I
sleeps when I ain't 'ad much luck. Though I 'ad a
room all to meself once; I ain't always bin out o'
luck. I wouldn't mind bettin' you've got two rooms,
dearie, ain't yer? Yer look as if yer might 'ave. Wot
I mean, anyone might mistake yer for a real gent,
the way you talk an' all. Reminds me rather of an
engineer wot I took up with once – though 'e was a
dirty bahstad 'e was. Treated me real dirty. You are
comin' along o' me, dearie, ain't yer?'

I reassured her.

'Yus,' she continued, reminiscently, 'I 'ad a room
once; an' a canary. A real live canary in a cage wot
used to sing. When you 'eard 'im you might almost
fancy you was in Eppin' Forest. But I lost 'im. I fell
out o' luck, as you might say, an' 'ad to pawn 'is cage
an' let the pore little bahstad loose. A cat got 'im.
– I didn't 'arf 'owl when a cat got 'im. I often think

o' that canary. — Like Eppin' Forest 'e was.'

We had by now come into Hanbury Street and my guide led me into a doorway. 'Don't make a row,' she whispered.

I did not know it at the time, but I took extraordinary risks that night. I learned later from the newspaper reports that nineteen persons lived in that house, and that the landlady's son often came into the yard at the back at unforeseen times to eject tramps and other undesirables. And it was into this back yard that the woman took me; a narrow, littered place approached by a few steps.

'We shall be quiet 'ere, dearie,' she whispered. And she was perfectly right.

On the morning after the Hanbury Street episode the joke occurred to which I have alluded.

I had reached home without mishap, found the door unbolted as I had left it, let myself softly into the house, bolted the door and gone up to bed. I did not know, and my landlady had forgotten, that my fellow-lodger was out.

This man, who occupied the two rooms above my own, was a middle-aged man of a shy and retiring disposition. He was short and of poor physique, rather consumptive-looking, and had a thin layer of ginger-coloured hair turning grey. He wore very high collars round a long, thin neck, and his eyes

were magnified to a goblin-like size by thick-
lensed spectacles. I think he was a solicitors'
clerk, but of this I am not certain.

On the evening of the 7th September, this
individual had gone to visit some friends or
relatives living in an outer suburb; he either
omitted to advise the landlady or she, in the mild
excitement of her ministrations to me, forgot his
absence. She bolted the street door in the usual
way. I, on my return from Whitechapel at about five
on the following morning, also bolted the front
door for I was, of course, ignorant of my fellow-
lodger's absence.

But he managed to miss his last train and had to
walk home from his friends' house.

Soon after I had got into bed, and just as I was
dozing, I heard a stealthy knocking at the front
door. I will confess that the sound filled me with a
momentary alarm; it flashed into my mind that by
some extraordinary chance I had been seen and
followed. That, in fact, the police stood without.
That is one of the penalties of unconventional
conduct like mine: even a knocking in the small
hours may promote uneasiness.

I listened to the repeated knockings which
gradually grew louder as they drew no response. I
had no intention of going down. Then I heard my
landlady's footsteps passing my door, followed in a

few moments by the sound of bolts being withdrawn
and a murmur of conversation. Steps ascended the
stairs and then I heard movements in the room above
me and realized, with some relief, the truth. It was
my fellow-lodger whom I had bolted out.

In the morning, when I was taking a late
breakfast, my landlady burst into the room. She was
panting and the normal mauve of her complexion
had changed to a pasty white.

'Oh my Lord, sir!' she said in a kind of intense
whisper. And, sinking into a chair, she began
thumping her chest as though with the intention of
counteracting her asthmatic breathing. 'Oh my
Lord, sir!'

'Whatever is the matter, Mrs —?' I enquired; and
again a thrill of uneasiness ran through me.

'Another of them pore creatures was cut to bits
last night, sir!' she cried.

I was puzzled; how did she know that already? The
affair had been too late, I felt certain, to gain
notice in the morning papers.

'The milkman's just told me,' she went on. 'And
they say — but there, I can't tell you what they say
has been done to her, sir!'

She paused, while I continued to wonder at her
extraordinary distress.

'But that's not the worst, sir!' she continued. And
she made stabbing motions towards the ceiling,

trying to muster her breath. 'He – he was out all night! And what do you think; I went to his bedroom to tidy up, and his left-off shirt and handkerchief are soaked in blood, sir! Soaked!'

I stared at my landlady, and the thought passed through my mind that my innocent-looking lodger was, perhaps, afflicted by a craving similar to my own. And that he was plagiarizing me. But I dismissed it as preposterous. The coincidence that such a fellow-worker should be living in the same house was not one to be entertained. I guessed the explanation of the blood.

'What on earth shall I do, sir?' my landlady asked. 'I can never live in the same house with a homicidal lunatic!' (She had got that phrase pretty pat.) 'Do you think I ought to tell a policeman? Thank Heavens I've got another man in the house!'

'Is he up there?' I asked.

'Yes, sir. It's his Saturday morning off.'

'Very well,' I said, rising. 'I'll go up and look into this!' And I went up.

My fellow-lodger was taking his breakfast, and when I taxed him with committing atrocities in the East End, and wagged my finger at him reproachfully, he was first aghast then, when I had explained, highly amused. It appeared that, as I had guessed, his nose had bled badly as a result, he thought, of his unusual exertions in walking the

long distance home. We both roared with laughter;
he thought I was a great wag.

It was really a good joke, but my landlady could
not be persuaded to see it. I think she still felt
slightly suspicious that she was harbouring the
'Whitechapel Murderer'.

Chapter 21.

The Hanbury Street affair took place in the early
morning of Saturday, September 8th, and on the
Monday following I awoke to find myself famous.
Until that morning I had not fully realized the
amount of interest and speculation which had been
aroused by the George-yard and Bucks Row cases; but
on opening my usual paper on this morning I
gathered that the whole nation had been working
itself into a pitch of mild excitement over these in
association with the assault upon Emma Smith in
April. The identity of the unknown craftsman
appeared to be the question of the day.

I had not been prepared for this wave of interest
though reflection showed me that I should have
been prepared for it; for the smug and respectable
British public loves nothing so much as a
mysterious murder, particularly a murder which
carries with it a suggestion of eroticism. Yet I will
admit that when I savoured this unlooked-for

publicity I experienced a thrill.

The satisfaction derived by many persons from any kind of public notice, be it in the form of fame or notoriety, is not, perhaps, such a curious phenomenon. Most of us like to talk about ourselves; to each of us there is nobody so important as 'I'. To read about that 'I' in a public print, to realize that one has attributes sufficiently distinctive from other members of the common herd to warrant mention in a paper printed for the interest and entertainment of many thousands, provides a peculiar pleasure to certain types of mind. The actress gloating over the critic's reference to her over-night performance; 'Paterfamilias' chuckling over his witty letter published in the 'From our Readers' column; the man pridefully clipping from the newspaper the smudgy portrait of himself appended to his testimony regarding the virtues of Somebody's Skin Ointment — all are moved by the same kind of reaction. They are all possessed by a form of superiority complex.

And I am doubtless similarly possessed, for I was thrilled when I read my newspapers on that particular morning; I was unable to enjoy the full measure of satisfaction since I could not hoard my 'press-cuttings' and exhibit them negligently to friends. I could not even cut out the accounts and paste them into a scrap-book; it would have been

indiscreet. Nevertheless, the thrill was there.
Whether it was engendered solely by the accounts of
my doings, or whether it was due to my feeling of
being the sole possessor of an exciting secret — the
knowledge that I alone, of all the millions of my
fellows, KNEW the identity of this mysterious
individual — I cannot say.

In the course of my reading I was startled to find
that a police-description of the 'wanted man' had
been issued, based upon information supplied by
someone who saw a man entering the Hanbury Street
premises in the early morning of the 8th September.
But my momentary uneasiness gave way to relief
when I read:

> Description of a man wanted who entered a
> passage of the house at which the murder
> of a prostitute was committed at 2. a.m. on
> September 8th. Age 37; height 5ft. 7in.;
> rather dark beard and moustache. Dress,
> dark jacket, dark vest and trousers; black
> scarf and black felt hat. Spoke with a
> foreign accent.

I knew then that the giver of the information had
not seen me; the height agreed, and I was dressed in
dark clothes, but I was clean shaven and I do not
speak with a 'foreign accent'. I was to learn later

that there was no dearth of persons able to give information to the police on the matter of my identity, and I believe that such is usually the case when a notorious malefactor is 'wanted'; most of my readers will be able to recall that a wealth of information was forthcoming as to the whereabouts of my late colleague, Dr Crippen.

Wherever possible the police appear to have been diligent in acting upon information, and this is well illustrated in the matter of the unfortunate 'Leather Apron'. When I first read of this man in the newspapers I supposed him to be a figment of hysterical imagination, but I learned later that he actually existed. He was a Polish Jew named Pizer and was probably a harmless individual, if an eccentric one. He was said to walk about Whitechapel wearing a leather apron and brandishing a knife; it was also said that his appearance was ferocious, that he was often soiled with blood, that he terrorized women, and so on and so forth. Such an original character was bound to arouse suspicion at that period of hysteria. The police arrested him and, in fact, produced him at the inquest on Mrs Chapman where he was questioned by the coroner; but, of course, he was ultimately released.

Pizer was but one of many arrested at this time; if my memory serves me it was on the 9th that the

great round-up of suspects commenced. On that first
day alone quite a considerable number of persons
were detained and questioned, and within a few days
the number had swollen to several dozens. One poor
neurotic even came forward and gave himself up as
the author of the 'atrocities', but a little
investigation soon convinced the police that he was
perfectly innocent — in that connection, at least.

I chuckled at first, but presently I became
slightly awed as the excitement grew more intense. I
felt rather like a man who has given a push to an
unattached cart standing on top of a hill; and now
the cart was progressing on its way, increasing its
velocity and causing the wildest consternation not
only to those in its path but to mere lookers-on.
And the bottom of the hill was not in sight.

Needless to say I was mainly concerned with this
wave of popular feeling in estimating its bearing
upon my own safety. Would the extraordinary
notoriety accorded to me, as the Unknown, increase
my risk of discovery? I thought the matter over and
decided it would not. Had I been less level-headed I
might have been overcome by panic, for it is a
fearsome thought that a whole population, urged
and inflamed by the unreasoning herd instinct, is
thirsting for one's blood. However, a mob must have
an actual objective: a Bastille to sack, a Negro to
lynch. It cannot launch itself against an

abstraction, and I was little more than an
abstraction. I must not confuse that which would
happen to me if the outraged citizenry laid hands
upon me, with the likelihood of its being able to do
so. Insofar as my past exploits were concerned,
since I had not been seen, had left no personal
traces and had acted with an entire lack of motive
(as that term is commonly understood), how could it
matter whether my identity was being speculated
upon by thirty-thousand policemen or ten-million
amateur policemen? Clearly the numerical factor had
no bearing whatever.

So much for the past; but what of the future? This
was a different matter, for when it comes to watching,
ten pairs of eyes are more efficient than one. They
can focus between them on a larger area. If I
continued my operations I should be moving in an
alert, hostile country; I should be plunging into an
area in which everyone was waiting and watching
for me. Every window, every street corner, might
harbour a lurking and enthusiastic spy. No mean
achievement to get through that cordon!

I read in my newspaper that a number of public-
spirited East Enders had formed themselves into
'Vigilance Committees' for the purpose of
patrolling the streets during the hours of
darkness. I read of the supine incompetency of the
police which rendered such precautions necessary;

but somehow I did not quite believe in that alleged incompetency; I felt fairly certain that the police were working steadily with mole-like efficiency even if they omitted to boast about it.

However, the newspapers pointed out, in so many words, that in the matter of the Whitechapel Murderer the police were clearly broken reeds; unkind things were said about them. The Commissioner was a retired General, but even the glory of his past vocation did not save him from epithets and innuendoes of a regrettable kind. The very Home Secretary himself was not spared.

I read all this and more, for pages could be filled with an account of the wave of excitement caused by the Whitechapel Atrocities; such waves do ride over our civilization at times, though they are usually due to a war or a football match. I have neither the time nor the inclination to give a more detailed account, but I cannot refrain from touching upon the 'comic relief' furnished by the bloodhounds. Bloodhounds were suggested by some bright mind as being peculiarly fitted to the task of tracking down the Whitechapel Murderer. The mere idea of employing bloodhounds in Whitechapel is funny, but the outcome was funnier still. For the grotesque idea caught on to the ignorant public mind, and the clamour for bloodhounds became insistent. In order to quieten this clamour

234

(presumably), bloodhounds were produced; they were tried out on Tooting Common before being loosed in the Whitechapel area. But the ingenuous hounds missed this opportunity of fame by getting lost; in fact, they got lost so thoroughly that the Police Stations had to be advised before they were recovered. Very amusing.

But, again, what of the future? Should I take the enormously increased risk attendant upon a continuation of my operations? I hesitated; and the Voice, the mystical 'X.', again became insistent.

I say mystical, but not mysterious. He was no longer that, for I knew his personality; had I not been granted a sight of him on that dreadful night when I had parted from Julia? And that first meeting must have been something like a conventional introduction for now he seemed no longer diffident about coming forward. He was no longer a mere Voice, he was a definite, visible presence.

On several occasions X. appeared in my sitting-room. I was intrigued when this first happened, but I was not alarmed. I was also extraordinarily interested. I am not proposing to offer any explanation of this; I have my views, and the reader may form his. I only recount that which happened.

He was always clothed as I had first seen him, in

tight-fitting black, and he always carried his coil of hard, black cord. He had a partiality for one special chair in my sitting-room, a deep arm-chair with a low, sagging seat. He would compose himself in this, his long, bony legs crossed, his elbows resting on the wings of the chair, and his finger-tips pressed together. His coil of rope he either hung on the back of a chair or dropped carelessly on the floor.

He was an entertaining but cynical conversationalist, and he spoke in an ordinary colloquial manner; his origin may have been mediaeval, but his speech and outlook were perfectly modern. I quite looked forward to his brief visits.

He always opened the conversation in the same manner. 'I'm damned tired,' he would say, sinking into his chair. 'Had a busy day.' And he would go on to tell me the details of that day. I do not think it politic to repeat any of these, for this is a weak-stomached generation.

'And when are you going to work again, young fellow,' he would say, eyeing me with a grin.

During the period when I was hesitating as to the wisdom of penetrating again to the East End, I put my doubts before him. He listened with an indulgent smile, and then waved away my objections. 'Yes,' he said, 'it may seem risky to you; but, you see, the point is that you will not be caught.'

'You mean, you know I shan't be caught?' I asked, curiously.

'You – will – not – be – caught,' he repeated, slowly and distinctly, pointing a finger at me.

Was I reassured by this? I think I was. Without pursuing a matter which may strike the stolid, unimaginative reader as grotesque, I may say that my chats with X. certainly did much to decide me. I resolved to continue my operations.

Chapter 22.

On Saturday September 29th I set out upon another
expedition. My previous plan of leaving my lodgings
after Mrs D. had retired to bed had proved so
successful that I repeated it; but I did not wait
until such a late hour for now that I knew the East
End was an armed and watchful camp I could no
longer rely upon the normal settling down of the
inhabitants. The success of my exploit must now
depend upon my own resource and ingenuity, and it
was therefore desirable that I should allow myself
time in which to spy out the land.

I left home just before eleven, for my landlady
went early to her room and my fellow-lodger was
passing the week-end with some friends.

I soon perceived that the newspaper reports of
the watchful activity in Whitechapel were greatly
exaggerated. There certainly seemed to be more
police about, but I saw no one who seemed likely to
be a member of the Vigilance Committees; at least

there were no indications of an organized patrolling of the streets. There seemed, in fact, to be fewer people about than usual; possibly the menace of the Unknown had developed a discretion which had urged many to remain indoors.

I met the woman whose name I afterwards learned was Mrs Stride near a fruit stall in Berners Street. She accosted me in the usual terms and then suggested that I should buy her some grapes. I was not, at that early hour, actually looking for my subject; nevertheless, acting upon impulse, I stopped and spoke to her. And we moved over to the fruit stall where I bought half a pound of grapes.

I caught the stall-keeper's eye upon me as he passed the paper bag over to me. It was not a suspicious, but a contemplative eye; yet it sent a sudden pang of uneasiness through me. I knew that I had been stupidly reckless in courting his notice. The woman at my side was certainly impossible as a subject; she and I had been seen together.

We walked away down the street together, she munching from the bag she held, I pacing thoughtfully at her side. I did not regard her as a possible subject, but it occurred to me that if I had to walk the streets for long I was no more conspicuous with her than I should have been as a solitary prowler.

The memory of that early evening is somewhat

hazy; I cannot recall exactly where we went, but I recollect our sitting under an archway while the woman talked in a rambling way of her affairs. She spoke with a foreign accent which I was, at the time, unable to identify; I thought she was probably a Dane, though it turned out afterwards that she was a Scandinavian. She told me, amongst other things, that she had had two children, both of whom had been drowned in the Princess Alice disaster. I listened sympathetically to her discourse; I felt sympathetic, for she struck me as being extraordinarily miserable. And I think it was this realization which decided me to ignore my earlier pang of nervousness at the fruiterer's glance, and to make this woman my subject. Here was clearly one who had nothing to hope for from life.

I abruptly rose to my feet. 'Come along,' I said, 'it's cold here.' This might be the woman but it was certainly not the place. Several people had passed while we had been sitting there, and although we were in shadow and I had no fear of subsequent recognition, the risk of operating there was too great for me to take. The woman must lead me to a better spot.

She struggled to her feet, still clutching her paper bag with the remnant of the grapes, and we resumed our walk.

Presently we found ourselves again in Berner

Street; the woman looked hastily around the deserted street and then turned suddenly into an alley, motioning me to follow. I did so and saw in the semi-obscurity a large gate. I paused momentarily as I caught sight of this, for there was something more. Leaning negligently against the gate was the black figure of X. As our eyes met, he pulled himself upright and made a grotesque, scraping bow, motioning towards the half-open gateway as he did so. Then he vanished into the black aperture. The woman appeared to have seen nothing; she took my sleeve and drew me beyond the gate into a dark yard.

At a spot near the gateway she sank down against a grimy wall and a rustling of the paper bag informed me that she was finishing her grapes. I sat down beside her and watched curiously as she ate the fruit, crunching the skin and spitting the seeds on to the ground around her. The sight and the attendant sounds suddenly aroused in me a rush of irritation; deliberately I rose to my feet. The woman paused in her eating and looked up at me in surprise, a grape held half-way to her mouth. Before she had time to guess my purpose I bent down and grasped her by the throat. Her eyes widened so that a rim of white surrounded the pupils; her mouth slopped open disclosing a mass of half-chewed grapes and, dropping the paper bag, she

clutched my wrist. Then her staring eyes shifted
from my face to my right hand groping in my breast-
pocket. I tightened my hold as I felt the muscles of
her throat writhing beneath my hand in an effort
to scream; then I pulled out my scalpel and plunged
it into her neck. She collapsed and sank to the
ground as I released my grip.

At that moment I heard the grinding of wheels
and the slither of hooves just outside the gate.

My mind switched abruptly from the huddled form
before me to that sinister sound, and I looked
quickly around me; in spite of the obscurity of the
yard I could see that the gateway was the only
egress. I was trapped.

I confess that in that moment of panic my nerves
all but failed me, though only for a second.
Everything went black before my eyes and down my
spine shot a cold thrill like a stream of icy water.
Then the panic passed and I recovered my self-
possession. I was trapped, but I would break the
trap. Whoever entered the yard need never live to
tell of what he had seen; one quick stab of my
scalpel from the shadow of the half-open gate as he
entered, and I should be free to depart unhindered.
The gate opened inwards and was swung half-way to
the wall; I tip-toed across the yard and crept into
the blackness behind the gate.

A pony and cart drove into the yard.

There came a clatter and scraping as the animal shied at that which it had seen upon the ground — or was it at that which it sensed behind the door? The driver muttered something under his breath and, peering from my hiding place, I saw him climbing down from the cart. He was not a yard away from me. As his foot reached the ground and he turned his back towards me, I slid from the shadow, passed between the gate and the cart and crept silently into the alley-way. I tip-toed along this into Berner Street and then broke into a run. Berner Street was deserted and I sped along it to another street and then turned into another. In a few seconds I was in a familiar thoroughfare. Nobody was in sight and I slackened my progress to a walk.

I found myself wet with a cold perspiration. I was still grasping the scalpel and my left hand was brown and sticky. I put away the weapon and tucked my left hand into my overcoat-pocket.

I set off home; I was rather pleasantly elated at the neat manner in which I had evaded the intruder, not because I was conscious of any particular skill on my part in doing so, but because it seemed that 'luck' had not deserted me. X. had assured me that I should not be caught, and this narrow escape tended to confirm his assurance, or so it seemed to me at the time. I became conscious of a feeling of increasing boldness.

But I was slightly disappointed with my night's work; the mere slitting of the woman's throat had not been very satisfying. My thoughts took a new channel and, in my mind, I cursed the unknown man who had come so inopportunely into the yard.

I had been walking towards home, and now found myself in a lighted thoroughfare; it was Houndsditch. The night was close and oppressive and seemed to promise thunder. Neither moon nor stars were visible, and the houses rose grimy and mottled in faintly illumined silhouette like buildings in a drawing by Sime. Here and there their surfaces were broken by oblongs of yellow light, or oblongs broken into patterns of light varying in density where the windows had been partially screened by ragged curtains or their glass-work repaired with patches of paper. The pavement gleamed slimily in the yellow glow of the street lamps and the muddy and garbage-littered roadway looked like the treacherous surface of a swamp in wait for the footsteps of the unwary.

A number of people were about. A man went by me wheeling an empty barrow which rattled over the stones of the roadway. A group of rough-looking youths, caps pulled over their faces, lounged at the entrance of a passage; they turned as I passed and cast curious glances upon me. A Chinese slid by; a drunken sailor lurched against me and stumbled on. And then a woman stumbled from an alley-way and stopped before me, grinning into my face. In the light of a street lamp I looked her over.

She was more or less drunk. She was a short, elderly woman dressed in a black jacket with a moth-eaten collar of imitation fur and three grotesquely large metal buttons. Her skirt looked like a piece of window-curtain; it was of dingy green print patterned with a faded design of flowers. She wore broken men's boots and her head was covered by a black straw bonnet trimmed with black beads and green velvet; once it might have looked coquettish, now it looked merely pathetic.

I had half intended to go home, but the sight of this grotesque, leering creature made me hesitate. My experience that evening had been disappointing, but here was another subject ready to my hand.

I looked around; nobody seemed to be observing me and I followed her away from the light and into a side-street. Here I talked to her for a few moments; she was not too drunk to understand me and presently led me back towards the direction from which I had come. I should not have gone far that way, for I had no intention of returning to the neighbourhood of the earlier affair; however, she turned again into another street, and so through others until at last we emerged into a dark, deserted square.

A footstep broke the silence and I drew the woman into a dark corner as a policeman strolled by.

As soon as he had passed the drab uttered a sort of chuckle and gave me a playful shove. ''E didn't see us that time, dearie,' she said.

I grinned at the woman's words and at the thought of how she would have dashed after the constable, imploring his protection, at a revealing word from me. I looked sideways at her and saw that her face bore a silly smirk; she caught my eye and laboriously winked. I regarded her curiously; I wondered whether she had been suffering under the universal nervousness and panic; whether she had ever considered the possibility of meeting the Whitechapel Murderer. Had she just heard of him as she might hear of an earthquake in a remote country – something interesting and exciting but never likely to touch her? Did she exercise no caution in the plying of her trade? Evidently not, for she had accepted me with hardly a second glance. What nonsense we hear about the intuition of women!

A spirit of impishness impelled me to remark: 'You haven't met our friend the Murderer yet then?'

'Garn,' she said, contemptuously, 'I ain't afraid of no murderer, I ain't. I reckon there ain't no such person. 'E's only somethink got up by the noospapers. Let's go over to that corner.'

I followed her to the spot indicated. 'So you don't believe in the mysterious killer?' I persisted. 'But how about these women who've been killed?'

'Give over!' she replied. 'A sailor done that; we know all about 'im round 'ere. There ain't no one else, you take my word. 'E's bin got up by the noospapers. And the bobbies,' she added after a pause. She sat down on the pavement.

I looked around the square. It was a small one, paved with cobbles and enclosed on three sides by what I took to be warehouses. On the fourth was a dwelling-house. I observed several entrances to the square, and was reassured; never again would I operate in a cul-de-sac.

By way of answer I leaned down and took her by the throat while my right hand groped in my pocket for the scalpel. At that instant the side of the square on which we were was dimly illuminated by the moon as it now burst through the clouds which had concealed it during most of the evening. This was very convenient, and I took full advantage of the moonlight. And as I was able to work without hurry I made quite a good job of this affair.

I reached home relatively early, feeling extremely tired, but satisfied with my evening's work. I had

not only done that which I had set out to do, but I
had done it in spite of the alleged Vigilance
Committees; I looked forward, with some excitement,
to the newspaper uproar I knew would follow.

Chapter 23.

My sobriquet 'Jack the Ripper' was chosen not by
myself, but by another. And the circumstances were
such as to require special mention.

During the first few days of October I learned
from my newspaper that the Central News Agency had
received a letter written in red ink and smeared
with dried blood, purporting to come from the
unknown assassin and referring to a prospective
campaign in Whitechapel. It was signed 'Jack the
Ripper'. On the morning following the Berners
Street and Mitre Square affairs the Agency received
a second communication, a postcard, similarly
signed.

Since great excitement was caused by these
missives at the time, and much discussion has taken
place since regarding them, I may state definitely
that I was not the author. They were written, I
judge, by a practical joker of eccentric humour who
doubtless derived much entertainment from his

innocent pleasantries. But this unknown poet gave me my name; henceforward I was 'Jack the Ripper'.

But Jack the Ripper became something more than a name; he began to take on a definite personality built up from scraps and smatterings of inaccurate and purely imaginative 'information'. Dozens of people were able to describe a man they had seen in 'suspicious circumstances'. Sometimes he had accosted women who, feeling frightened at 'something in his manner', had escaped in time. He had distributed tracts to women; he had appeared in many circumstances which aroused suspicion in the minds of the witnesses — when they came to think it over. But for some reason which I am unable to explain, all the evidence tallied on one point: J.R. always carried a shiny black bag.

Now I never carried, nor even possessed, a black bag; but many men did, and some of them attracted such unfavourable notice by their simple equipment that they were chased by the outraged citizenry. One or two clerks or working men narrowly escaped lynching. This sounds almost Gilbertian, read today; but at the time of the Terror it was nothing to laugh at. I recall hearing that a certain woman opened the door of her cottage in response to a knock and immediately fell dead upon catching sight of her visitor. This is a result which few of us can hope to achieve, but this man happened to be carrying a black bag.

'The Man with the Black Bag' and 'Jack the Ripper' were terms uttered fearfully, as less enlightened nations pronounce the secret name of a testy deity. They were meat and drink to good Mrs D. my landlady.

But I can state with authority that no one did see J.R. with a black bag, and that only one person, other than his subjects, saw him in 'suspicious circumstances'; that incident I will now mention.

I have already described how, in the company of the woman Stride, I bought some grapes, and how I caught the fruiterer's ruminative eye upon me. In the later excitement of the evening I forgot this, and I will confess that in this respect I was guilty of a piece of reckless oversight.

A few days later I read in the newspapers of a message which, it was alleged, had been chalked upon a wall by Jack the Ripper. According to the report the legend read: 'The Jews are not the people to be blamed for nothing'. (Incidentally I may remark that a section of the public favoured a theory that the Unknown was of Jewish extraction.) I was curious to see this message and decided to go to Whitechapel. When I arrived at the spot indicated by the papers I found that the writing had been erased by the police; and I was retracing my steps when I passed the fruiterer's stall, and again saw the fruiterer.

And he saw me; recollection came to me as I caught his eyes upon me, and in that eye I saw a sudden interest and fixity. He remembered me, and he remembered when and in what company he had seen me.

I passed and continued my walk without, as I thought, hastening my pace; but I felt, rather than saw, the man leave his stall and take a few steps in my direction. At the corner I gave a brief glance backwards; the fruiterer was speaking to a boy and pointing towards me. I turned the corner and rapidly increased my pace, and in a few minutes I found myself in a main street thronged with people and traffic.

Here luck was with me, for a tram had stopped and was just re-starting within a few yards of the end of the street from which I had emerged. I jumped on to the platform, and as the conveyance jangled on I looked back through the doorway and saw the boy, who had obviously been instructed to follow me, standing on the pavement and staring after.

Yes, luck had been with me; luck or Destiny. But what an escape! As I sat in the tram something in my expression must, I think, have betrayed my uneasiness; I at least imagined that several fellow-passengers were casting curious glances upon me, and the conductor certainly looked sharply into my face as he punched my ticket. He had seen my hasty scramble on to the platform; had he also noticed my follower?

I was seated in the corner of the tram and now I examined my fellow-passengers more carefully; and I became aware, for the first time, how extraordinarily self-conscious one can become in a public conveyance. Here were a dozen or twenty people sitting together, passive, free for a brief space from the necessity of action, their limbs at rest but their minds ceaselessly busy with the gnawing worries of their individual affairs. Each an individual 'I' to whom all others were merely units of environment. And yet the mere presence of this group of silent, passive people, their roaming fish-like eyes, made me self-conscious.

Despite the suggestion conveyed that each of these travellers was shut away and isolated, indifferent to his or her fellows, the eyes would wander from trifle to trifle; the attention would be caught occasionally by an object of sufficient passing interest to drag the mind from its ruminating to a consciousness of surrounding things. A text pasted on a window of the tram; a gaping wound in the boot of a woman; a bundle of rough wood held between the knees of a workman; an intriguing brown-paper parcel clutched under the

arm of a flashily dressed Jewess. Or the relatively
respectable black suit and hat of a sallow, quick-
breathing man in the corner.

I looked cautiously along the row of people
facing me, and caught one or two pairs of eyes
resting meditatively upon me. I turned my head and
stared out of the back of the tram; then I glanced
stealthily back again. Several persons were now
looking at me, though most of them turned their
eyes away as they perceived my observation. But a fat
woman seated in the corner opposite my own, her lap
encumbered with a large basket filled with
vegetables and one or two newspaper packages,
maintained her stare. She sat there heavy, motionless,
a sagging mass of fat, one side of her face persistently
twitching as she sucked at a tooth, her little pig eyes
fixed steadily upon my face.

I looked above her head at an advertisement
pasted on the roof of the tram, but I could see,
without actually looking at the woman, that her
attention was still fixed upon me. Or was it
attention? Was it not perhaps the mere fixed,
unthinking gaze of one entirely absorbed by inward
thoughts? Was she really seeing me at all? I looked
quickly downwards and then back again at the
advertisement. Yes, the woman was really observing
and studying me; there was intelligence and
interest in those pig eyes.

And then, as I tried to ignore the woman by concentrating my attention upon the advertisement, I was suddenly possessed by an extraordinary feeling. It seemed as though a telepathic message was emanating from the fat woman, a message addressed to her fellow-travellers and catching their attention one by one. 'Here's a funny-looking fellow,' the message said. 'There's something about him I can't quite make out. Have a look at him; what do you all think? Doesn't he look nervous as though he was afraid of something? Have a look at him. Doesn't he look scared? Have a look at him. Have a look.' And I could feel other heads turned in my direction one by one, feel other eyes studying me covertly as I tried to fix my attention on the advertisement.

I longed for something to break the spell of that silent scrutiny; if only someone would speak! Any trivial muttered remark to show that these staring creatures were human. Something like panic obsessed me. I turned abruptly to the conductor at my elbow and addressed him with the first words which came into my head. 'They don't seem to have caught this fellow yet,' I said.

'Ah, they'll catch him all right,' replied the conductor sagely. 'Don't you worry.' He knew at once who 'this fellow' meant, and so did everyone in the tram. Every head turned swiftly in my direction;

even the travellers on my side of the tram craned
their heads forward to look at me.

That break in the silence was sufficient to
unloose a flow of talk. Each traveller turned to
his unknown neighbour; half a dozen conversations
commenced. 'This fellow' was a topic to set every
tongue wagging; no one but could advance some
theory, recount some hearsay incident, suggest what
ought to be done to the 'fellow' when caught.

'They say they're sendin' out tecs dressed as
women —'

'The papers say —'

'No, she sez to me. I daren't go. Not at this time o'
night —'

''Eard 'em we did. Footsteps creepin' like up the
stairs. An' my missus sez to me —'

'They say they couldn't find out oo she was, she
was so cut to bits an' all —'

'No, it's more than six. It's eight. 'Ow about that
one down by the river —'

'They knows right enough. You take my tip.
Waitin' to cetch 'im red-'anded, that's wot they're
doin' —'

'Yus, they say 'e carries away bits in that there
bag —'

'Dirty — ! That's wot 'e is. 'Angin's too good fer
'im. If I 'ad my way —'

'Any more fepisss-s!'

'They say —'

'The papers say —'

But the fat woman spoke no word: only eyed me steadily, sucking at her tooth. I could stand it no longer and, jumping up, I jerked the cord in the roof and left the tram. On the kerb I looked back at the retreating vehicle and through the door caught a glimpse of that heavy face, bent forward and turned in my direction.

For five weeks I pursued a quiet and uneventful life with my books and my drawing. I eschewed newspapers and offered no encouragement to my landlady's chatter. I knew that my craving had led me into recklessness, and in that direction lay detection. I managed, by concentrating upon other things, to still my craving. For five weeks.

Chapter 24.

The streets again, long rows of monotonous houses
grimy and glistening with an unhealthy sweat
where the recent rain had swept them; the windows
patched with boards, newspapers and scraps of
ragged clothing. Here and there through an
aperture a subdued light could be seen, and on
screens of ragged fabric moved figures in
grotesquely elongated silhouette, their pathetic
attempts at privacy betrayed by the light behind
them.

Occasional street lamps, naphtha flares on
barrows and the illuminated windows of shops cast
patches of light upon the pavements and walls,
intersecting in triangles of varying brightness,
while the bluish moonlight played upon the shiny
roofs forming patterns with the black shadows of
the chimney-stacks.

And a ceaseless mutter and the shuffle, shuffle
of innumerable feet upon the greasy pavements.

I stood on a kerb before a fried-fish shop curiously regarding its steady flow of customers. The shop was brightly lit by several gas-jets and, from my position, I could see the counter behind which a sweating man in shirt-sleeves and cloth cap strove to serve fairly in turn each of his clamouring customers. Men and women elbowed each other in efforts to reach the counter before the supply of fish gave out; for within a short time the shop would close for the night. The fortunate ones broke with difficulty from the crowd around the counter and emerged from the shop clutching their purchases. Some paused outside to open their newspaper-wrapped packets and then proceeded slowly, their faces bent over their repasts, their fingers picking. Others shuffled quickly away bearing home their suppers.

From the shop came a buzz of chatter, and a penetrating odour of fried fish.

Outside the shop a man stood, monotonously rocking backwards and forwards a home-made perambulator in which a baby slept. Presently a young woman pushed her way from the shop holding a packet of fish; she took her husband's arm and they went off, pushing the perambulator before them.

A rough-looking man came out holding some fish on a slip of newspaper upon his upraised palm; he

picked at the fish, his jaws working, while he stood
by the window of the shop. He wore a large cap
which shadowed his bent face. He remained there
eating, and I saw his eyes upon my motionless figure
by the kerb, running up and down my person. I wore
a very old suit and a pair of broken, muddy boots,
and my attitude and appearance must have suggested
a person fascinated by the sight and smell of the
fish-shop yet without the means to buy. The man
suddenly advanced and thrust his paper of fish in
front of me. ''Ave a bit, mate?' he invited.

I was startled and declined with some mumbled
words of thanks. Then I turned on my heel and went
off down the street.

I wandered on through streets and alleys, crossed
Whitechapel High Street still rumbling with
traffic and plunged into another network of slums.
It was a raw night in early November with a
suggestion of mistiness in the air, and I mended my
pace for I was feeling chilly. As I went I examined
furtively the people I passed. Some were hurrying,
intent upon reaching their homes; others were
loitering, while some were even lounging in
doorways or the shadowed recesses between walls.
Some of the latter I guessed to be police officers in
plain clothes, for the newspapers had informed me
how closely the streets had been watched since my
double exploit.

Many women of the 'unfortunate' class were
about, but few were walking singly.

I walked about the streets until what must have
been, I think, the early hours of the morning, and
then I came suddenly upon an elderly drab
crouching in a doorway. As I paused and looked down
at her she grinned into my face and greeted me with
the grotesque endearments with which I was now
familiar. I turned my head and looked around;
the slum was deserted. Then I went closer to the
woman.

Did my action in scanning the street arouse
suspicion in the woman, or did an expression on my
face warn her? I do not know. But in a moment her
leering smile vanished giving place to a look of
surprise and horror. She leaned there against the
door, her hands stiffly outstretched, the palms
resting against the blistered paintwork. For an
appreciable interval neither of us moved. Then she
ducked, slipped by me and set off down the street at
a shambling run. At the corner she turned and
looked back at my still motionless figure. Then she
disappeared.

Chuckling I resumed my walk. The sense of power
aroused by this creature's tribute to my
personality offset my slight disappointment. And,
very soon, I saw another female figure in front of
me; it seemed to be that of a younger woman and,

from the uncertainty of her walk, I thought that
she was probably drunk. I followed her into a
narrow court where she mounted a step and pushed
open a door; as she did so she looked back over her
shoulder and perceived me.

I advanced from the shadowed entrance to the
court and she regarded my approach with a grin. She
was no elderly drab, I saw, but a woman of, perhaps,
thirty years, her face heavily powdered and her
clothing flashily smart. She was not so bad-looking
and as she stood there smirking I experienced a
wave of excitement. Here was a 'subject' differing
greatly from the others: a certain novelty was
promised. She winked and jerked her head towards
the open door and then, seeing me step forward
again in response, entered.

In the darkness within the entrance I felt her
hand upon my arm, and she turned from the passage
and drew me into a ground-floor room in the front
of the house. I could see nothing but the grey
oblong of the window draped with a thin muslin
curtain.

I heard movements in the darkness and the
scraping of a match; a rush of feeble yellow light
as the woman lit an oil lamp revealed the interior
of the room.

In an earlier chapter I have referred to that
curious habit my memory has of recalling

outstanding incidents in purely visual form. I can picture now that scene in the room in Millers Court, but I cannot re-capture the first conversation and can do no more than assume its purport. Nothing of what was said with the exception of the few sentences at the last comes back to me.

The room was a small square one, its walls covered with faded wall-paper which, here and there, hung in torn fragments where it had peeled away, revealing beneath another grimy paper of different pattern. Near the floor, and up to a height of a couple of feet, strips of the paper had been torn vertically; it seemed as if a child or a mischievous puppy had been at work.

Of furniture there was little. A large iron bed-stead with one remaining brass knob and frowsty-looking bed-clothes occupied much of the space. A small wash-hand stand of thin deal bearing remnants of brownish paint stood against one wall beneath a lithographed 'supplement' from a Christmas annual; near it was a chair with a broken back and a padded seat oozing grey flock. The oil lamp which the woman had lit stood on a flimsy little table near the bed.

I think the young woman and I must have talked for some time but I cannot, as I have said, recall our early conversation. I sat on the broken chair and I can picture her perched on the edge of the bed, or moving about the room. I remember that soon after our entry to the room she screened the window by pinning up a piece of tattered rep curtain, and that I was grateful to her for this precautionary act. And, in the course of our talk, she, in a very leisurely way, completely undressed.

I had not noticed it at first but now perceived on the wall beside the bed a square of mirror suspended in a narrow wooden frame. Some movement of my own must have attracted my attention, for I caught a reflection of my own face. For some extraordinary reason I can remember clearly what was said from that point onwards.

'What's your name, dearie?' the woman said. She was not drunk but, on the other hand, she was not sober. She sat there immediately beneath the square of mirror so that, to my fancy, my face hung above her own. In that moment a thrill of nervous excitement shot through me and I felt my hands wet and clammy; I slowly rubbed the palms on my knees. I did not immediately reply to the woman's question; I was absorbed in my sensation of excitement and anticipation. I remained silent, staring at her and mechanically rubbing my palms backwards and forwards.

'What's your name, dearie?' she repeated.

I found that my lips had gone stiff and dry; I

passed my tongue over them and replied, slowly:
'What do you want to know for?'

She gave her head a toss. 'Oh, I don't want to know
particular.' She grinned at me. 'I don't care what
yer name is. So long as it ain't Jack.'

I rose slowly to my feet and as I did so caught a
glimpse of my reflection in the mirror. I can
visualize the expression now. I thrust my face
forward towards the woman, and as I did so I felt,
rather than saw, my image blur and expand. Ghost-
like suggestions of other faces peered, distorted,
around my head; mouthed over my shoulder. And then
I spoke, clearly and distinctly.

'As a matter of fact,' I said, 'my name is Jack.'

She gave a single cry of 'Murder!' as I reached out
and clutched her throat. That cry, I afterwards
learned, was heard by an inmate of the house who
did not, fortunately for me, trouble to investigate.
I stood rigid for a few seconds, grasping her throat
with both hands and listening intently. Not a sound
broke the silence without; I was conscious only of
the blood drumming in my ears and a low gasping
and wheezing from the woman as she squirmed and
struggled under my grasp.

I was able to work quietly and at leisure.

I had no premonition as I set out for a walk on the
following day of that which was awaiting me. I

could not foresee that on that day Jack the Ripper would practically cease to be. I went briskly along the pavement, picking my way between the pedestrians and not observant, to any extent, of my surroundings. I was 'licking the chops of memory' to quote one of Stevenson's expressive phrases; pondering the events of the night. But in a crowded thoroughfare the cry of a newsboy attracted my attention. The raucous and familiar cry: 'The Ripper Again!' drew me out of the past to the immediate present.

I fumbled for a copper and stepped unthinkingly into the road towards the lad on the other side. "'Orrible discovery in Whitechapel!' was the last thing I heard before there came a jangle of bells, a shout and a jarring crash; and with that consciousness abruptly left me.

I cannot fix any definite time at which I returned to a perception of life; its dawning was too gradual. I was dimly aware of unfamiliar bare walls and rows of beds with ghost-like figures flitting amongst them long before I was able to correlate these impressions into the realization that I was in a hospital.

When a measure of intelligence returned to me I discovered that my head was swathed in bandages; and I was conscious of a dull throbbing in my right leg.

They told me I had been knocked down by a hansom and that the wheel of a dray had passed over my leg. My right leg. That throbbing was deceptive; I had no longer a right leg to throb.

Part 3

Chapter 25.

When I commenced this record, some months ago, it
was my intention to conclude it by the description
of my Millers Court exploit and the subsequent loss
of my limb. This seemed to me a natural conclusion
because the woman of Millers Court was my final
'subject' and the accident put an end to my active
life; while the many years which have since elapsed
have brought to me no more than the trivial
incidents of a hum-drum existence — certainly
nothing worthy of inclusion in this
unconventional autobiography. Forty years of
hum-drum existence, mark you, gentle reader; it
hardly seems right, does it? You, who can look back
upon a blameless life entirely free from bloodshed
except, perhaps (if you are a man), a few years of
purely patriotic bloodshed, may quite justifiably
feel a certain resentment at the dilatory behaviour
of Nemesis; in my case, at least, the daughter of
Erebus is hardly what our American friends would

call a fast worker. In fact if I die peacefully in
bed, as I hope to do, that melancholy event will
hardly seem to square with your ideas regarding the
prevalence of right and justice. I know that I
should have, according to your lights, an extremely
unpleasant end.

Yet perhaps I am being unduly cynical in
assuming in you an entire lack of understanding — I
will not say sympathy — which I can hardly expect.
For I have tried, in the course of this record, to
convey my sense of being a mere plaything of
Destiny; an instrument in some scheme of Fate. Yet
what, may well be asked, can that scheme have been?

We touch here upon one of the most elusive
problems of the universe. A baby is born; he is
carefully tended and cherished, nursed through
illnesses, educated and fed to the end that he may
become a useful member of society. He gradually
develops under the loving and marvelling eyes of
his parents to that miraculous and efficient
organism a man. And then at the age of twenty he is
killed in a futile war. Why?

A city is painfully and laboriously built; for
many years, centuries perhaps, princes, architects,
artists and slaves lavish upon it their wealth and
toil until at last it stands completed, a monument
to man's energy and efficiency. And an earthquake
destroys it in a day. Again why?

Ask our philosophers the purpose of such cruel and wanton events; they will tell you they do not know. Ask our parsons; they will tell you that God moves in mysterious ways; or, in other words, that they do not know. But I, who am less competent to judge than the philosophers, though more competent, I think, than the parsons, will make bold to suggest that the catastrophes visited upon suffering humanity, as individuals or in the aggregate, are simply the caprices of a malevolent and irresponsible Power. This is admittedly a depressing doctrine, but what other can a reasoning and unprejudiced man hold?

The theory I advance is, at least, not one to be readily upset by the test of human experience. In the light of it we may cease to wonder at the tribulations of mankind. And certain 'laws of nature' would seem to lend support to my belief, since most of these clearly tend to the discomfort, rather than to the comfort, of humanity. Take, for example, the 'laws' of heredity.

A man is the product of heredity and environment. If he is born in a slum of thievish parents, descendants of rogues and doxies, the chances that he will grow up to be other than a dishonest scoundrel, a nuisance to himself and others, are so trivial as to be negligible. But he is merely the sport of demons; he is perfectly helpless.

His fate has indeed been hung about his neck.

Are we to blame that wretched product of heredity? We may imprison or even hang him, since he is a nuisance to other citizens whose parents happened to be respectable; but we ought to do it kindly and sympathetically because, you know, he would have chosen respectable parents himself had he been allowed the chance. And I would respectfully remind you, reader, that it is due to the caprice of chance and not to any merit of yours that you were not similarly handicapped at birth.

'Ah!' you may say, yawning behind your hand, 'I can see what this fellow is driving at. He is trying to make out that he couldn't help being a filthy assassin because he was born like that.'

Well, after all, I was 'born like that', O reader. Do you really suppose that if your ancestors had engaged, through generations, in the daily avocation of cutting, ripping and rending their fellow humans; investigating, and inventing perhaps, ingenious dodges for killing with the maximum amount of discomfort to their victims; blood and torn flesh the ordinary accompaniments of their everyday life; do you really suppose that with such forebears you would have been the nice person you are? Like the baby mentioned in 'Punch', you have always 'kept yourself respectable', but do not take too much credit to yourself.

So much for my theory of Providence, which you may accept or reject according to your circumstances and your capacity for thought. Paradoxical as it may seem, my own latter years have been rendered more comfortable by the belief in malevolent Destiny to which I have referred; it has freed me so thoroughly from responsibility. I have been actuated not by a deliberately cultivated wish to do evil in the sight of others; I have been driven, willy-nilly, along a course mapped out for me. The fate of every man, etc.

And as my latter years have been comfortable I might have ended this record on a note of smugness; a tame ending and very disappointing to a reader accustomed to a proper climax in his literature. But you are not to be disappointed after all; you shall have your final burst of excitement. For it has been brought home to me, quite recently, that even at this eleventh hour I may make the acquaintance of the hang-man in his business capacity unless I bestir myself very thoroughly.

You find me then, after a hiatus of forty-two years, living in rooms in a street not far from Russell Square. It is a tall Georgian house with window-boxes, a green door and a highly polished brass knocker; a house respectable in every sense of the word. My living-room is on the first floor; my bed-room at the back of the third.

The latter arrangement is my own choice, and this choice was not dictated by reasons of economy; for although my means have been depreciated by the war and subsequent taxation, I am sufficiently comfortable, financially, to be able to avoid pinching. The room immediately below my bed-room was occupied when I first came to the house; I could have had a room in the front, but I preferred that at the back for the reason that one of its windows communicates with a fire-escape. And I happen to have a morbid horror of fire.

My landlady's name is Hamlett. My mention of her name would appear to be inconsistent with my earlier declaration that I proposed to avoid mentioning the name of any person at present living; I hope, however, that the conclusion of this record will show that there is no such inconsistency.

Mrs Hamlett is, so far as I know, an excellent woman, and her efforts for the comfort of myself and my fellow-boarder have been unceasing. She is tall and thin and although well past her prime has been sufficiently infected by the virus of modernity to bob her hair, which hangs beside her face and occasionally over her eyes in a series of rat-tails. She is lugubrious in manner but is fortunately free from the garrulous propensities

of her tribe – a great advantage in my eyes. She is
assisted by a maid-of-all-work named Minnie – a
typical post-war product complete with
indifferently shingled hair and artificial silk
hose. She is chatty, but her chattiness may be
stemmed by hints. I have rather taken to Minnie;
she is a fair example of a decent English board-
school girl whose education has been completed by
the American 'talkies', and although she shows a
tendency to lapse, occasionally, into the diction of
the Bowery I believe that she has a streak of shrewd
and kindly common-sense. I have a feeling that, in
emergency, Minnie would show up well.

Of my fellow-boarder I need say but little. He is, I
believe, a retired civil-servant addicted to the
collection of stamps; this hobby he pursues with such
unnatural zest that he frequently absents himself
for days at a time in order to attend sales. Sales, at
least, are the ostensible reason for his absences.

As for myself, you may picture an elderly and
comfortable bachelor, hampered, it is true, by the
loss of a leg and inclined at times to testiness and
irritability. But so far as my testiness is
concerned, my helots, like my associates at the
club, 'make allowances'; they derive, I think, a
certain spiritual satisfaction from 'making
allowances'. I wish I were a sufficiently 'nice'
person to appreciate this, but I am not. Accustomed,

as I have been, for many years to my affliction,
sympathy, expressed or implied, still mildly
irritates me.

And now, after this brief introductory chapter,
let me begin the relation of those events which are
to be, I think, the 'last lap' of a not uneventful
career.

Chapter 26.

I admitted, earlier in this chronicle, an interest in the cinema, but at the time of writing I had, of course, no inkling that I might be personally affected by this popular invention. I find it strange and rather uncanny that my peace and security may be affected, after forty years, by 'the pictures'. Yet so it is.

I am a frequent visitor to the cinema and for this there are several reasons. In spite of my recent literary activities and a certain amount of bridge-playing at the club, time hangs heavily upon me; the cinema is a convenient form of amusement and, for a man of my age, an innocent one; and my experience in drawing has led me to take an interest in the technical side of the film.

This is neither the time nor the place for a dissertation on my part on the cinema, but it is desirable that the following be mentioned:

My technical interest was developed almost

entirely by the study of German and Norwegian
films in those halcyon days, all too brief, which
now appear to have passed. The false and childish
sentiment and the blatancy of the average American
film used to distress me until I found the cure; I
disliked the distorted impressions, conveyed by
these films, of the American people. I happen to
have visited America, I have met many educated
Americans, and I can state quite definitely that
good-class citizens of the United States are grossly
libelled by the American film. I disliked, also, the
grotesque ethical values exhibited in these films, I
was distressed by their lack of accuracy in
historical detail and, above all, I resented the
American film-producers' distortion of English
masterpieces of fiction in order to bring such
works within the boundaries of what they doggedly
and ignorantly assume to be popular taste; the most
glaring offence in this connection being, of
course, the introduction of an alien or wholly
unsuitable 'love interest'.

As I say, I disliked all this until I found the
cure; and as, doubtless, I am not alone in my
prejudices I will do a good deed and pass the cure
on. It is simply to cease to regard an American film
of the baser sort as a drama, but to view it as a
satire or a farce. Once this attitude of mind has
been acquired it is surprising what a lot of

pleasure can be derived from an American film; for myself I have experienced the greatest enjoyment from certain films whose alleged pathos has induced unrestrained weeping in the less enlightened female portion of the audience.

Nevertheless my serious interest in the cinema has been centred mainly in the German films, and it was only by an oversight that I missed the first showing in this country of a particularly effective production called 'Waxworks'. But, quite recently, this was revived and I was able to see it.

'Waxworks' was divided into three distinct episodes dealing, respectively, with three notorious characters: Ivan the Terrible of Russia, the Khaleefeh Haroon Er-Rasheed and Jack the Ripper. As to the historical treatment meted out to the first two worthies I am incompetent to judge; I can only testify to the artistic interest of the two parts of the film concerned. But as regards the episode of J.R., I am able to state, from definite knowledge, that it bore not the slightest resemblance either in person, scene or action to the reality; of course I should have marvelled had it been otherwise. But I was extremely interested; technically it was perfect; as a glimpse of the macabre it left nothing to be desired even by the most unwholesome intelligence.

It will be appreciated, of course, that I do not

refer to this film simply for the personal satisfaction of expressing my views; I mention it because of what it led to. For, knowing my landlady to be a film-addict, I recommended her to see 'Waxworks', but without giving her any description. She took my advice.

A few evenings later I was reading in my sitting-room when Mrs Hamlett entered with a glass of hot milk, which I am accustomed to take before going to bed. I looked up and perceived that her eyes were red with weeping.

'Why, Mrs Hamlett; has something upset you?' I asked.

'Oh, Mr Carnac; that horrid film you sent me to see!' she said. 'If I'd known what it was about I wouldn't have gone near it!'

'Well, perhaps it was a trifle gruesome,' I admitted. 'But I had no idea it would upset you, Mrs Hamlett, or I would not have advised you to see it.'

'Gruesome isn't the word, Mr Carnac. But it wasn't that quite; I've seen films as bad. It was that horrible part about Jack the Ripper. You see, sir, it set me thinking. There are some things I thought I'd forgotten; or at least left off thinking about, if you understand what I mean. But when I saw that horrible thing on the pictures to-night it brought it all back to me as if it was yesterday.'

'But I'm afraid I don't understand, Mrs Hamlett,'

I said. 'Why should a recollection of Jack the Ripper worry you? Those affairs have been forgotten years ago; and you could have been no more than a young girl at the time. I should hardly have thought you would have remembered them.'

'My poor sister,' she said. 'It set me thinking of her.' And she drew out a sodden morsel of handkerchief and began to dab her eyes.

'What about your sister, Mrs Hamlett?' I asked. I was conscious of a sudden rush of eager curiosity, for I had more than an inkling of what was coming.

'She was murdered by that horrible wretch, Mr Carnac,' she continued. 'They said she was cut about in a shocking manner. Of course I was only young at the time, but they couldn't keep it from me, what with the police in the house, and the papers and everything. And then my poor mother never got over it. She wasn't strong, for we had a hard life when I was a child, sir. She died soon after, and everyone said it was the dreadful shock.'

I stared at my landlady as she dabbed at her eyes, and my mind was mainly concerned with the extraordinary coincidence. It seemed to me, at the time, remarkable that I should have been on familiar terms for several years with this good woman without suspecting, for a moment, that she was related to one of my 'subjects'. And yet I do not see why I need have been surprised; after all, some of the women I had disposed of must have had living relatives. Rather remarkable, perhaps, that I had not before encountered one during the past forty years.

'Do sit down, Mrs Hamlett,' I said. 'Perhaps you'd care to tell me about it, if it's not too painful a subject. I need not say how sorry I am that I suggested you should see that film; of course I had no idea.'

'I don't mind telling you about it, sir,' she replied. 'I shall probably be awake all night thinking about it, as it is. The harm's done now, – not, of course, that I mean I blame you, Mr Carnac. You were not to know, of course. And I don't suppose you can understand me carrying on like this for something that happened so long ago. We all have to bear the death of someone we're fond of, sooner or later, and try to forget it. But when it's a natural death it's somehow different. It's knowing that the person ought never to have died, Mr Carnac; what I mean: not died young. That they might still be alive if it were not for a horrible brute. I know I can't explain properly, sir, but perhaps you'll understand what I mean. And then there's the feeling that the beast who murdered her has never been caught, and the thought of what you'd like to do to him if you only could. It's all very well to talk about 'Vengeance is mine, said the Lord', but most people don't know what it is to want revenge as I've wanted it; to lie awake at night thinking about it. And never getting it. I don't suppose you've ever felt like that, sir.'

'Well, no, I haven't, Mrs Hamlett. But perhaps I can understand it.'

And, in fact, I was just beginning to envisage a point of view which had hardly occurred to me before. The degradation of the women with whom I had dealt so many years ago had been such as to preclude the thought that they might possess decent relatives; and I, who rather prided myself upon my imagination, had taken the women entirely at their face value as though they had evolved from the slime. Even the appearance of respectable witnesses at the various inquests and their identification of the bodies had not held for me a definite significance; I had ignored that universal phenomenon, the inter-relation of individuals, as of events; I had regarded those women as separate and disconnected unities. And now, for the first time, I was face to face with one of those repercussions which I had not had the wit to imagine.

'I was brought up in a Christian home, Mr Carnac,' Mrs Hamlett went on, 'and before that thing happened to my sister I never thought to set myself against the ways of Providence. But when months and years went by and still the wretch was not

caught I couldn't see the justice of it. It seemed to
me that it must be all lies about everything being
for the best, and God's goodness, and all that. For
how was it that He allowed such things to happen;
how was it that he allowed that wretch to go on
living? It's not as if my poor sister was a
thoroughly bad girl like some of the other victims;
I wouldn't have you think that. She was a good,
respectable girl; if she hadn't been one might have
understood it. Or, at any rate, it wouldn't have
seemed quite so dreadful.'

Here was news; I tried to keep the interest from
my voice as I asked: 'What was your sister's name,
Mrs Hamlett?'

She mentioned a name; and, as I did not catch it,
repeated it. And it was not the name of one of my
'subjects'. I was conscious of a feeling of relief;
after all, I had not been responsible for this good
woman's distress. This had doubtless been one of
those cases wrongfully and unwarrantably
connected with my exploits by popular excitement.
There had been several such, as I have already
mentioned.

'Well, I don't want to upset you with my troubles,
Mr Carnac,' said my landlady, rising. 'But when I
saw that film this evening it not only brought it
all back to me, but I had another feeling as well. It
came into my mind that I may still live to see the

wretch caught, even after all these years. And if I could have just one wish, before I go, it would be that. The wish that the murderer of my poor sister should be caught and hanged.'

'But he's probably dead long ago, Mrs Hamlett,' I suggested. 'I don't think you ought to let your mind dwell on it like that.'

'No, Mr Carnac, he's not dead. I know he's not dead. You can call it woman's intuition, or whatever you like; but as sure as I'm standing here I'm certain that the wretch is still alive. And it's knowing that that makes me still hope.'

After Mrs Hamlett had left me I sat for some time and pondered her revelation. I found something a trifle grotesque in her 'woman's intuition'. It told her that J.R. was still living; and it was perfectly right. And yet J.R. was not responsible for her sister's death; unless, of course, the girl's name had been wrongly given at the inquest. I resolved to look this up immediately.

I possess a number of scrap-books in which I have pasted innumerable 'press notices' of J.R.'s exploits: reports of inquests, letters to newspapers composed by amateur criminologists and, in fact, all those press references to the 'Whitechapel atrocities' which had come under my notice. The majority of these cuttings date back to the time of the affairs, and are yellow with age, but some —

mainly consisting of 'popular' journalistic
articles – have been published more recently. In
order that these cuttings might not attract
unwelcome attention if seen, they are liberally
interspersed with cuttings referring to other
crimes. So that in the event of a curious person
examining my scrap-books – and I have never
attempted to conceal them – the contents would
suggest not that I am a student of J.R. in
particular, but a student of general criminology.

I now took from the book-case one or two of these
volumes, and applied myself to a diligent study of
their contents.

In a short time I found what I sought. The name
given me by my landlady was that of a girl who had
been murdered some months after my last exploit; an
official view had been expressed that this murder
had not been committed 'by the same hand' as the
previous affairs, but in spite of this it had been
associated, by journalists and the public at large,
with the J.R. campaign.

As I replaced the volumes I reflected that since
Mrs Hamlett so definitely shared the popular view,
my innocence – in that particular connection –
would be of no help to me in the event of her
suspicions being aroused. Not that her suspicions
were likely to be aroused; nevertheless I felt
slightly uncomfortable. Here was I, living in the

same house with a woman who would leave no stone unturned to bring me to the gallows if, in some unforeseen manner, she obtained the slightest inkling of my unconventional past. And in the small safe in my sitting-room reposed a potential bomb in the shape of this manuscript.

I must confess that for a few moments I actually contemplated the destruction of the manuscript; but, after reflection, calmer counsels prevailed. Though I will admit that it is, possibly, a mere indulgence to my egotism, it represents many hours of labour; and anyone who has devoted some months of spare time to the painful composition of a work of literature will appreciate my unwillingness to destroy this manuscript. After all, it was, I felt, as inaccessible as it would be in the Bank of England, for the key of the safe never leaves my person. Its presence, also, lends a satirical – and even a dramatic – touch to my situation; the fact that Mrs Hamlett daily perceives, and possibly dusts, the repository of the secret she would give so much to learn rather appeals to my peculiar sense of humour.

No, I decided; I would leave things as they were and trust to Fate. Of course I should have known, after years of experience, that Fate is not to be trusted; she has a vindictive habit of letting one down at crucial moments.

Chapter 27.

When a man reaches the age of sixty his internal machinery usually begins to show signs of wear; and so it is with me. During the past year or so my heart has developed a slight weakness; normally it does not trouble me, but on rare occasions I have had attacks of syncope. Quite recently such an attack occurred to me in a cinema, causing some inconvenience to my neighbours in the audience and to the management; I was brought back to consciousness, in fact, in the manager's office.

But I have never been finicky over my health and, like many other people, I obstinately ignored the possibility of really serious trouble developing. True, I consulted a doctor and listened blandly to his advice on 'taking things quietly'; but my occasional fainting-fits seemed to me so trivial that I left them out of my calculations when reviewing my position in the house of Mrs Hamlett.

This negligence on my part afforded an

opportunity which Fate eagerly embraced. I had an attack one evening in my sitting-room. In the ordinary way this would have been unimportant, but it occurred while I was revising this manuscript.

I regained consciousness to find myself in my bed-room, whither I had been carried. I was lying on my bed fully clothed but with my collar and waistcoat loosened, and my doctor stood by the bed-side with the rubber tubes of a stethoscope hanging from his ears. Mrs Hamlett was near him, looking anxious, and the girl Minnie hovered in the doorway.

I was hazy, with that slight feeling of nausea and 'emptiness' which oppresses me after these attacks, and I did not immediately realize what had happened. In fact, quite an appreciable interval elapsed before I recollected the circumstances of my seizure; when I did I was hard put to it to conceal my apprehension. For I knew that this manuscript lay open upon my sitting-room table.

My doctor's professional attitude is of the genial and chatty variety, and on some occasions I have found him not unamusing; but now I wished him to the devil. All I wanted was to be left alone in order that I might descend to the sitting-room and lock away my manuscript. I assured him that I felt all right, and so great is the influence of mind

over body that I actually believed it; but he did
not believe it, and he showed no signs of departure.
His conscientious attentions irritated me, and when
I had again told him I was feeling quite well, and
suggested that I might be keeping him from more
necessitous patients, he insisted upon remaining to
help me undress, while Mrs Hamlett and Minnie left
the room to make me a 'nice cup of tea'. Finally,
after what seemed hours of fussing, the doctor left
with a promise to call on the following morning; I
had consumed the tea, and Mrs Hamlett had
withdrawn leaving me alone for the night.

For some time I curbed my impatience and lay
there listening intently. After the sound of my
landlady's descent into the lower regions of the
house I heard nothing; and at last I decided to make
an attempt to reach the sitting-room. Mrs Hamlett
had turned out my light, but I levered myself up in
bed and, feeling for the switch beside me, turned it
on again. The slight movement made me feel faint
and giddy, but after sitting on the edge of the bed
for a few minutes my head cleared, and I looked
round for my crutch. It was not there, and I cursed
softly; evidently it had been left behind when I had
been brought up to bed.

I should explain that I do not wear an artificial
leg, but I can make shift to move about without my
crutch if solid objects are to hand which I can hold

292

to; and I was sure I could manage to get down the two flights of stairs with the aid of the banisters. But I was feeling far from fit, and I wanted to make no noise. I stood up on my one leg and held to the head of the bed; immediately the room began to swim round and I nearly fell. But I mastered my weakness and, with a sort of hopping pirouette, reached the foot of the bed and, by aid of a chair, the door. There I took down my dressing-gown, struggled into it and, leaving it flapping open, cautiously unlatched the door.

The lights were burning on the landing outside and also, apparently, upon the landing below, and this surprised me for it was unusual after the household had retired. But I assumed that Mrs Hamlett had forgotten to turn out the lights in the excitement caused by my performance of the evening. I began my descent by clinging to the balustrade and hopping from step to step; but I could not avoid a slight noise, so I sat on the stairs and, getting the necessary leverage with my arms, slid myself down, one stair at a time. I had to rest occasionally on account of my giddiness. Looking back to that night it strikes me that the affair must have been a horridly grotesque one, such as would have appealed to a German film-producer. A one-legged elderly gentleman, lightly clad and with an expression of apprehension on his face, bumping

himself down from tread to tread of an ill-lit
stairway on his posterior in order to conceal that
which might send him to the gallows.

I finally reached the threshold of my sitting-
room where I found that the door was open and the
room lit. Without pausing to reflect that the room
might not be unoccupied, I struggled upright and,
clinging to the door-frame, hopped inside. There I
paused aghast. Mrs Hamlett was standing by the
table reading my manuscript.

Some slight sound on my part must have attracted
her attention, for she looked up in the act of
turning a page. No doubt the figure she saw must
have startled her; clinging to the side of the door,
its dressing-gown hanging open and its light-
coloured pyjamas with one empty leg fluttering. She
gasped, but she did not move; simply stood there
holding the page and staring fixedly at me.

For what seemed an eternity we stood without
movement gazing into each other's eyes. The table
was illuminated by a shaded stand-lamp; the shade
itself cut a broad bar of shadow, but the manuscript
and Mrs Hamlett's hands were brilliantly lit, and
the upper part of her face was bright from the
upper opening of the shade, so that she seemed to be
wearing a luminous mask. From this patch of light
her two pale eyes gazed unblinkingly into mine, and
in that moment I perceived that Mrs Hamlett knew.

Concurrently with this perception there flashed into my mind a visual recollection of that other dramatic scene with my uncle so many years ago. Then two eyes had stared into mine in the relatively dim light of a candle, while I waited above him, a poised scalpel in my hand. The vision dimmed and the room before me swam; I felt faint again, doubtless the shock of this present revelation acting upon my weak state. I must have tottered, for my landlady left the manuscript and darted forward, grasping me by the arm. I drew back my head abruptly and stared again into her eyes, now at close quarters, for I wanted to confirm what I felt was a certainty. Yes; she did know.

But she addressed me in what seemed almost her usual tone; or was it her usual tone? Was it not rather a carefully controlled tone?

'Come, Mr Carnac, this won't do,' she said. 'You ought to be in bed, you know. What have you come down for?'

I did not reply immediately; I continued to stare. Then I wrenched my eyes from her face and pointed to the table.

'I left some important papers out,' I replied; and found that my voice was dry and hoarse. Twitching her hand away I swung myself, by aid of a chair, to the table, seized the manuscript and hopped with it to the safe. I thrust it in and slammed the door; and then remembered that the key was in the pocket of my trousers upstairs.

'Would you mind fetching my keys, Mrs Hamlett?' I said.

She hesitated, still standing by the door; then, without a word, left the room. In a few minutes she returned with my bunch of keys. I locked the safe and, without again looking her in the face, suffered myself to be helped upstairs to bed.

Strange that I should have slept that night, but I did; or, at least, I passed the night in some form of coma approximating sleep. But when I awoke, early next morning, I felt reasonably well again, and my brain leapt instantly at the problem confronting it.

I had no doubt that my landlady knew that I, her respectable lodger, was none other than Jack the Ripper, whom it was her dearest wish to meet. And the fact that she did not really wish to meet Jack the Ripper, but a plagiarist, had no bearing upon the situation. I say that I had no doubt; I knew, but I cannot explain how I knew, beyond putting forward the unsatisfactory statement that I had read it in the woman's eyes.

The human eye is an extraordinary thing. It is limited in movement and its actual form is immutable with the exception of the variation in

size possible to the iris. We talk of the eye
'flashing' but, in reality, the eye never does flash;
that is a mere novelists' cliché. Neither does it dim,
nor grow soft. Yet, in spite of its limitations, the
human eye is the most expressive and revealing part
of the body; it can convey a meaning only secondary
to that conveyed by speech. It can betray the fraud
and the liar — I do not mean that it always does, but
that it can to the discerning; it can betray the
slightest traces of fear, anger and other emotions.
And those eyes of Mrs Hamlett seen in the bright
illumination of a stand-lamp had betrayed
to me the possession of certain undesirable
knowledge.

And now what was I to do? For Mrs Hamlett to
know, and for Mrs Hamlett to prove were two
entirely different things; and though a ray of
comfort might exist for me in this it was offset by
the unfortunate fact that my doings during the
vital period concerned would not bear suspicious
investigation — or so I thought. My safety in the
past had been due largely to an entire absence of
suspicion on the part of anyone. And now I had been
fool enough to set down in black and white my
private thoughts and actions for all the world to
read; and the most undesirable person possible had
promptly read. Yes; I was a blind, egotistical fool.
I recognized that now. And a bigger fool still not to

have destroyed my effusion under the recent
prompting of sanity.

However, self-recriminations would not help me;
this was a case for calm, self-controlled thinking
if ever there was one. I settled myself more
comfortably in bed, while I gazed at the blank
whiteness of the ceiling and reviewed the problem.

What would Mrs Hamlett do? She was not of the
thoughtlessly excitable type and would not,
therefore, dash poste-haste to Scotland Yard. She
had no evidence to offer beyond her allegation that
she had read a confession which could very well be
explained as an essay in fiction. She would be
laughed at or shown the nearest way out, and she
must know that quite well. And, after all, she does
not know all because of her reading of my
manuscript, but because that reading set her mind
working in the right direction and because she
correctly interpreted my look when I found her in
the act of discovery. It was almost as though she
had said last night: 'I have been reading this
confession of yours; can it possibly be real?' and I
had replied: 'I was afraid of this, Mrs Hamlett;
that's why I came down. Yes, it is true.' This is how
Mrs Hamlett came to know; by a species of telepathy
functioning in particularly favourable
circumstances.

Of course in a legal sense she does not know; she

possesses no provable knowledge, but she entertains strong suspicions.

And, again, what would Mrs Hamlett do? As I estimate her character she is of the slow and sure type. She will bide her time, nosing into my affairs until something else comes to light sufficiently definite to justify her taking legal assistance. And, knowing as I did the uncanny capacity of the female of the species for rooting up tit-bits of hidden scandal, I was not inclined to underrate the potentialities of Mrs Hamlett. I did not know which part of my manuscript she had read nor, therefore, what incident in my life had been revealed to her as a starting-point for investigation.

Of course all this will doubtless seem very vague as a basis of anxiety to a reader who may have no more than a few trivial peccadillos to conceal, but my position was such as to force me to take even trivialities seriously. Yes, even after forty years of exemplary living. 'Conscience makes cowards of us all' you will quote, dear reader; but it was not conscience in my case. You 'get me wrong' (as Minnie would say) if you think that. I have never been troubled by conscience in the sense you mean; but I was now seriously troubled by the fear of being found out. Which is quite a different matter.

I pursued my thoughts, as I lay in bed, though as confusedly as I have, I fear, presented them here. I tried to envisage Mrs Hamlett's point of view and to estimate her line of action, and was still so occupied when the good lady entered the room bearing my breakfast-tray. I looked at her carefully; I felt I was looking furtively, but hope that was not the case. She glanced swiftly at me and then turned her eyes away as she bid me 'Good morning' and enquired after my condition.

I told her I was perfectly well again, and apologized for the trouble I had caused her. She began a formal chatting as she arranged the breakfast-tray upon my knee, and while she was doing this I was thinking: 'She has not apologized for prying into my manuscript. She is ignoring the manuscript. That shows that I am right. She does know, and that is why it is impossible for her to refer to the manuscript.'

As I interpreted her manner it said: 'All right, I know who you are now. I can't prove it, but I shall soon be able to do so. Just wait. In the meantime I must not let you know I know. I am going to carry on as usual as the considerate landlady. But it will be a bit of a strain.'

The door closed behind Mrs Hamlett and, over a poached egg, I applied myself again to the problem. My own side of the question this time.

What could I do? I could sit still, do nothing and hope for the best. This I instantly dismissed. The best would probably be weeks of suspense terminating in the appearance in my sitting-room of two (or more) large gentlemen in navy blue and bowler hats, accompanied by a triumphant Mrs Hamlett.

As an alternative I could flee, as many other potential clients of the hang-man have fled. But this did not appeal to me at all. It would confirm Mrs Hamlett in her conviction and, moreover, it is extremely difficult to flee successfully, particularly when one is plainly labelled by a noticeable physical disability, which renders identification easy. And was I, an elderly gentleman of settled habits, to pass his declining years in hopping about the planet on one leg, looking for a non-extraditional country and expecting at any time the feel of a policeman's hand on my shoulder? This scheme was obviously out of the question.

There remained, then, but one alternative, and I admit that I considered it with distaste. Mrs Hamlett possessed knowledge which was inimical to my safety; therefore Mrs Hamlett must be eliminated.

Chapter 28.

My active life as J.R. ceased at the time of my
accident forty years ago; not only did the loss of my
leg result in that sudden termination of the series
of 'atrocities' which puzzled the authorities, but it
also resulted in a definite change in my feelings.
My craving to slay departed, leaving me in peace. I
am still interested in knives, those useful
implements devised by man for the cutting of his
food and his fellows, but I have no longer a desire
to use them in a way repugnant to respectable
society. Whether my craving atrophied through my
sheer inability to move about and slay, or whether
the crack upon my head at the time of the accident
resulted in some trifling mental change, I cannot
say.

However, when I began to contemplate the removal
of Mrs Hamlett, I was actuated by none of those
feelings which had driven me to unconventional
behaviour in the past. I did not propose to kill her

because I experienced a purposeless desire to kill,
but because I regarded her as a menace to my safety.
I wish to be perfectly honest, and I state,
therefore, that no parallel existed between my
former cases and that which I now intended. The
killing of Mrs Hamlett would be plain murder – a
murder of expediency – as serious a crime as any
other murders for which men have been executed,
and without justification or excuse in the eyes of
any member of the community. I felt justified,
because it was her life or mine, but no one else
would be likely to share that view, and I confess
frankly that I commenced a consideration of the
project with some repugnance.

But no other course than the elimination of Mrs
Hamlett would, I was convinced, solve my problem;
so I stifled my scruples and began to grapple with
the problem of ways and means. And, in my planning,
I lost some of my first feeling of distaste and even
developed a certain jest as the excitement of the
thing took hold of me.

During the past few years an enormous growth of
'detective' literature has developed, and probably
very few means of murdering one's fellow-citizens
have lacked exposition. I, myself, am by no means
unfamiliar with this class of book; but when I
began to review as many as I could recall of the
various methods invented by writers of crime novels

I realized that the majority of those methods were impracticable. They were too ingenious. And the plans evolved by the fictitious criminals for evading detection were based, in most cases, upon extremely complicated alibis in circumstances specially devised by the authors.

I could gain no hint whatever from my recollection of any of the books which I had read, and none of the methods seemed adaptable to my present case.

I considered first of all the relatively crude murder followed by concealment of the body. Well, obviously, this would not work in my case because my physical disability would not permit the activity necessary to conceal the body; without going into unnecessary details I may say that the labour involved in any scheme of concealment seemed to be outside my capacity. The circumstances and routine of the household also disallowed me the necessary leisure; and, furthermore, the inexplicable disappearance of Mrs Hamlett, a person of regular and settled habits of life, would immediately lead to investigation.

In my early exploits it had, of course, been entirely unnecessary to conceal the bodies; but in the case I contemplated, the only circumstances in which concealment need not be attempted would be those attendant upon a killing in some place remote from the house. And I could see no prospect of arranging such circumstances.

My thoughts then proceeded to the more subtle methods of murder, of which poison is a leading example. I examined this idea despite a strong repugnance, for the medium is one which I would only use in the last resort. Although, perhaps, a man of few principles, I share the popular abhorrence of the poisoner.

Now there are no advantages whatever, from the point of view of the murderer, in the use of poison unless an entire absence of suspicion as to the cause of death obtains. Once suspicion has been aroused, the cause of death is easily discoverable. It is true that many people have doubtless been poisoned whose death has been ascribed to natural causes; but it must always have been a gamble for the criminal. I did not dwell long upon the possibilities of safely poisoning my landlady.

There remained, then, the ingeniously staged 'accident', and this field I considered thoroughly, for I felt it was the one which offered most scope to my abilities. Something must happen to Mrs Hamlett which would appear to be an obvious accident, and one such thing occurred to me immediately. She might fall downstairs and break her neck. A black string judiciously stretched at the head of the stairs?

I pursued my cogitations for several days, but without arriving at any satisfactory decision; and during that time the relations between Mrs Hamlett and myself were peculiar. Outwardly they were as usual, but it seemed to me that the good lady was hard put to it to keep them so. In innumerable small ways she betrayed the strain under which she was labouring: the occasional stealthy glance, the forced normality of tone, the rather excessive politeness, the pointed avoidance of any reference to German films – a subject on which we had often chatted. And I am fairly certain that she must have observed a similar constraint in me.

On several occasions my landlady betrayed signs of definite distress, entering my sitting-room with eyes red from weeping. It would have been too crude had I endeavoured to conceal my perception of this; my policy in our cat-and-mouse game was to pretend that our relationship was entirely normal. Mrs Hamlett might suspect – be almost certain, in fact – that I was aware of her knowledge, but while some sort of pretence was maintained it was possible for the status quo to continue, albeit precariously. Mrs Hamlett was either planning or waiting – I was not sure which – and I admired not only her patience but also her pluck. How many women would care to remain in constant touch with a (supposed) desperate criminal until such time as they could

trap him? But once the gloves were off, the good
lady would doubtless be driven to some reckless
procedure which would definitely end my brief
period of safety.

In reply to my enquiries Mrs Hamlett informed me
that she was suffering from almost constant
neuralgia, and I professed sympathy. The same
explanation was evidently given to Minnie, for the
girl mentioned to me the discomfort of her mistress,
and discussed possible remedies. And in the course
of our chat Minnie gave me the germ of my great
idea.

'Don't it seem awful, sir?' she said. 'She's said
several times that if it goes on much longer she'll
feel like putting her head in the gas-oven. I can't
make out why she doesn't see a doctor or a dentist or
something. I know I would.'

'I shouldn't worry, Minnie,' I told her. 'Your
mistress won't put her head in the gas-oven. A lot
of people talk like that, but they don't mean it.'

'Oh, I know it's all talk, sir,' said Minnie. 'I'm
not worrying because I think she will. She always
says that sort of thing when she's upset. But to see
her going about like that fair gives me the pip.'

I replied in an absent-minded manner as Minnie
left the room; I was turning over in my mind that
phrase: 'put her head in the gas-oven'. If Mrs
Hamlett only would; what an end to my problem!

And then the thought logically followed: why should not Mrs Hamlett gas herself? Or appear to do so. Could it possibly be arranged? The ground was prepared. If Mrs Hamlett was discovered dead of gas-poisoning, Minnie, as a witness, would testify to the frequent threats of her mistress to gas herself. So far as I could see a verdict of suicide would follow as a matter of course provided the affair was arranged with care and ingenuity.

This seemed a promising line of thought, and I pursued it. I considered the conditions of the household. Mrs Hamlett sleeps on the ground-floor next door to a small room occupied by Minnie. It seems a curious part of the house for sleeping-quarters, though not uncommon, I believe, for landladies who prefer to reserve the upper bed-rooms for actual or prospective lodgers. Mrs Hamlett had a gas-fire in her room I knew, for I had noticed it through the open door on more than one occasion. In fact there are, so far as I know, gas-fires in most of the bed-rooms, though my sitting-room is heated by a coal-fire.

Of course if my landlady did decide to commit suicide she would not 'put her head in the gas-oven', she would retire to her bed-room, turn on the gas and lie down. At least, I suppose she would. If, therefore, I wished to assist her in carrying out her professed desire, it would be necessary for me to enter her room while she slept and turn on the gas-fire for her.

But Mrs Hamlett is accustomed to locking her door at night, I have heard her turn the key. And she would certainly not refrain from doing so now with a lodger of my supposed propensities at hand. But would not another key from another door in the house fit her lock; or if not, could not a duplicate be obtained? And would it be possible to use a duplicate if Mrs Hamlett's key remained in the lock inside?

I sat there and continued to cogitate.

My problem is solved. The solution is one of those simple and obvious things which, by their very simplicity and obviousness, are liable to escape attention in a system of ingenious planning; like those large-type headings on placards which we fail to see because they are so much in evidence.

This, the final chapter of this record, I am writing during the period which must elapse before I can put my plan into execution. Let me go over the events of this evening.

I heard Mrs Hamlett go out soon after tea, leaving Minnie in charge of the establishment. My fellow-lodger is away on one of his alleged stamp-collecting expeditions. It is a bitterly cold night.

At about nine I heard the sound of Mrs Hamlett's

return and, soon after, she entered my sitting-room with the glass of hot milk which I am accustomed to take at that time. I saw at once that she was developing the first symptoms of a cold.

Now within limits I have certain sympathy with my fellows — strange, perhaps, though that may seem — and when I heard my landlady sneeze and perceived her running eyes I was moved to suggest the best course for her to pursue. Be it remembered that I had no grudge against Mrs Hamlett in the sense which that term usually conveys. On the contrary, I admired her qualities and rather liked her.

As a measure of expediency I thought it necessary to eliminate her, but I did not wish her to have a bad cold.

'You seem to have a cold, Mrs Hamlett,' I said.

'I'm afraid I have, Mr Carnac,' she replied. 'I ought not to have gone out this evening. It's bitter. But there was something important I had to see about.'

'Now I'll tell you what you want, Mrs Hamlett,' I continued. 'A glass of strong whiskey and water, hot. Have you any whiskey?'

'I'm afraid I haven't. I don't keep it in the house as a rule.'

'Then I will mix your medicine for you, Mrs Hamlett*,' I said. 'I insist. Supposing you ask

*In the original Manuscript this read Mrs Carnac.

Minnie for some hot water and a lemon?'

With a half smile Mrs Hamlett left the room and I heard her call down the stairs to Minnie. When she returned I insisted upon her sitting beside the fire. She sneezed once or twice and then commenced a desultory conversation.

'And what have you been doing with yourself this evening, sir?' she asked. 'I suppose you've not been out?'

'No, Mrs Hamlett. I've been cleaning a picture which I picked up a few days ago on a stall.'

'Not in your bed-room I hope?'

'Yes, in my bed-room. It was cold up there, certainly, but I couldn't bring petrol down here with the fire. And then I have been doing a little writing – and thinking.'

'It's really too bad of me taking your whiskey, you know, sir,' said Mrs Hamlett. 'I expect I shall be all right in the morning.'

'Not without the whiskey, Mrs Hamlett. That may stop the cold.'

Then Minnie entered, grinning, carrying a small, steaming kettle, and a lemon on a plate.

'Thank you, Minnie,' I said, rising. 'Now you leave this to me, Mrs Hamlett,' And I rose and hobbled to the side-board.

'I lit your gas-fire an hour ago, mum,' said Minnie. 'So your room will be lovely and warm.'

I was raising the whiskey-decanter as I caught
the words and in some inexplicable manner the
solution of the problem which had been troubling
me leapt to my mind in that instant. In a flash of
inspiration I saw what I had to do. And so rapid is
the course of thought once the right path has been
reached that in that brief period between my
raising the decanter and pouring out the whiskey, I
realized the desirability of increasing the dose
which I had intended. I poured out nearly half a
tumbler-full of the spirit, added a slice of lemon, a
lump of sugar and some hot water. Then I took a tea-
spoon from the drawer and, turning, handed the
decoction to Mrs Hamlett.

She took the glass with a word of thanks and
turned to the door.

'Good night, Mr Carnac,' she said. And, 'Good
night, sir,' added Minnie, following her out. My
response was delayed for a fraction of a second . . .
I was overcome by the excitement of my idea. And I
was thinking: 'The next time I see her she will be
stiff and cold and motionless. Minnie will be
looking scared, and probably weeping. I shall be
acting the part of the sympathetic and shocked
lodger. And then a doctor will come, and probably a
policeman with a note-book. And I shall be free of
my incubus.'

'Good night, Mrs Hamlett. Good night, Minnie.'

I sat for a long time, as it seemed, by the fire and listened. I heard them both descend the stairs. Then, after an interval, Mrs Hamlett's steps going to the top of the house, and their return. Another interval; and the closing of a door followed by the faint click of a lock. I found, to my surprise, that I was trembling.

I must continue to sit here for some time before I can carry out my plan; and my plan is based upon a simple fact which, previously, I had quite overlooked. There are two taps to a gas-fire; that within the room, and the main-tap. And the main-tap of this house is accessible; it is in a cupboard under the stairs on the ground floor. I know, for I saw an official manipulating it on a recent occasion in connection with the installation of a new geyser.

In nearly everything the simplest is the best. In art, in invention; in the conduct of life and — it has now occurred to me — in the conduct of death. Mrs Hamlett's gas-fire is alight; her door and window are shut. All I have to do is to wait until she is soundly asleep — and the whiskey will insure the soundness — descend cautiously to the hall and turn off the main gas supply. I shall wait for a few minutes and then turn it on again, after which I shall go peacefully to bed.

The scheme is so simple that I could almost

convince myself that it will not be a murder; at the most a sort of teetotal murder. The mere turning on and off of a tap — as though in absent-mindedness! It is so simple and yet so effective that I feel sure some writer of detective fiction must already have thought of it. But, if so, I have not read his book, and I claim the original invention of the idea.

And who, at the inquest, will remember that a gas-fire goes out when the main-tap is turned off; and that the gas begins to escape when the tap is turned on again? Or would pursue the idea even if it occurred to him?

I am now completing this manuscript; I know the last chapter will show signs of haste, and may appear slovenly to the fastidious reader, but I am anxious to finish it before embarking upon my last important enterprise. I have read somewhere that 'the supreme gift of the artist is the knowledge of when to stop'; I make no claim to being an artist, but I do know when to stop. Shall I spoil a good, decisive climax by wandering on into an unnecessary description of the inquest, of my after-thoughts, and so meander aimlessly on until my writing peters out like a trickle of water which gradually dies away into the dust? No; I will finish this manuscript to-night, and seal it up; then I am less likely to be tempted to embellish or extend it.

At this eleventh hour I am conscious of an

uncomfortable lurking doubt as to whether I am not, after all, acting hastily. I cannot disregard the possibility – the very slight possibility – that my instinctive feeling that Mrs Hamlett knows who I am is wrong. Supposing the whole thing is due, on my part, to that which the conventional person calls 'conscience'? Supposing she had read but a trivial and unrevealing section of my manuscript? Supposing she really has had neuralgia? Supposing, in short, that the whole thing is due to my imagination? I cannot think that it is; I cannot convince myself that it is, and yet I am just conscious of that little doubt.

However, the risk is too great for me to carry; I must give myself the benefit of the doubt, for is not self-preservation the first law of nature?

And, writing of 'nature' reminds me that here is something which will confirm by actual test the truth of my belief regarding the malevolence of that Destiny which shapes our ends. If, contrary to my opinion, we are, individually and in the mass, watched and guarded by a benevolent Providence, surely one might expect some kind of miraculous hitch to my proceedings; Mrs Hamlett will not be 'allowed to' succumb to my evil machinations. 'Right and truth shall prevail' says the righteous man, entirely unconscious of the teaching of history. Well, let right and truth prevail here. Let

Providence step in and confound me; the installation of the Gas Company is doubtless efficient, but surely Providence could get over that difficulty!

But I am getting excited and, perhaps, a trifle incoherent. The time is near and I must make an end. I shall now seal up this manuscript and place it, as I originally intended, in a second envelope addressed to my executor. I shall lock it in the safe, and there let it remain. After that I shall take my rubber-shod crutch and creep softly, softly down the stairs. Am I sorry for what I must do? I do not know, I am too excited. I may be sorry tomorrow; who knows? But of the outcome of this night's work I am confident; and in that confidence I append to this manuscript the one word: Finis.

J.W. Carnac.

Epilogue.

A Coroner's Charge to a Jury.

Well, gentlemen, you have heard all the available
evidence and it now remains for you to decide how
this unfortunate gentleman came by his death and
to return a verdict accordingly.

As to the identity of the remains: I think you
will agree that no doubt exists that they are those
of Mr James Willoughby Carnac. I need not point out
to you that direct identification has been
impossible; it has been your very unpleasant duty
to view the remains, and you know that they are
quite unrecognizable. But in this matter of
identification you have the following to guide you:
Mrs Hamlett, the landlady of the house, has told us
that at the time of the fire the only occupants of
the house were herself, the maid Minnie Wright and
Mr Carnac. Mr Carnac was not saved. This, alone,
renders it practically certain that the charred
remains are those of Mr Carnac; and it is supported

by the evidence of Dr Short who has stated that the
remains are those of a man of approximately Mr
Carnac's build and with a right leg missing. And we
have been told by Mrs Hamlett and Minnie Wright
that Mr Carnac had lost a right leg.

Now as regards the cause of death. Mrs Hamlett
has given her evidence very clearly and directly,
but I will just run over the main points again. It
appears that on the evening of February the third
Mrs Hamlett was suffering from a cold, on account
of which she retired early, Mr Carnac having kindly
mixed her a glass of grog.

Mrs Hamlett drank the mixture and retired to her
bed-room on the ground-floor; she found the room
was unduly hot, as the gas-stove had been alight for
some time, and she turned the gas out. It then
occurred to her that Mr Carnac's bed-room would be
extremely cold; she passed upstairs, lit his gas-
fire, closed the door and returned to her own room.

Now up to that point, gentlemen, the evidence is
perfectly clear. Mrs Hamlett states quite
emphatically that she lit Mr Carnac's gas-fire;
that it was burning at about half the full strength
when she left the room. You have seen that lady and
heard her give evidence, and if your impression is
similar to my own you will agree that she is not the
sort of person who would carelessly turn on the gas
and leave the room without lighting it; in fact it is

a little difficult to see how any sane person could do such a thing. We can take it, I think, that the gas-fire was burning, and that it ultimately went out. It is possible, of course, that the flame was turned rather lower than Mrs Hamlett thought, and that it 'popped out' as the girl Minnie Wright suggested. In fact that seems the only reasonable supposition. We have most of us had experience of gas-fires and we know that such things do infrequently occur. However, from whatever cause — a draught or a 'back-fire' — it would seem that the gas-fire went out, and of course the gas would at once begin to escape and would gradually fill the room, — you will recall Mrs Hamlett's evidence to the effect that the windows were closed.

Now we know, from the same witness, that it was the habit of Mr Carnac to light himself up to bed with a candle in a tall brass candlestick; for although electric-light was laid on, the switch controlling the staircase light was situated in the hall, and it usually fell to Mr Carnac, as the last member of the establishment to go to bed, to turn out this light. This is perfectly clear, and explains the presence of the brass candlestick beside Mr Carnac's charred body.

I think, gentlemen, you will easily visualize the train of events. Mr Carnac passes upstairs with a lighted candle, places the candlestick on the floor beside the door — remember that he was a one-legged man; one hand would be engaged with his crutch, and he would have to put down the candlestick before he could open the door — and when he did fling open the door the gas with which the room was filled ignited, causing a terrific explosion and the subsequent fire. And there can be little doubt that the fierceness of that fire — sufficient to gut the upper part of the house — was, to some extent at least, due to the bursting of a large bottle of petrol which, as Mrs Hamlett tells us, Mr Carnac had been using for the purpose of cleaning a picture, and which he had left in his bed-room.

I wish we could think, gentlemen, that this unfortunate man was killed by the force of the explosion; unhappily the evidence suggests only too clearly that he was endeavouring to drag himself towards the staircase when he was overcome by the flames. But I need not dwell too long upon that very horrible circumstance.

There is only one small point, and I need barely refer to it. Mrs Hamlett told us that for several days previous to the disaster Mr Carnac's manner had become — 'peculiar' was, I think, the word she used. It appeared to her that he was perhaps suspicious or upset, and she thought this might be due to his resenting her discovery of the fact that he was writing a novel. This may, of course, have been so; one cannot always estimate the feelings of an elderly person. But, whatever the cause, I do not think we need consider this change in Mr Carnac's manner. It might possibly be suggestive were there any suspicion of suicide in this case; but no such suspicion is warranted by the circumstances surrounding the tragedy.

I think that is all, gentlemen; and now perhaps you will let me have your verdict.

Appendix I

Paul Begg's Analysis

This manuscript was found among the effects of a man who died in the early 1930s and in a brief introduction called 'Explanatory Remarks' he claims to have known Carnac and been appointed his executor, and that he had received the manuscript along with Carnac's effects. It was 'in a sealed packet and attached to the exterior of this was a letter' addressed to him in which Carnac asked that it be sent to a specified literary agent, who were rare beasts back then. Fearing that compliance with this request might create problems with the probate authorities, the package was opened and the contents read. Some particularly revolting material was apparently removed, but otherwise it was intended that the manuscript be presented to the literary agents as requested. Whether this was actually done, and the manuscript returned, or whether something stopped Carnac's wishes being complied with is unknown.

Was this story even remotely true? Or is the author of the Explanatory Remarks, this supposed friend and executor of James Willoughby Carnac, really the author of the whole manuscript, using the well-established literary device of claiming it to have been a bequest to give his narrative verisimilitude? If so, might he have been Jack the Ripper? Fortunately, he could not. Not unless Jack the Ripper was a babe in arms, which could explain how Jack the Ripper escaped detection but is too ridiculous even for a subject which feeds off ridiculous suggestions, so at least one reputation will remain intact and unsullied. But was he the actual author of the manuscript?

On the face of it, it is about as likely as Elvis living on Mars. The man who wrote that introduction was Sydney George Hulme Beaman, a sometime actor, an artist, and a superb and distinctive illustrator. Almost forgotten today, he was once as famous as Enid Blyton. He enjoyed an all too brief personal celebrity and a lasting immortality as the creator of Larry the Lamb and all the characters of Toytown.

All of Hulme Beaman's literary output was for children, so writing a novel about Jack the Ripper – writing *anything* about Jack the Ripper – would have been an extraordinary literary diversion, perhaps as shocking in its way as discovering that Enid Blyton secretly penned explicit sex novels. So this book is extraordinary and immensely valuable even if it is a novel by Hulme Beaman.

And it would be an extraordinary and immensely valuable novel even if it wasn't written by Hulme Beaman because it must surely be an early attempt to tell a crime story from the criminal's perspective, and as an attempt at character analysis it is rather perceptive, avoiding all the almost stereotypical motives suggested at the time, such as religious fanaticism, an insane doctor or an escapee from a lunatic asylum, and instead presenting James Carnac as a man who kills because he likes it, an image far more in keeping with what we know about serial killers today.

Carnac is also an unlikeable man, attracted by the macabre and grotesque, cruelly cynical, and with an acid-tongued sense of humour, as revealed in his dedication – 'Dedicated with admiration and respect to the retired members of the Metropolitan Police Force in spite of whose energy and efficiency I have lived to write this book' – and occasionally encountered elsewhere in the book.

Sydney George Hulme Beaman

A person is the product of many influences, and Sydney George Hulme Beaman had an interesting family heritage, one which was normal to the point of being staid, yet also bohemian and artistic.

His great-grandfather was George Hulme Beaman, a doctor who enjoyed an extensive private practice and was Parochial Surgeon to St Paul's in London. He was one of the founders of the New Equitable Life Assurance Company and for many years was its Deputy Chairman. He was also Chairman of the renters and debenture holders of the Drury Lane Theatre. Today he is chiefly remembered, if he is remembered at all, for being called by the police on 5 November 1831 to examine the body of a 14-year-old, fair-haired, grey-eyed boy.

The boy's body had been brought by John Bishop and James May to the dissecting room of King's College with the intention of selling it to the anatomy department. There was a severe shortage of cadavers suitable for the study and teaching of anatomy, and a fresh corpse could fetch as much as 12 guineas. There were rules about where the bodies could come from, but a blind eye was generally turned to the corpses of the recently dead that had been dug up from their graves. The gangs who undertook this gruesome but profitable work were politely known as resurrectionists, or more commonly as body snatchers. Bishop and May would later confess to having stolen and sold between 500 and 1,000 corpses in a career lasting twelve years.

On this occasion the suspicions of the anatomy demonstrator, Richard Partridge, were aroused by the freshness of the body, which he thought showed no signs of having been buried. He called his superior, Herbert Mayo, Professor of Anatomy, who agreed that the police should be called. Bishop and May were arrested, and later so were two other members of the gang, Thomas Williams and Michael Shields. They were charged with murder. They had in fact taken the boy from the Bell in Smithfield to a house in a part of the East End known as Nova Scotia Gardens, where they had drugged him with rum and laudanum and then drowned him in a well. The boy was later tentatively identified by the police as an Italian lad named Carlo Ferrari, but Bishop and Williams eventually admitted that he was a cattle drover from Lincolnshire, name unknown.

George Hulme Beaman was called upon to examine the body of the boy, concluded that the body had never been buried and deduced from the empty chambers of the boy's heart that death had been very sudden and almost certainly from a blow to the neck. Hulme Beaman had made a particular study of death from spinal injuries; he had killed numerous animals by hitting them on the back of the neck and afterwards dissecting them to observe the results, so he considered himself something of an expert. Partridge and Mayo, who joined him in conducting the post-mortem in the first-floor room of the tiny watch-house in St Paul's graveyard, concurred, and the police minutely searched Nova Scotia Gardens, finding clothes from numerous other victims.

The trial was one of the first in which not only the detective techniques were publicly on display, but also the medical detective work (or forensics), and it caused a sensation. Bishop and Williams were found guilty and publicly hanged at Newgate on 5 December 1831 in front of an estimated 30,000 spectators. The corpses of both men were duly dissected by anatomists. But at the end of December 1831 a professor of medical jurisprudence named John Gordon Smith published a blistering letter in *The Lancet* in which he denounced Hulme Beaman's conclusion that sudden death was indicated by the chambers of the heart being empty, which he said instead suggested a lingering death. And Bishop and Williams' admission that they had drugged and drowned the boy also called into doubt Hulme Beaman's confident claim that death was caused by a blow to the back of the neck. These criticisms did nothing to enhance Hulme Beaman's reputation.

At some point there may have been a rift in the Hulme Beaman family.

George Hulme Beaman and his wife Mary Ann Offley had a large family, among their children being S.G.'s grandfather, George Hulme Beaman, who also became a doctor and for a while shared a practice with his father. Another son was Ardern Hulme Beaman, who was a Surgeon-General with the Army in Hoshangabad, India. One of his sons, the unusually named Emeric Hulme Beaman (1864–1937), was a writer who in partnership with William Senior Ellis wrote four mystery novels under the pseudonym Ben Strong. These were published between 1925 and 1928.

George Hulme Beaman's daughter, Henrietta Hulme Beaman (1831–1895), was also an interesting person. In 1851 she married Joseph Robins, a young and successful businessman who was wooed by the smell of the greasepaint and the roar of the crowd and took to the stage. He was a comedian, but not a successful one, and his career declined to doing small parts in the provinces, which was where he met Henry Irving, perhaps the greatest of the Victorian actor-managers. Engaged in some small way to do a pantomime one bitterly cold Christmas, he was pained to see a fellow actor shivering and suffering in poverty and thin, summer clothing. Pawning most of what he owned, he laid before his fellow actors a memorable Christmas dinner at his cheap lodging and to the shivering actor gave a suit of thick, warm and heavy underclothing. Irving was that actor and never forgot Robins' generosity.

In 1874 Joe fell ill and Henrietta, who had joined him treading the boards, appealed in the theatrical newspaper *The Era* for help to pay his medical bills, which amounted to £60. As her father and family could have paid this money, the appeal in *The Era* suggests that Henrietta and her father were estranged. Sadly Joe never got better and in 1878 he died. Destitute, Henrietta again turned to *The Era*, advertising for theatre work or a job as a housekeeper. The theatrical cavalry evidently rode to her rescue because the 1891 census records that Henrietta was an 'Actress with own Company'. She died on 18 April 1895.

Her brother, S.G.'s grandfather, George Hulme Beaman Jnr (1825–1863), was admitted to the Royal College of Surgeons on 17 May 1850. He married Jane Elizabeth Oakley and they had four children, two daughters, Emily Jane and Kate Julia, and two sons, George Hulme Robins Hulme Beaman, who was S.G.'s father, and Arthur Henry. For a time George shared a practice with his father at 32 King Street, Covent Garden, but the *London Gazette*, 6 January 1860, records that the partnership was dissolved. This may reflect a rift in the family, especially as Joe Robins' surname was given as a forename to S.G.'s father.

George Hulme Beaman died in 1863 aged only 38

years and his wife was left with four young children to raise, the youngest only ten months. It appears that she was supported by *her* family, possibly further evidence of a rift, and struggled alone for six years before she met Augustus Grain, manager of the Petersfield branch of the Hampshire Banking Company. The couple married in 1869 and had five children, sadly only three making it into adulthood.

S.G.'s father, George Hulme Robins Hulme Beaman, was born about 1855 in Westminster, London, and was educated at Epsom College, Surrey, a relatively new school opened as the Royal Medical Benevolent College by a Dr John Probert (1793–1867) with the express purpose of giving assistance to the widows and orphans of members of the medical profession. Originally it catered for just a hundred boys, but an extension in 1862 increased the intake to two hundred, of which ten were day scholars and the rest residential. The college register records that Hulme Beaman won several prizes.

He became a surveyor and risk assessor for an insurance company and early in 1881 married Eleanor Nicholls, who hailed from St Albans, Hertfordshire. At one time she had run away from home to become a singer and actress, adopting the stage name Nellie Leslie. She and G.H.R. lived at 11 Woodstock Rd, Hornsey, but moved to Tottenham where their children were born: Sydney George Hulme (1887), Dorothy Eleanor (1889) and Winifred Gladys (1892).

By the 1911 census the family was all still together; S.G., now 24 years old, was an insurance clerk. His sister Dorothy was a private secretary to a chartered accountant, and Winifred was presumably a scholar, no occupation being given for her.

S.G. wanted to be an artist, but his father was not supportive – something he had in common with James Carnac – and wanted him to use his talents as an architect, but his mother settled the matter and he was enrolled in the famous Heatherley's School of Art, founded by Thomas Heatherley in 1845. Among the pupils who had studied there were Burne-Jones, Rossetti, Millais, and sometime Jack the Ripper suspect Walter Sickert.

S.G. also indulged his taste for the theatre and per-formed in music halls and at smoking concerts – these were very popular all-male live concerts, usually musical, the music invariably providing a background to dis-cussion about politics and such like. S.G. formed an amateur group called the Dickensian Fellowship, acting assorted parts as diverse as Fagin and Mr Peggotty. He was good enough to be invited to perform professionally. It was through his performing that he met Maud Mary Poltock, who played piano for his recitals. They married in April 1913 in Fulham. She and S.G. would have two children, Geoffrey S. Hulme Beaman (born in 1914) and Betty Hulme Beaman (born 1918).

The end of the First World War in 1918 saw a changed Britain in which music halls and smoking concerts were to all intents and purposes things of the past, and new entertainments were emerging. There was a shortage of toys and S.G. turned an upstairs room in his house in Golders Green into a studio with a work bench, drawing board, tools, paints and a pot of resin glue almost permanently bubbling on a gas burner, and there he began carving figures for model theatres, starting with Mr Noah and the animals of his Ark. They were blockish, angular figures, and he adapted the style for a comic strip called *Philip & Phido*, which began appearing in the *Golders Green Gazette* in 1923. Two years later, in 1925, he wrote and illustrated two children's books, *The Road to Toytown* and *Trouble in Toyland*, several of the characters in these and subsequent stories having their origins in the *Philip & Phido* strips, such as the self-important Mr Mayor, who developed from a character called the Admiral.

The books were seen by May Jenkins, then better known as Aunt Elizabeth on a radio series called *Children's Hour*, who recognized their dramatic potential.

Children's Hour became a national institution. It had begun on 23 December 1922, just a month after broadcasting started, and by November the following year *The Times* reported that it had almost one million listeners and said there were discussions about broadcasting programmes on different wavelengths so that listeners would be able to choose between *Children's Hour* and speeches in Parliament. This might suggest why *Children's Hour* became so popular. It was broadcast between 5 p.m. and 6 p.m. every day, the anticipated audience range being from five to fifteen, and *Toytown*, first broadcast on 19 July 1929, soon became a firm favourite. It was narrated by Derek McCulloch (1897–1967), known to millions of children as 'Uncle Mac', a persona he maintained until the 1960s. He also provided the tremulous voice for Toytown's most famous animal resident, Larry the Lamb.

S.G. also developed a model stage show called *The Arkville Dragon* – Arkville was a neighbour of Toytown – and Pathe Films turned this into an animated film, but S.G.'s premature death prevented the development of the project. But Toytown lived on without S.G., his friend, the writer and producer Hendrik Baker, turning four of the Toytown stories into a stage play entitled *The Cruise of the Toytown Belle*, a film version of which was broadcast under the title *Larry the Lamb* by BBC Television on 10 May 1947. In 1956 the BBC broadcast a series of 20-minute marionette plays featuring Larry, and in 1962 and 1964 the animators Halas & Batchelor produced *The Showing Up of Larry the Lamb* and *The Tale of the Magician*. About this time Baker released through HMV some Larry the Lamb stories on 45rpm EPs, four of the stories later being released as an album called *Stories from Toytown*. Between 1972 and 1974, twenty-six animated shows were made by Larry the Lamb Ltd for Thames Television.

Sadly, Sydney George Hulme Beaman would never realize the huge success of his creation or enjoy the profits that were surely his. He died from pneumonia in February 1932 at the age of 43. He left £979 in his will and is today very largely forgotten; not even his respectably suburban home in Sneath Avenue, Golders Green, bears a blue plaque, which unquestionably it should do. But it is a testament to the man that Larry the Lamb and the population of Toytown are still loved by thousands of people over eighty years after they were created.

Thankfully, there is no suggestion whatever that S.G. Hulme Beaman was Jack the Ripper, but the question whether or not *The Autobiography of James Carnac* was his work remains. As said, it would have been a step outside his normal writing and also alien to what we know of his character. In fact, the only hint that there was a dark side to Hulme Beaman is a 1930s edition of Robert Louis Stephenson's *The Strange Case of Dr Jekyll and Mr Hyde*, for which he was commissioned to provide the illustrations. As a professional artist and illustrator, Hulme Beaman accepted commissions from publishers so he can't be held responsible for the choice of subject, nor is there anything about his illustrations that's remotely violent or bloodthirsty. Indeed, they draw heavily on early Expressionism, being beautifully stylized and strikingly atmospheric, and are among the finest twentieth-century illustrations for Stephenson's classic.

336

James Willoughby Carnac

As for James Willoughby Carnac, nobody of that name has so far been identified, so either he is a fictional creation or the name is a pseudonym, either adopted by Carnac himself or bestowed upon him by someone else. Although the *Autobiography* is largely concerned with the Whitechapel murders, it provides a detailed and engaging account of Carnac's life up to the commission of the crimes. Writing shortly before his death, he says he was 69 years old and he variously describes the murders as having been committed 40 or 42 years earlier. This means that he was born between 1859 and 1861, and wrote and died between 1928 and 1930.

He was born in Tottenham and lived in a double-fronted semi-detached house in a row of six houses. Next to his home there was a field owned by a dairy farmer. His father was a doctor named John Louis Carnac, but an inclination to over-drinking kept his practice from flourishing and the family never achieved financial security until he inherited a considerable sum of money from an aunt named Madeleine.

At the age of 12 years, James Carnac attended a day school which was run by a religious fanatic named Dr Styles – a 'hateful, narrow-minded, ignorant bore' – whose principal success seems to have been turning over a large number of staff. The school was in a private house about one mile from Carnac's home, and it was there that he developed an interest in art and an early preoccupation with blood, being particularly attracted to the slaughter of a pig by the father of a school friend.

He also recalled an attraction for three books he discovered in his father's library, Roberts' *Treatise of Witchcraft* and John Cotta's *Triall of Witchcraft*, also an 1875 edition of Edgar Allan Poe's complete writings. I assume the first of these was a book by Alexander Roberts, a preacher of King's Lynn in Norfolk who was a witchfinder contemporary of the notorious Matthew Hopkins. John Cotta escapes me, but the Poe was presumably the edition by John Henry Ingram, published initially in Edinburgh in 1874 and 1875 and which must therefore have been a relatively recent acquisition by Carnac's father.

Both his parents died when he was nearly 18 years old, putting the event between 1877 and 1879, and he went to live with his uncle, a bookmaker in Peckham. Although the uncle was very good to him, Carnac developed an overwhelming desire to cut his throat and one night very nearly did so. He fled his uncle's home never to return and thereafter had very little contact with him, although his uncle did on one occasion supply him with a family tree which had been found among the papers left by his father, which he thought might suggest that Carnac's blood lust was hereditary. The tree traced his ancestry back to the Sanson dynasty of Paris executioners.

This dynasty existed. Indeed, it is notorious because its later members executed Louis XVI and Marie Antoinette.

The dynasty appears to have begun with Charles Sanson (Longval; 1658–1695), a soldier in the French royal army who was appointed Executioner of Paris in 1684. He was succeeded in turn by Charles Sanson (1681–1726), and Charles Jean Baptiste Sanson (1719–1778). It was through Charles's brother, Nicholas Charles Gabriel Sanson (1721–1795), that the Carnacs apparently claimed descent.

Nicholas Sanson was the executioner at Reims and achieved a degree of notoriety in 1757 when he assisted his nephew, Charles Henri Sanson (1739–1806), in the execution of Robert-François Damiens, who had attempted to assassinate Louis XV. Damiens, who had managed to inflict a minor wound but caused no significant injury, and who was probably insane, was subjected to a long period of the most excruciating torture, then tied to horses with the intention of having them wrench his arms and legs from his torso, but his limbs refused to part and Sanson had to separate them with an axe. The horrendous execution was witnessed by Giacomo Casanova, who left an account in his memoirs in which he recorded his horror: 'I was several times obliged to turn away my face and to stop my ears as I heard his piercing shrieks, half of his body having been torn from him . . .'

Nicholas Sanson resigned his position as executioner of Reims thereafter, but his nephew, Charles Henri Sanson, continued as executioner of Paris and, despite claiming that he disliked the family business, executed nearly three thousand people during his career. He was the first person to use the guillotine, of which he was a firm advocate, the earliest customer being a robber named Nicolas Jacques Pelletier. He was publicly executed at 3.30 in the afternoon outside the Hôtel de Ville in the Place de Grève, but the excited crowd was not satisfied with the fast and clinical method of execution, which altogether lacked the spectacle and entertainment value of a hanging or breaking on the wheel.

Charles Henri went on to achieve immortality as the executioner of King Louis XVI. His second son, Henri Sanson (1767–1840), executed Marie Antoinette, who accidentally stepped on Sanson's foot as she mounted the scaffold, saying, 'Pardon me, sir, I meant not to do it.' They were her last words.

The last of the dynasty was Clément Henri Sanson, who served until 1847.

Meanwhile, Nicholas Sanson, who had resigned his position as the executioner of Reims, had a rather grandly named son, Louis Cyr Charlemagne Sanson, who in turn had a son named Pierre Louis Sanson, who in his turn had a son named Charles Louis Sanson. The *Autobiography* claims that this man also had the surname Carnac and was the father of John Louis Carnac, James Willoughby Carnac's father.

After fleeing his uncle's home, Carnac, having inherited a sum amounting to £250 a year, rented accommodation in New Cross and began desultory studies to be a doctor, which he quickly abandoned. He moved to Tottenham Court Road and by the summer of 1888 had moved to rooms in a house in Henrietta Street, near Covent Garden Market (which had connections with S.G. too, it being where George Hulme Beaman and his son had their medical practice). In the early part of 1888 he met Julia Norcote, the sister of a friend from his days as a medical student, John Norcote. Neither appears in the 1881 census, but then Carnac states that he will not use the real names of people. Towards the end of July, after they attended the theatre, he proposed marriage and she accepted, but the demon within him – the tiger, as he called it – awakened, and he realized that he could never enjoy a happy married life. It also set him on the course that would create Jack the Ripper.

After the last murder, that of Mary Kelly, Carnac suffered an accident which resulted in the amputation of a leg, putting an end to his mobility and his killing.

The Manuscript

The manuscript was found among the effects of S.G. Hulme Beaman, bequeathed to his daughter Betty, who in turn bequeathed it to her cousin, Jean Caldwell. The collection included some of S.G.'s wooden carvings of bandsmen from Larry the Lamb's Toytown and figures from *Faust* which he used for his illustrations, copies of the children's books he wrote and illustrated, and this manuscript. Mrs Caldwell knew about the manuscript but wanted to keep the collection together and hoped that whoever bought it would publish the manuscript. Appreciating the potential value of the Larry the Lamb material, she approached Bonhams auction house, who recommended she offer the collection to Alan Hicken, the proprietor of the Montacute TV, Radio and Toy Museum in Montacute, Somerset. When Alan Hicken read the Carnac manuscript he felt he had to get it published, with Mrs Caldwell's full approval and encouragement.

The manuscript appears to have been written between 1928 and 1930 – this date being calculated from the author's claim to have been 69 years old at the time of writing and for the murders to have been committed 40 or 42 years earlier. This date agrees with some of the statements made in the manuscript, such as the author's observation that detective fiction was a relatively new genre and enjoying considerable popularity. The 1920s and 1930s were indeed the Golden Age of detective fiction and are generally recognized as such today, having produced Margery Allingham, Agatha Christie, Ngaio Marsh, Dorothy L. Sayers, and Josephine Tey. The date also fits S.G. Hulme Beaman's life. Hulme Beaman, of course, died tragically young in 1932, so the manuscript can't have been written after that date. However, 1928–1930 was also the time when Hulme Beaman was hard at work with Larry the Lamb and Toytown.

The manuscript is in three parts with an 'Explanatory Note' by S.G. Hulme Beaman and an 'Epilogue' recounting the inquest and inquest verdict into Carnac's death.

The Explanatory Note is perhaps the most curious part of the whole manuscript. It runs to one and a half single-spaced pages and ends with the initials 'H.B.'. It was typed on a typewriter different from the rest of the manuscript. S.G. explains that he was executor of the will of James Carnac and in that capacity had received Carnac's effects, among which was the manuscript. It was 'enclosed in a sealed packet' – an important point to note – and that attached to the packet was a letter requesting S.G. to send the manuscript to a specified literary agency whose name we are not told. Fearing legal complications from giving an unopened package to a literary agent without first knowing the content and having the sanction of the probate authorities, S.G. explains that he opened and read the contents and that having done so it is his intention to hand the manuscript over to the literary agent. He does not say he had done so, which is another important point.

In the nine paragraphs he explains that he knew Carnac and along with others who knew him had regarded him as 'unpleasantly eccentric' and as a man who held 'unorthodox and peculiarly offensive views on certain vital matters', who had a vitriolic tongue and a cynical or macabre humour. He put all this down to a personality soured by the loss of a leg in Carnac's youth, but even so Carnac sounds such an unlikeable person that one wonders how S.G. could ever have become sufficiently close to him to be appointed executor of his will.

What is perhaps highly important about the manuscript is that it is unclear to whom the 'Explanatory Remarks' are addressed. S.G. states that he intends to send the manuscript to the literary agent, as Carnac had requested, so the 'Remarks' are not directed at the agent. It is also obvious that they are not intended for a publisher or for a general reader such as you or me. In fact, the tone suggests that they are directed at someone known to S.G. and with whom he had discussed the manuscript, albeit not in any detail.

S.G. also claims in the 'Explanatory Remarks' that he had removed and destroyed 'certain portions of the manuscript which contained details particularly revolting to me', but that otherwise the manuscript is 'presented exactly in the form in which it came to me . . .'.

It is tempting to assume that the material S.G. found offensive were descriptions of the bodies of Jack the Ripper's victims, but this need not be the case.

S.G. says the passages were sufficient to convince him that Carnac was insane, but he prefaces this by remarking that he possesses 'little medical knowledge'. Why would medical knowledge have been a requirement for finding the passages offensive? And wouldn't the fact that Carnac murdered and mutilated six women in the most brutal fashion have been sufficient to show that Carnac was insane? What S.G. seems to be saying is that Carnac wrote things which S.G., though lacking medical knowledge, thought made Carnac insane. The offensive material could have therefore involved the victims, but equally could be blood-lust fantasies, or the occult or blasphemous descriptions which we see in the manuscript.

However, it is questionable whether any material was removed from the manuscript. There are no gaps in the manuscript where material was removed, therefore either S.G. has completely rewritten the manuscript to provide a flowing, uninterrupted narrative, or S.G. did not remove any material.

All of the above reasoning assumes that the manuscript is 'genuine', at least in the sense that S.G. received it from someone else and did not write it himself. What lends some support to this assumption is the fact that the 'Explanatory Remarks' are written on a typewriter different to the rest of the manuscript. However, this could be because S.G. bought a new machine, borrowed a machine or typed the 'Remarks' away from his office, and whilst we should be cautious about reading too much significance into it, it does raise a question we should stop to examine.

Claiming that a manuscript has been found among the possessions of a dead man, or been bequeathed, or discovered in an attic or in a sales room is, as I said at the beginning, a device used by authors to give verisimilitude to their stories. Perhaps the best known and loved use of the device was that by George MacDonald Fraser, who claimed the Flashman Papers were found in an antique tea-chest in a Leicestershire auction room in 1965.

However, there is rarely any pretence that the fiction is actually genuine. There are occasional instances where that is not the case, where an author intentionally presents his fiction as genuine and does what he can to make his narrative look authentic. Could this have been what S.G. was doing by using different typewriters? Interestingly, in the 'Remarks' S.G. dates the Jack the Ripper murders to 1880, which could be a typing error, but at the start of Part 11, where the murders are correctly assigned to 1888, the year is underlined and there is a large, ostentatious question mark in the margin. Could this have been done by S.G., part of an elaborate and very subtle way of making it appear that he was questioning the date?

Or was he really questioning the accuracy of the date?

Trying to make sense of this manuscript is impossible, the questions too numerous, the permutations too many, the desire to dismiss the story as Hulme Beaman's invention too great a temptation, the inclination to think of it as real an equally great temptation, all leading to a feeling that a sign should be hung on the opening page of the *Autobiography* saying 'Insanity This Way Lies', but what we *can* say is that the 'Explanatory Remarks' seem to have been written for somebody other than a literary agent, publisher or general reader, that S.G. Hulme Beaman claims to have known James Carnac, that he claims to have removed personally offensive material (but the manuscript doesn't have any gaps showing where the material could have been removed), and that the whole of it is written on a typewriter different to the rest of the manuscript.

Part 1 of the manuscript provides the biographical background of James Carnac already discussed and brings his life story up to 1888. The page number is typed in the centre at the top of the page, except for the start of every new chapter.

Part 11 consists of chapters 12 to 24. The opening page looks older than Part 1, the page being creased and with tiny tears along the page edges. This page is not numbered, but one would not expect it to be as the start of new chapters are not numbered. However, none of the subsequent pages are numbered until the numbering resumes with chapter 15. Page numbering thereafter continues until chapter 21, when it ceases altogether. This is not a slip of memory. The page numbering stopped with page 72 and resumed again with page 77, so if it was a slip of memory we'd expect there to be four unnumbered pages. In fact there are 24 pages, so it is clear that a substantial addition has been made.*

The numbered and unnumbered pages were written on the same typewriter, from which it seems clear that the author was responsible for them all. What cannot be

---

* These page numbers refer not to this printed book but to the original manuscript, some pages of which are included in Appendix 2.

determined is whether the unnumbered pages are older than the numbered pages or vice versa. In other words, was there an original manuscript consisting of un-numbered pages which the author expanded by adding Part 1 and the other numbered pages?

Part 11 opens in the summer of 1888. As already noted, somebody has underlined '1888' and put a large, ostentatious question mark in the manuscript's margin, evidently questioning the date. The most obvious person to have done this is S.G. because in his 'Explanatory Remarks' he assigns the murders to 1880*.

Carnac is living in rooms in Henrietta Street, Covent

---

*Hulme Beaman dated the murders 1880; on the first page of Part 11 they are correctly dated 1888 but someone has put a question mark in the margin (the original page is reproduced in Appendix 2), so was obviously questioning the date of the murders. That Hulme Beaman dated the murders '1880' in the Explanatory Remarks seems to be too big a coincidence to be dismissed as a typo, but instead suggests that Hulme Beaman was questioning the date himself. If so then that is good for the manuscript *not* having been composed by Hulme Beaman, because anyone having researched the murders would certainly know the date of the crimes and would neither have written '1880' nor questioned the date '1888'. (It's possible that somebody else questioned the date, and presumably that person would have to be the person to whom the Explanatory Remarks were addressed.) On the other hand if Hulme Beaman did write the manuscript then he either intended it to be published as a work of fiction or he planned to pass it off as the genuine confession of Jack the Ripper. If the latter then I'd expect to at least find some things about the manuscript intended to 'distance' Hulme Beaman from his fake and also to bestow some verisimilitude upon it. One such would be to pretend

Garden, one of two lodgers in the house of a 'Mrs D.'. Financially independent, he devotes himself to reading and art. His literary tastes were for the occult, on which he claims to be an authority, and his art took him across London looking for subjects to draw, being particularly 'attracted by the grotesque and the macabre' of the East End. He had done some drawings to accompany his book – the manuscript – but doubted they would be good enough for publication.

He describes falling in love with Julia Norcote, the sister of a friend, and proposing and being accepted, but then the manuscript diverts into an extraordinary tale which reads like a drug-induced fantasy. It begins quietly enough with a reference to hearing voices and one more than the rest which he calls 'the Voice'. He then recounts an evening with Julia in which he sees a vision in a small wall mirror of her throat cut, a circlet of red around her neck and drops of blood on her white bosom. Excited by the sight and at the same time horrified by his emotions, he rushes from the house, the 'tiger', as he called his urge to kill, having reawakened inside him.

Carnac notes that the experience and his reaction is 'like a scene from a "Surrey" melodrama'. This is a reference to the Surrey Theatre in Blackfriars Road,

that *he thought* the murders were committed in 1880 and to question the date 1888 in the text, then on it being established that the murders were committed in 1888 he'd be shown to have a poor knowledge of the crimes and the manuscript would be shown to be accurate.

which had a long history of producing melodramas. From 1881 until 1900 it was owned by George Conquest (1837–1901), who famously produced a string of melodramas there, but after his death from heart disease in 1901 the theatre's popularity rapidly declined and it was turned into a music hall and by 1924 had closed.

Having fled 'like a scene from a "Surrey" melodrama' from the Norcote house, Carnac plunges into a bizarre and surreal account of being taken by a man in black with Carnac's features to a torture chamber and seeing an unconscious woman strapped to a wheel. He leaves the house and meets other wraith-like but real men (or so Carnac claims), all dressed in black, all with his face, and he wanders through the streets dazed until he reaches home. Carnac says he had not seen a torture wheel, but had read of one in *The Cloister and the Hearth*, an historical novel set in the fifteenth century by Charles Reade and published in 1861, and about twelve years later had seen one in an exhibition in Earl's Court and recalled a fracas being reported in the newspapers when two men connected with the event had a fight and the one removed the wax dummy on the wheel and hoisted the other man on to the wheel.

Chapters 15–20 are page numbers 77–109.

Chapter 17 has what reads like a first-hand account of a visit to the Opera Comique to see the first-night performance of a much-discussed version of *Dr Jekyll and Mr Hyde* staged by Daniel Bandmann.

The Opera Comique had opened in 1870 and some of Gilbert and Sullivan's early operas had been staged there, but after their departure for the Savoy Theatre its fortunes declined. A refurbishment in 1885 led to a short-lived period of popularity, which it was enjoying in 1888, but it was a false summer and within eleven years it was closed. The Bandmann production was perhaps typical of the sort of productions in what the theatrical paper, *The Era*, described as the theatre's 'singularly eccentric and mostly disastrous career'.

Both Daniel Bandmann and Richard Mansfield had come to London with productions of *Jekyll and Hyde,* and Mansfield's transformation from Jekyll to Hyde was widely acclaimed and is what he is largely remembered for today. Bandmann was an actor-manager of note and distinction, but his much-awaited version was a disaster. His transformation consisted of little more than disturbing his wig and putting in a hideous set of false teeth whilst the lights were turned down, and, according to *The Times*, Bandmann as Hyde then 'hops about the stage after the manner of a kangaroo, emitting a wheezing sound like a broken-winded horse . . .'. The *Daily News* likened Bandmann's hopping to that of 'a galvanised frog' and referred to the audience laughing aloud and that 'unseemly tittering' even accompanied a murder scene.

'As tedious as it is puerile', according to the *Pall Mall Gazette*, the play lasted only a few performances.

Carnac describes the play briefly, but accurately, and, as

said, it feels like a first-hand account. S.G. Hulme Beaman could not have seen it and in some respects it is surprising that he'd even heard of it, so reference to it could indicate that the manuscript is not his. On the other hand, it *was* something of a theatrical cause célèbre at the time and he could have heard of it from his mother or another family member.

What is also interesting, if Hulme Beaman was the author of the *Autobiography*, is that he connected the first night of Bandmann's *Jekyll and Hyde* with the night on which Martha Tabram was murdered. In many ways it is inspired.

Carnac briefly describes the murder of Martha Tabram, whom he calls Martha Tabron. He also denies having murdered Emma Smith and refers to reading accounts of the crime and mentions Dr Killeen and Dr Phillips.

Chapter 19 briefly describes the murder of Mary Ann Nichols and describes it as 'a somewhat dull affair', which of all the Whitechapel murders the murderer might well have retrospectively felt it was. It certainly lacked the risks the murderer took in the later cases.

Chapter 20 describes the murder of Annie Chapman, who is portrayed as a very chatty Cockney whose main achievement, at least as Carnac recalls, is having once possessed a canary in a cage. She recalled having to pawn the cage and release the canary, which much to her distress was eaten by a cat.

The real Annie Chapman had known much better than

that, having been married to a coachman and lived in a mews accommodation in the West End, and also for a while lived on the estate of the very wealthy Sir Francis Tress Barry at St Leonard's Hill near Windsor. She was often drunk and ultimately an embarrassment to all concerned, her husband separating from her, but she had enjoyed a lifestyle in which having a singing canary would not have been a high spot.

Chapter 22 refers to the murder of Elizabeth Stride. Carnac buys grapes for her, which is a controversial story concerning Matthew Packer who had a small shop in Berner Street and who claimed to have sold grapes to a couple and watched them standing in the rain eating them. Carnac says she had an accent, which some contemporary sources don't support, and relates her telling him a story about having lost her children in the *Princess Alice* disaster. This was a story Stride frequently told. On 3 September 1878 the Thames pleasure steamer *Princess Alice* collided with the *Bywell Castle* and sank within four minutes, over 650 passengers drowning. As far as can be told, Stride's husband and children were not among them, nor was Stride herself a passenger. Why she repeatedly told the story is not known. Carnac also refers to being disturbed by the arrival of a horse and cart. This was a man named Louis Diemshutz who was returning home.

The account of the murder of Stride is by far Carnac's most detailed. The murder of Catherine Eddowes is mentioned almost in passing.

Chapter 23 claims he did not write the famous Dear Boss letter which gave the world the name 'Jack the Ripper'.

Chapter 24 tells the story of Mary Kelly and afterwards of an accident which deprived him of his right leg and ended the career of Jack the Ripper. There are some curious details about the account.

Carnac states that Kelly's room was at the front of the house, whereas it was at the back. This is particularly interesting because Carnac claims to be unable to recall any of the preliminary conversation with Kelly, but to have the image of place firmly in his mind.

Carnac describes Kelly's face as 'heavily powdered' and her clothing as 'flashily smart', but this better fits a 'theatrical' perception of the big-hearted, feather-boa-ed prostitute and is perhaps more suited to the demimonde of the 1920s than to the destitute and alcoholic prostitutes of the East End in 1888. It certainly doesn't ring true about Kelly at all, there being no references to Kelly possessing face powder or flashy clothes.

As well as telling us that he took Kelly into a room in the 'front of the house', when in fact it was in the rear, Carnac says that the window was 'draped with a thin muslin curtain', when in fact it was covered by an old coat; that 'The woman lit an oil lamp', but the only illumination was a penny candle stuck in a broken wine glass; that the bed was metal with one remaining knob, when from the photograph it is clearly wooden and is so described in *The Star* on 12 November 1888.

On the basis of these errors one would have no hesitation about dismissing the account as a piece of poorly researched fiction, but perversely the opposite conclusion can also be drawn because these details were widely and accurately reported in the press and anyone doing even minimum research would have probably got them all correct, the bed being a possible exception. It could be argued that these errors therefore suggest that the manuscript was written by somebody misremembering the details, as, one can suppose, the actual killer might have done.

Curiously, Carnac refers to a small mirror at the head of Kelly's bed which acquires a special significance for him and he writes in some detail about it. As far as I can tell, and I cannot claim to have gone through every newspaper, no English newspaper refers to this mirror, which is mentioned only in the *New York Herald* (10 November 1888). *Prima facie* this is a very important detail, which shouts loudly from the page, 'How did the author get so much else wrong, but know about the mirror?' Such are Ripper studies, people will probably be littering internet message boards or the Ripper periodicals with example after example of this mirror being mentioned, but as of the time of writing it is curious.

What emerges from this is the intriguing possibility that the author may have had a very basic text lacking any detail and that rather than research out the facts for himself, he used embellishments of his own imagination, picturing Annie Chapman bemoaning the loss of her singing canary, picturing Mary Kelly as an over-made-up tart with a heart, and so on, but retaining what was to the author of the original document the all-important matter of the mirror.

Part 3 contains Chapters 25–28, and the Epilogue. The opening page shows that it was fastened separately from the rest of the manuscript. It was written on a different type-writer and the line length is longer, stretching almost to the edge of the page, affording little or no right-hand margin. Also it is called part '3', whereas both parts 1 and 11 use Arabic numerals, '1' and '11'. There are no page numbers at all.

The author claims that Part 3 was written 'some months' after Part 11 and says he had originally intended to conclude his story with the murder of Mary Kelly and the end of his killing imposed by the loss of his leg, but that the manuscript had been discovered and read by his landlady, Mrs Hamlett, and he had resolved to kill her. He explains how he intended to do this and then ends the manuscript confident that his plan will succeed, and, if S.G.'s 'Explanatory Note' is to be believed, Carnac then packaged and sealed the manuscript and affixed a letter to S.G. requesting the delivery of the package to a specified literary agent.

This is all very fortuitous because Carnac's plan back-fires and he is killed, the short 'Epilogue' being a typewritten summary of the inquest hearing and verdict.

The style of Part 3 does not seem the same as the rest of the manuscript and jars quite badly, having the look and feel of a work of fiction. There is evidence of crude plotting, an example of which is a reference by Carnac to a morbid fear of being burned alive, which lo and behold is precisely how he does die. It's too corny, too much of a just retribution to be real. And so too is Carnac ending his manuscript on the eve of a murder and in anticipation of its success. Would a murderer really have done that, or would he have completed the manuscript after the murder and when assured of its success? Would Carnac have sealed his manuscript in a package and affixed a letter to his executor at a time when he had no expectation of dying? And if he sealed the manuscript, as S.G. claimed, how did the 'Epilogue' with its account of the inquest into Carnac's death get inside and who wrote it?

And why is the 'Epilogue' written on the same type-writer, with the same line length, as the rest of Part 3?

Part 3 reads like fiction, looks like fiction and smells like fiction, which, applying the old adage 'if it barks like a dog', means it probably is a fiction.

The manuscript can therefore be separated into three parts: the 'Explanatory Notes', Parts 1–11 with the numbered and unnumbered pages possibly representing an original manuscript and later revisions, and Part 3, the stylistic differences suggesting that it was written by somebody else and is probably fiction. Whether Carnac, if he ever existed, actually did die in a fire is unknown.

The Sources

Whether or not the manuscript is authentic, it is likely that the author will have used sources, either as research or to refresh his memory. Carnac confesses to having read about his crimes in the newspapers, and the accident which cost him his leg was caused through inattention whilst trying to get to a news vendor to buy a copy of a paper reporting the murder of Kelly. Anyone writing later would have visited a library, probably the Newspaper Reading Room in the British Museum in Great Russell Street. Only London and overseas newspapers were available there, all others were stored at a special newspaper repository built in 1905 at Colindale, and these had to be ordered in advance and were transported to the British Museum. By 1928 the repository at Colindale was full and as a result of a recommendation by the Royal Commission on National Museums and Galleries a new newspaper library was built, providing a public reading room (for just over fifty people) and other facilities. This was completed in May 1932. I don't know how much disruption this would have caused to the easy availability of newspapers at the time *The Autobiography of James Carnac* was written, or, indeed, whether all newspapers would have been available for consultation.

Information about the Ripper crimes was otherwise available from books, although between 1888 and

1928 these were mainly police autobiographies or commentaries. For the most part these books either claimed that the identity of Jack the Ripper was utterly unknown, or proffered one of a fairly standard number of theories.

The Suspects

L. Forbes Winslow (1844–1913), probably the most controversial psychiatrist of the late Victorian period, wrote about or otherwise gave interviews about the Ripper crimes whenever the opportunity offered itself, and in his memoirs published in 1910 told for the umpteenth time the story which he had convinced himself was true: Jack the Ripper was a religious fanatic whom he'd have caught on the steps of St Paul's if the police had rendered him the assistance he'd requested.

In March 1910 the memoirs of the head of the CID at the time of the murders, Sir Robert Anderson, were published in serialized form in the monthly *Blackwood's Magazine* and later in the year as a book. Anderson made the extraordinary claim that Jack the Ripper's identity *was* known and that he was a Polish Jew who we now know was called 'Kosminski'.

The chatty memoirs of Sir Melville Macnaghten, another senior CID officer, were published in 1915 and claimed that Jack the Ripper was a doctor who was drowned in the Thames at the end of 1888. (This man was actually a teacher cum barrister and was named Montague John Druitt.)

Charles Kingston, in 1925, in his book *The Bench and the Dock*, also wrote of doctor suspects, this time a well-known West End doctor (who was discounted because he was in Italy at the time of the murders) and an insane young medical student at St Bartholomew's Hospital.

In *Masters of Crime*, published in 1928, Guy B.H. Logan postulated that Jack the Ripper was a man of some surgical experience who was killing and murdering prostitutes because of a blood-lust, and that he had a secret lair in Whitechapel. Logan also claimed that some blood-soaked clothing was found months after the murder of Mary Kelly. It was in a locked trunk in the bedroom of the East End lodgings of a man whose movements had aroused some vague suspicions and who had left the lodgings in a hurry. He was an American, as was suggested by the buttons on a blue serge suit which bore the name of a Chicago tailor. A close secret at the time, said Logan, was that a Scotland Yard detective named Andrews had gone to America in December 1888, in search of the Ripper.

That Jack the Ripper was an American or had fled to America was offered by another detective, Tom Divall, in his 1929 book *Scoundrels and Scallywags*, where he claimed that Sir Melville Macnaghten had received information that the murderer had died in an asylum there.

A close analysis might reveal that some information was provided by these books, but nothing has leapt from the page. Otherwise there are some very vague hints, such as Carnac's self-professed authority on the occult which might reflect the just-circulating story about the Ripper's blood-stained ties being found in a box belonging to a student of the occult (a story that we now know related to a man named Robert D'Onston Stephenson). And there was the story about R.J. Lees who had allegedly followed a man he believed from a psychic vision was Jack the Ripper, but who turned out to be an eminent physician.

Leonard Matters

The most obvious inspiration and source for Carnac's memoirs is the first English-language book about Jack the Ripper, *The Mystery of Jack the Ripper* by Leonard Matters (1881–1951). He was an Australian journalist who appears to have been talented and widely respected, and who in 1929, the same year as his Ripper book was published, was elected Labour MP for Kennington, a seat he held for two years. He afterwards became the London correspondent for the Indian newspaper *The Hindu* and remained active in politics. In *The Mystery of Jack the Ripper* he told the story of the murders and ended with a claim to have discovered the identity of Jack the Ripper whilst editor of the *Buenos Aires Herald* in Argentina. According to Matters, he came across a Spanish-language Argentinian journal which gave a lengthy account of the deathbed confession by a distinguished London doctor. Matters called him 'Dr Stanley' and said that 'Dr Stanley' had committed the murders whilst searching for the prostitute from whom his brilliant son had caught syphilis and died.

Matters had first proposed the theory in *The People* newspaper on 26 December 1926, in an article called 'Jack the Ripper Sensation. Noted Murderer A London Doctor? Dying Confession'. The book was published in May 1929. Because no subsequent researcher has traced the article, Matters' 'Dr Stanley' has been generally dismissed as a fictional creation to provide a plausible motive for the murders, but as a respected journalist and a politician there is no obvious reason why he should have lied (except that he was a journalist and a politician).

The publication of the articles in 1926 and the book in May 1929 could have inspired S.G. Hulme Beaman to write the 'autobiography' of James Carnac. Equally, of course, it could have pre-empted him and stopped him from sending the manuscript to a literary agent or publisher. There are some slight similarities between the *Autobiography* and Matters' book: for example, both are supposedly based on something else, a manuscript in Hulme Beaman's case, an article in a Spanish-language journal in the case of Matters, but otherwise there is no hint that the former was aware of the latter, there's no discernible stylistic similarity, and no evidence that it was used for research, in fact quite the opposite.

Leonard Matters' murderer was a prominent West End doctor. Carnac had studied medicine, but very soon abandoned it, and as we have seen, the theory that Jack the Ripper was a doctor was a common one, even as far back as 1888, so one can't attribute Carnac's abandoned medical studies to Matters or anyone else.

There are other significant differences. Carnac says that he met 'Martha Tabron' – called Martha Tabram by Matters – in Commercial Street, whereas Matters says the Ripper met her in Osborne Street.

Carnac says he met Mary Nichols in Court Street, a street which Matters mentions as one of two 'narrow bridge roads' across the railway from Buck's Row and leading into Whitechapel Road, and Carnac left the scene by way of Bakers Row, whereas Matters pictures the murderer leaving by way of Brady Street.

Carnac refers to buying grapes for Elizabeth Stride, but Matters doesn't mention these at all.

There were varied reports of what was written on the wall, among them, 'The Juwes are not the men that will be blamed for nothing' (Daniel Halse, who saw the writing), 'The Juwes are not the men who will be blamed for nothing' (Mr Crawford, who wrote down what he saw), and 'The Juwes are the men who will not be blamed for nothing' (PC Long, who found the writing). Matters followed the version given by Daniel Halse, but Carnac differs from all of them, and a quick perusal of the newspapers has so far produced only one instance of his phrasing and that is in *The Globe* on 17 March 1910, in a short article about Anderson's claim that the Ripper was a Polish Jew. Carnac, incidentally, says he didn't write it, whereas Matters says it was 'alleged' that the Ripper wrote it.

Curiously, the writing was noticed because a piece of bloodied apron, later found to have been torn from an apron Catherine Eddowes was wearing, had been discarded below it. Matters refers to it, Carnac doesn't. This is odd because the piece of apron was almost unquestionably dropped by Jack the Ripper, so why doesn't the author refer to it? On the other hand, would the real murderer have recalled where he disposed of the scrap, or even necessarily have remembered that he'd torn it from the victim's apron and used it to wipe his knife, or even thought it sufficiently interesting to mention?

Carnac says Kelly was murdered in the downstairs *front* room of a house; Matters, who visited the house, now long demolished, says the murder was committed in the downstairs rear room.

These differences suggest that the author of *The Autobiography of James Carnac* did not use Matters as a primary source, and probably didn't use him as a source at all.

One *could* argue that a work of fiction written after the publication of Matters' book in May 1929 would have used it for research or inspiration and that the author of the *Autobiography* either didn't do so because he didn't have to – his work was genuine! – or because he wrote before Matters' book was published. Equally, of course, the author may not have known about Matters' book.

Ripperature

The rather silly but witty and useful word for the factual and fictional writings about Jack the Ripper is 'Ripperature', and whilst it doesn't contain many literary confessions, they are not unknown, and the earliest dates from late November 1888, only days after the murder of Mary Kelly. The confession was published in a newspaper and was supposed to be the diary of Charles Kowlder, a New Yorker in London on business, who awakes from a dream – 'a condition of hypnotism' as the newspaper calls it – to discover himself in Mary Kelly's room, a blood-dripping knife in his hand. There is no pretence that it was other than fiction, but another story published less than a month later did purport to be true, though was obviously a fiction, and was allegedly found in a little book given to its customers by a London tailor's.

Within a month of the murder of Catherine Eddowes on 30 September 1888, long, narrow posters distinguished by a blood-red splash at the top appeared on walls around London, advertising a shilling booklet called *The Curse of Mitre Square*. Written by John Francis Brewer, the short story claimed that Mitre Square had been cursed ever since the murder of a woman on the altar steps of Holy Trinity Church (which stood on the same site) by a mad monk, Brother Martin, during the

JAMES CARNAC

reign of King Henry VIII. Even at the time it was
published the story was recognized as being a far-fetched
fantasy, and its reputation hasn't fared better over the
years, but it tried, as so many authors have tried since, to
provide an explanation for the crimes. In this case it was
a supernatural one.

Other standard ideas were reproduced in fiction:
slaughtermen were a class common in the East End and
police suspicion fell on them with the first murder. In
1889 Margaret Harkness, who wrote socialist novels
under the name John Law, published *In Darkest London*,
which featured Jack the Ripper as a Gentile slaughterman
hiding among the Jewish immigrant community in the
East End.

Possibly the single most successful fiction about Jack
the Ripper and one which could have influenced the
Autobiography was Marie Belloc Lowndes' story
The Lodger. Published in *McClure's Magazine* in 1911
and as a novel in 1913, the book ingeniously examines
the changing emotions of a landlady, Mrs Bunting, as she
grows to suspect her lodger of being a murderer called
the Avenger, but who in all other respects was Jack the
Ripper. The story could have had an influence on
the *Autobiography* in two respects. One is that it attempts
a psychological portrait of suspicion, of getting inside the
head of Mrs Bunting, and the *Autobiography* tries to get
inside the head of Jack the Ripper – and does so remarkably well. The other is that Part 3 of the *Autobiography* is

almost a reverse of the Mrs Bunting story insofar as Mrs Hamlett is the landlady and Carnac is the lodger, and Mrs Hamlett is the one with suspicions and Carnac is the one to take action.

Lowndes did not originate the lodger story; there were stories circulating in 1888 and afterwards in which land-ladies expressed suspicions about lodgers, and L. Forbes Winslow's suspect emerged because of a landlady's suspicions.

Summing up

Overall, though, the *Autobiography* doesn't seem to have taken inspiration from anywhere, or it took inspiration from everywhere, and it is this singularity, almost uniqueness, which makes this manuscript so intriguing. Carnac embodies many of the traits or facets of other 'suspects' – a lodger, medical experience, an interest and perhaps an expertise in the occult, and so on – but he is his own man, a murderer who is driven to kill by a passion for blood, who kills because he enjoys it.

I have often thought that Jack the Ripper touches our primal fear of the unknown, that the desire to know who he was is so that we can give him boundaries: an insane doctor killing prostitutes as he searches for the one who gave his son syphilis means that the vast majority of people need not fear him. The religious fanatic killing prostitutes to clear the world of immorality likewise means that the victims belong to a small group and that everyone else has little to worry about. What is so frightening about Jack the Ripper and is so frightening about serial killers in general is that they move among us unrecognized, killing with no discernible motive. Whilst almost every other commentator on the Whitechapel murders, even John Francis Brewer, was trying to make Jack the Ripper comprehensible, the *Autobiography* cut across the grain and presented a murderer who is today far more real.

The question is: was he real?

Although this manuscript could be dismissed as entirely the work of S.G. Hulme Beaman – and it would be a fascinating document if that was the case – many things draw one into wondering if it is a far more complex document than that.

To begin with, this manuscript is such an extraordinary and improbable departure from his usual output that it requires a leap of our imagination to suppose that Hulme Beaman would have taken it, and not simply because it's an adult crime book, but because it is a first-person narrative from the killer's perspective and, apart from the oddly fictional Part 3, it offers no even slightly redeeming motive. The proposed date when it was written also rests uneasy with the direction of Hulme Beaman's career, his models and stories really taking off and inevitably absorbing his interest and time.

This is followed by the oddities of Hulme Beaman's 'Explanatory Remarks', which appear to have been directed to somebody unknown to us and *prior* to contact being made with a literary agent. The tone suggests that Hulme Beaman had already discussed the book with that person, albeit not in any great detail.

It is probably reading too much into the wording, but his concluding comment that the 'narrative is presented exactly in the form in which it came to me' could be interpreted as meaning that the manuscript is not what was received from 'Carnac', but was a rewritten, possibly fleshed-out document which *sans* some offending material nevertheless followed the story (narrative) as received.

Although it is a common literary device for an author to divorce himself from a manuscript by claiming that it is a bequest or something found in a dusty attic or bought as a curiosity from a small, provincial auction house, the explanatory introduction is usually directed at you or me, the reader, or takes the form of a letter to an identifiable person such as a publisher or literary agent. Hulme Beaman's 'Explanatory remarks' do not take that form. Instead they are directed at somebody unknown, somebody with whom, from the tone, he has already discussed the manuscript, but not the literary agent or publisher or readers like us. This strikes me as distinctly odd, almost as if the manuscript *is* something he was bequeathed.

I am as a general rule wary of reading more into what an author says than was probably intended, but it is also worth observing that Hulme Beaman ends by saying that the 'narrative is presented exactly in the form in which it came to me'. Why didn't he simply say that the manuscript is as it was received? Could the use of 'narrative' be taken to mean that the story, not the manuscript, is intact? Such an idea opens the intriguing possibility that what we have is not the manuscript received from 'Carnac', but a rewritten, fleshed-out document which incorporates all that Carnac said, but with biographical details added by somebody else.

Other questions arise from an examination of the manuscript, particularly the use of three typewriters. Maybe nothing should be read into this – I had a portable and desktop typewriter and frequently wrote on them interchangeably – but what does prompt question is that these machines were *not* used interchangeably. The introduction used one machine, Part 1 and Part 11, including the unnumbered rewrite pages, were all written with another machine, and Part 3 and the Epilogue were all written on yet another typewriter. Either this is because these were written at different times on different machines, or the author is trying to convey that impression.

Also, why is Part 3 not only written on a different typewriter and with different page layout to the rest of the manuscript, but also so stylistically different? It is such an obvious fiction, not least because the same machine was used to write the Epilogue. Odd, because it would have plotted better if the Epilogue had been presented as newspaper extracts appended by somebody, even by Hulme Beaman, to the sealed manuscript.

The questions arising from the manuscript are numerous and every time you think you may have theorized a coherent explanation for them, the explanation is checkmated by other problems. However one looks at it, the book you are holding is intriguing. Very intriguing.

Appendix II

Facsimiles of Original Pages
from the Manuscript Mentioned
in Appendix 1

EXPLANATORY REMARKS.

As executor of the will of the late James Carnac I feel it
incumbent upon me to preface the extraordinary narrative comprising the body of this manuscript by a few words of my own.   Primarily I desire to emphasize that which will, no doubt, be obvious;
namely: that I can produce no evidence touching the truth or
otherwise of what Mr. Carnac calls his autobiography.   I can accept no responsibility whatever for his statements.   His confession, or claim, to the authorship of those atrocities which horrified London in the year 1880 is not, I should imagine, susceptible to proof; though one or two of the incidents he records --
apartfrom the actual atrocities -- I know to be true.   And the
confession -- if it can be so regarded -- is valueless, I understand, from a legal standpoint inasmuch as it is unwitnessed; I
do not feel constrained, therefore to place it before the police
authorities.

I must admit to great diffidence in even attempting to obtain publication of the manuscript; firstly because it is not
unlikely that any publisher to whom I submit it may regard the
whole thing as a hoax either on my part or on the part of Mr.
Carnac -- though it is difficult to understand why Carnac should
have devoted the final periods of his life to a compilation designed to identify himself, untruthfully, with the most atrocious assassin of modern times; but secondly, and of more importance, is
the fact that, in my estimation at least, the narrative is in very
questionable taste.   Had this been a confession couched in terms
of contrition it would, I think, have been more acceptable, but it
clearly is not.   Throughout the whole runs a streak of cynical
and macabre humour or facetiousness which I find rather distasteful.   To me who knew the man this is typical of him, and I can
appreciate that if he was "Jack the Ripper" his terrible atrocities would have been carried out exactly in the spirit which his
style of writing suggests.

My personal view, for what it is worth and after carefully
studying the manuscript, is that James Carnac was in actual fact
"Jack the Ripper"; but with that belief I must couple the conviction that on one point at least he was insane.   I will not
labour this, but I feel sure that a similar opinion will be formed
by other readers of the manuscript.

In common with other associates of Carnac I always regarded
him as unpleasantly eccentric.   He held, we were frequently reminded, unorthodox and peculiarly offensive views on certain
vital matters.   I know that to speak thus of a man recently dead

375

is to be deplored, and I should not do so were it not that the
statements made or implied in his own manuscript render any reservation on my part unnecessary.

As he shrewdly surmised we ascribed his cynical outlook on
life to his physical disability; for he had lost a leg in early
manhood (as he explains in his manuscript) and on this account we
made many allowances for his vitriolic tongue.

The manuscript came to me, as Carnac's executor, with his
other effects; it was enclosed in a sealed packet and attached
to the the exterior of this was a latter requesting me to send the
packet unopened to a certain firm of literary agents· Clearly
I could not fulfil this wish blindfold; I could not accept the
responsibility of parting with a package of unknown contents without
sanction of the probate authorities. Such a course might have
entailed unforeseen legal complications. I therefore opened the
package and read the contents; and since it appeared to me to have
little intrinsic value I decided I could not shirk that other
responsibility imposed by my acceptance of the executorship.

I propose therefore to consult with the literary agents whose
names were specified by Carnac with a view to at least attempting
to fulfil his wishes regarding publication.

In conclusion I should say that I have, after due deliberation,
removed and destroyed certain portions of the manuscript which contained details particularly revolting to me. I have little medical
knowledge, but these passages were, apart from the general tone of
the manuscript, sufficient to convince me that if the narrative is
to be accepted as a truthful autobiography the writer must be regarded unquestionably as suffering from a form of insanity.

Apart from the deletions to which I have referred this narrative
is presented exactly in the form in which it came to me, even to
the cynical dedication.

                                        H.B.

PART 1.

7

it contained shelves bearing innumerable bottles of
varying size and fascinating appearance. The not unpleasant smell which proceeded from this Blue Beard's
chamber permeated the whole of the lower floor and could
occasionally be detected in the upper rooms.

My father, as I first remember him -- if such a
definite term can be applied to so indefinite a thing
as the gradually dawning perceptions of a child -- was
a tall, thin man, wearing a fair moustache which extended
into "mutton-chop" whiskers. Later he adopted gold-
rimmed spectacles, for his eyes were weak and his sight
was probably effected by his habit of poring over a microscope during his periods of evening leisure. When I cast
my mind back to those very early days I picture him crouching over the recently-cleared tea-table, one side of his
face red from the reflected light of the fire, the other
green from the illuminated shade of an oil-lamp standing
beside the microscope down which he was peering. Or I
see him fiddling with small tweezers and little circles
of almost incredibly thin glass, or, with a glass tube,
drawing up drops of dirty-looking water from a collecting-
bottle which, to my eye, contained nothing else but green
weed. When, these drops being placed in a reservoir slide
under the microscope, I was sometimes invited to look I
would never believe that the strange, moving creatures
which swam across my field of vision had come from the
bottle. My father's proficiency in producing these
things from nothing at all astonished me and yet, somehow,
it did not carry with it increased feelings of pride in him;
in some curious way I acquired the idea that the talent
he displayed in this magical procedure was one inherent
in all adults.

My father's microscopic hobby coloured the Sunday
morning walks which I took with him into the country lanes
near our house. A favourite walk was to a place called
Clay Hill, and my father always carried with him on these
occasions a telescopic walking-stick which I considered
a miracle of ingenuity. To the extended end of this
he would attach, by means of a screwed-on ring, a collecting-bottle and this he would dip into any pond or
ditch which lay along our course, transferring the "catch"
to one of the other bottles bulging in his pockets. He

73

PART II.

CHAPTER 12.

In the summer of the year 1888 I was living in rooms
in Henrietta Street, Covent Garden. I shall not mention
the number of the house, but it is one on the right-hand
side as one walks towards the Market. My landlady was an
elderly widow, rather stout, very talkative, but a kindly
and motherly soul. She kept my rooms spotlessly clean;
mainly by her personal efforts, for although a young maid-
of-all-work lurked somewhere in the lower recesses of
the building her contact with the "gentlemen" (i.e. I and
my fellow lodger) was limited to the carrying of coals,
water-jugs and heavy trays, and the cleaning and returning
of boots. Mrs. D., my landlady, dusted, made my bed and
carried in and arranged my meals.

Of her two lodgers I was, I think, regarded by Mrs.
D. with the most consideration, for I was financially
independent; and the moneyed drone is always, in this
world, treated with more respect than the worker. In the
popular view the possession of money would seem to postulate
intrinsic merit in the possessor. I had inherited my
uncle's savings in addition to my father's money, and the
combined capital was, and is, sufficient to provide me
with a comfortable income.

Technically I was, I suppose, a drone, but my time
was fully occupied. I did not live the life of the
"young man about town"; I was neither dissipated nor
extravagant. Although a comparatively young man I took
little pleasure in the flippances of youth; my disposition
was that of the student, and reading and drawing were my
principal interests.

I kept up my drawing. I have never had occasion
to practise as a professional artist and am quite aware
that such proficiency as I now possess is no more than
that of the average industrious amateur. I am not even
sure that the drawings I have made for this book reach the
standard of merit expected by a publisher.

In pursuit of my hobby of drawing I explored many

PART 3.

154

CHAPTER 25

When I commenced this record, some months ago, it was
my intention to conclude it by the description of my Millers
Court exploit and the subsequent loss of my limb. This seemed to me a natural conclusion because the woman of Millers
Court was my final "subject" and the accident put an end to
my active life; while the many years which have since elapsed have brought to me no more than the trivial incidents of
a hum-drum existence, -- certainly nothing worthy of inclusion in this unconventional autobiography. Forty years of
hum-drum existence mark you, gentle reader; it hardly seems
right, does it? You, who can look back upon a blameless
life entirely free from bloodshed except, perhaps, (if you
are a man) a few years of purely patriotic bloodshed, may
quite justifiably feel a certain resentment at the dilatory
behaviour of Nemesis; in my case, at least, the daughter of
Erebus is hardly what our American friends would call a fast
worker. In fact if I die peacefully in bed, as I hope to
do, that melancholy event will hardly seem to square with
your ideas regarding the prevalence of right and justice.
I know that I should have, according to your lights, an
extremely unpleasant end.

Yet perhaps I am being unduly cynical in assuming in
you an entire lack of understanding, -- I will not say sympathy,-which I can hardly expect. For I have tried, in the
course of this record, to convey my sense of being a mere
plaything of Destiny; an instrument in some scheme of Fate.
Yet what, may well be asked, can that scheme have been?

We touch here upon one of the most elusive problems of
the universe. A baby is born; he is carefully tended and
cherished, nursed through illnesses, educated and fed to the
end that he may become a useful member of society. He gradually develops under the lovingand marvelling eyes of his
parents to that miraculous and efficient organism a man.
And then at the age of twenty he is killed in a futile war.
why?

A city is painfully and laboriously built; for many
years, centuries perhaps, princes, architects, artists and
slaves lavish upon it their wealth and toil until at last
it stands completed, a monument to man's energy and efficiency. And an earthquake destroys it in a day. Again why?

Ask our philosophers the purpose of such cruel and
wanton events; they will tell you they do not know. Ask
our parsons; they will tell you that God moves in a mysterious ways; or, in other words, that they do not know. But ,

178

EPILOGUE.

A Coroner's Charge to a Jury.

Well, gentlemen, you have now heard all the available evidence and it now remains for you to decide how this unfortunate gentleman came by his death and to return a verdict accordingly.

As to the identity of the remains: I think you will agree that no doubt exists that they are those of Mr. James Willoughby Carnac. I need not point out to you that direct identification has been impossible; it has been your very unpleasant duty to view the remains, and you know that they are quite unrecognizable. But in this matter of identification you have the following to guide you: Mrs. Hamlett, the landlady of the house, has told us that at the time of the fire the only occupants of the house were herself, the maid Minnie Wright, and Mr. Carnac. Mr. Carnac was not saved. This, alone, renders it practically certain that the charred remains are those of Mr. Carnac; and it is supported by the evidence of Dr. Short who has stated that the remains are those of a man of approximately Mr. Carnac's build and with a right leg missing. And we have been told by Mrs. Hamlett and Minnie Wright that Mr. Carnac had lost a right leg.

Now as regards the cause of death. Mrs. Hamlett has given her evidence very clearly and directly, but I will just run over the main points again. It appears that on the evening of February the third Mrs. Hamlett was suffering from a cold, on account of which she retired early, Mr. Carnac having kindly mixed her a glass of grog.

Mrs. Hamlett drank the mixture and retired to her bedroom on the ground-floor; she found the room was extraordinarily hot, as the gas-stove had been alight for some time, and she turned the gas out. It then occurred to her that Mr. Carnac's bedroom would be extremely cold; she passed upstairs, lit his gas-fire, closed the door and returned to her own room.

Now up to that point, gentlemen, the evidence is perfectly clear. Mrs. Hamlett states quite emphatically that she lit Mr. Carnac's gas-fire; that it was burning at about half the full strength when she left the room. You have seen that lady and heard her give evidence, and if your impression is similar to my own you will agree that she is not the sort of person who would carelessly turn on the gas and leave the room without lighting it; in fact it is a little difficult to see how any sane person could do such a thing. We can take it, I think, that the gas-fire was

Appendix III

List of Victims

Whoever you may believe to be Jack the Ripper, what must not be forgotten are the very real victims of these brutal attacks of innocent women in Whitechapel, whose descendants are still alive amongst us today, and who have still not received justice for what happened over a century ago.

The victims of James Willoughby Carnac:

MARTHA TABRAM
Murdered Tuesday 7 August 1888 in George Yard Buildings (now demolished, off Gunthorpe Street), body discovered at 3.30am.

MARY ANN 'POLLY' NICHOLS
Murdered Friday 31 August 1888 in Buck's Row (now Durward Street), body discovered at 3.45am.

ANNIE CHAPMAN
Murdered Saturday 8 September 1888 outside 29
Hanbury Street, body discovered at 6am.

ELIZABETH STRIDE
Murdered Sunday 30 September 1888 in Duffield's
Yard, Berner Street (now Henriques Street), body
discovered at 1am.

CATHERINE EDDOWES
Murdered Sunday 30 September 1888 in Mitre Square,
body discovered at 1.45am.

MARY JANE KELLY
Murdered Friday 9 November 1888 in 13 Miller's
Court, off Dorset Street (now demolished and the site of
a car park), body discovered at 10.45am.

Picture Acknowledgements

Page 1:
Alan Hicken outside the Montacute TV, Radio and Toy Museum
© Emma Greenham-Hicken ATCL; Sydney George Hulme
Beaman © Alan Hicken.

Page 2:
Two images of Tottenham in the 1870s © Bruce Castle Museum
(Haringey Culture, Libraries and Learning).

Page 3:
Mortuary photo of Martha Tabram © The National Archives, ref.
MEPO3/3155; Martha Tabram's body is discovered at George
Yard Buildings by dock labourer John Reeves © Mary Evans
Picture Library/Alamy; George Yard Buildings in the 1960s
before their demolition © John Bennett.

Page 4:
Mortuary photo of Mary Ann Nichols © The National Archives,
ref. MEPO3/3155; Police Constable John Neil discovers Mary
Ann Nichols' body in Buck's Row (now Durward Street)

© INTERFOTO/Alamy; Durward Street in the 1960s © Trinity
Mirror/Mirrorpix/Alamy.

Page 5:
Mortuary photo of Annie Chapman © The National Archives,
ref. MEPO3/3155; the rear of 20 Hanbury Street where the body
of Annie Chapman was found © Mary Evans Picture
Library/Alamy; close-up of the murder scene © Trinity
Mirror/Mirrorpix/Alamy.

Page 6:
Mortuary photo of Elizabeth Stride © The National Archives,
ref. MEPO3/3156; the court in Berner Street where the body of
Elizabeth Stride was discovered © Mary Evans Picture
Library/Alamy; mortuary photo of Catherine Eddowes © The
National Archives, ref. MEPO3/140; a police sketch of Mitre
Square made shortly after the discovery of Catherine Eddowes's
body © Mary Evans Picture Library/David Lewis Hodgson.

Page 7:
The mutilated body of Mary Jane Kelly © The National
Archives, ref. MEPO3/3155; the outside of 13 Miller's Court,
Dorset Street, where Mary Jane Kelly was murdered, taken the
day after the murder © Mary Evans Picture Library/David Lewis
Hodgson.

Page 8:
An image of East End tenements in the 1870s taken from
London: A Pilgrimage by Blanchard Jerrold and Gustave Doré ©
The Print Collector/Alamy; Dorset Street, Spitalfields,
sometimes called 'The Worst Street in London', c. 1902 © Mary
Evans/Peter Higginbotham Collection.

Index

Letters sent from Jean Caldwell to Alan Hicken

3rd November 2009

Mr A J Hicken
Montacute Museum
No. 1. South Street
Montacute
Somerset TA15 6XD

Dear Mr. Hicken

Re: S. G. Hulme-Beaman

Many thanks for telephoning me yesterday: it was such a pleasure to hear from you and I was, of course, very interested to hear of "progress" for the Ripper book.

I confirm that Sidney's daughter, Betty, believed the manuscript to be true.

Sidney's father, George Hulme-Beaman (my grandfather) was a very talented artist. Painting was his hobby and I have many of his beautiful water colours. He was a Loss Adjustor for an insurance company in London. Sidney also was a "spare time" artist before it became his career, and I have some of his paintings, too, which are remarkably like his father's – from whom he clearly inherited his talent.

I thought you might like an example of each as a personal gift from me. Unfortunately, Sidney never signed any of his "hobby" paintings, although you will see his father did.

With best wishes for "the book" and all the Museum's enterprises and with kindest regards.

Jean

February 2008

Mr. A. J. Hicken
Montacute Museum
No. 1. South Street
Montacute
Somerset TA15 6XD

Dear Mr. Hicken

Re: S. G. Hulme-Beaman - Creator of the Tales of Toytown

I am very happy to know that my uncle Sydney's work now has a lasting home at the Montacute Museum.

His unique wooden figures, each hand made and painted, were the models for his colourful illustrations of Toytown and other children's books, but his remarkable imagination extended to the shuddering portraits for Dr. Jekyll and Mr. Hyde.

Due to ill-health and very little money before he finally achieved success – a struggle common to so many great artists he died whilst still a young man, otherwise he might well have ranked with Walt Disney, so varied and original was his talent.

He had two sisters, my mother and my Aunt Gladys (who had a son, now deceased), which left me as custodian of his inimitable art. I wish all who see it at the Montacute the wonder and delight it has given to me.

Yours sincerely

Jean Caldwell

(Mrs.) Jean Caldwell